American Country Furniture 1780-1875

By the same authors

DICTIONARY OF MARKS—POTTERY AND PORCELAIN

A DIRECTORY OF AMERICAN SILVER, PEWTER AND SILVER PLATE

To Harold and Jim who, like all older brothers,
never thought we could know enough to write a book,

and to

our children, Kim and Lee,
who always thought we knew enough to write a book
and who really made it possible by quietly leaving
the room while we were working.

American
COUNTRY FURNITURE
1780-1875

RALPH AND TERRY KOVEL

Over 700 Illustrations

CROWN PUBLISHERS, INC., NEW YORK

Acknowledgments

HUNDREDS OF HISTORICAL SOCIETIES AND MUSEUMS were consulted in the preparation of this book. We wish to thank all of them for their encouragement and assistance. We want to give special thanks to the many who did so much in helping us to gather the material for our book. Mr. James Keeney, Mrs. John F. Lyle, Mrs. Eos Petty Richardson, Mrs. Lilian M. Umbaugh, Miss Margery Dissette, Mr. Alex Orlowsh, Mr. Richard H. Howland, Lelia Abercrombie, Katherine Hagler, Mrs. G. L. Gray, Virginia Gunter, Clara S. Beatty, Robert F. W. Meader, B. Donovan, Mrs. Amos Struble, Ted C. Sowers, Martha W. McCann, Mr. Robert H. Jones, Charles C. Wall, Mr. William Pinney, Marvin D. Schwartz, Jerry MacMullen, Fenton Kastner, Daniel B. Reibel, Mrs. Eva W. Davis, Gertrude Carraway, Clifford P. Monoahon, John S. Walton, Ralph Thomas, Roy D. Prentiss, Albrecht A. Heyer, C. Dearn Blair, Mrs. Curry C. Hall, Harriet Schachman, Mildred Bahen, Marian Terry, Halver W. Getchell, Curtis Fields, Dorothy Facer, Gordon M. MacLaren, Sr., Mrs. Leslie V. Case, Wilbur H. Glover, R. N. Williams, 2nd, and Mrs. Cecilian Steinfeldt. The Parke-Bernet Galleries, New York Public Library, Cleveland Public Library, Dunham Tavern Museum, Western Reserve Historical Society, Index of American Design, and Garth's Auction Barn were generous with their time and information.

Our special thanks go to Dr. William Macey, Mr. Douglas Coffey, and our many friends who saw less of us and were understanding because they knew we were writing another book.

Introduction

WHILE EXPERTS are still debating the meaning of the term "country furniture," this book has been written to show the designs and influences of country furniture in the eighteenth and nineteenth centuries in America.

There are folk music and symphony music, folk painting and academic art, and there are formal furniture and country-style furniture. We have made no attempt to determine whether a piece of furniture should be classed as formal or country beyond including all the styles having the simplicity of design used by country makers. There is no doubt in the minds of any experts that a Philadelphia Chippendale chair of carved mahogany is a formal American style and that a nineteenth-century slat-back chair is a country piece. But what about the country version of the Chippendale chair? It had simple lines, a rush seat, and was made from local woods. Because it was the work of an unsophisticated country workman, we have included it in this book.

The painted Sheraton fancy chair of the nineteenth century has been included because it, like the Windsor chair, is used with the other country designs.

The history of each style of chair, table, or cupboard began with a formal design, so it must be understood that many "beginnings" shown are really the work of gifted city furniture makers. The most elaborate as well as the simplest of country pieces are shown with little attempt made to help decide which piece might be better. We feel that the country furniture was the work of an individual with a specific need

in mind, and the crudely shaped log often served as well as the more stylized chair or table. If any point is to be made, it might be that the more like the formal furniture, the more able the craftsman. We doubt, however, that all country craftsmen were trying to imitate the city design.

Dating country furniture is difficult because design ideas and methods of construction remained for many years in rural areas, while the style and construction methods changed in the city. The dates used in this book have been furnished by the museum or owner.

The term "early American" when used by a decorator has come to mean maple and pine furniture with a country flavor. Most of the designs are adaptations of New England antiques of the eighteenth century. We have included the early inspirational pieces as well as the nineteenth-century adaptations often found today. This book also includes furniture styles from the South, Southwest, and the Midwest areas, often ignored in the study of country furniture.

Mirrors and clocks have been omitted. On the other hand, a section is devoted to the cobbler's bench, pie safe, tools, and kitchen equipment that are now being used in some living rooms.

It has been impossible for us to list the values for country furniture. Prices are constantly changing. As this country becomes more aware of its heritage, antiques are more desirable. The informal ways of living have created a new interest in all country antiques. Each area of our vast country has a special type of country furniture that is in great demand. The majority of the country furniture pieces have been found in New England, New York, and the Pennsylvania areas. The southwestern furniture is rare and the number of collectors few. Price books about antiques are written each year, while several antiques magazines and newspapers carry advertisements regarding current prices of available antiques. It must be understood that the rarities and the fine examples will always cost more than the average antiques.

We deplore the now common practice of removing all paint from some of the nineteenth-century painted chairs and chests so that the "primitive" pine will be seen. Any piece of furniture with its original finish, particularly a stenciled or painted grained piece, is far more desirable than a refinished one.

Shortened legs, electrified candle stands, and other structural changes may make the furniture piece more useful, but the value to the true collector is not enhanced.

The study of country furniture is just beginning. Many parts of the country have ignored the local country workman and collected the Victorian formal furniture. Some historical societies have started collections but have not identified the work of their areas. All the information used here has been verified by the more than one thousand museums, historical societies, dealers, private collectors, and other sources consulted while writing this book. At times only a picture and a date, with very little other information, were available. We apologize for any errors, and will be most eager to gain any additional information that will help to shed more light on the American country furniture of the nineteenth century.

RALPH AND TERRY KOVEL

Contents

Introduction		v
1.	Beds	1
2.	Candlestands	17
3.	Chairs—Banister Back	25
4.	Chairs—Formal	30
5.	Chairs—Rocking	37
6.	Chairs—Sheraton Fancy or Painted	59
7.	Chairs—Slat-Back or Ladder-Back	83
8.	Chairs—Windsor	112
9.	Chests	132
10.	Cradles	151
11.	Cupboards	155
12.	Desks	169
13.	Tables	177
14.	Washstands and Commode Tables	200
15.	Workbenches, Kitchen Pieces and Other Items	207
16.	Pennsylvania Furniture	221
17.	Shaker Furniture	225
18.	Spool Furniture	228
19.	Furniture Construction	229
20.	Bibliography	232
Illustrated Glossary of Accessories and Terms		233
Index		246

1

Beds

History

The earliest beds used by American settlers were simple low wooden frames. Actually, very little is known about the bedsteads used by the Pilgrims. Those few that still remain and can be authenticated have plain frames, low posts, low headboards, and rails along the side. They were made to resemble the beds the craftsman remembered seeing and using in Europe.

Furniture styles never remain in a simple, crude form. The elements of structure required by the furniture dictate the elements of design. Thus, a bed must be long enough and wide enough to accommodate a sleeping person as well as being low enough to be easily accessible. In addition, it must be of a size that would be suitable for the room that it is to occupy.

The beds of the eighteenth century had a function that is no longer in demand. Colonial Americans, as well as Europeans, felt that the fresh night air was detrimental to health. With no central heating system, the rooms were always cold at night. Accordingly, many beds were made with large canopies and side curtains that kept the germs and cold night air out of the bed. These canopies required a specially shaped wooden form that helped to keep all the fabric in its proper place. Even after it was no longer fashionable to drape the bed, some of the wooden structure remained as an ornament.

Many of the houses of eighteenth-century America did not have a separate bedroom; consequently, a large bed was placed in the main room of the house. Even though the bed was fully draped for privacy, the housewife usually had the beds covered with embroidered linen or colored damasks or resist prints.

While the simple seventeenth-century Pilgrim bed was influenced by the needs of the bed, the eighteenth-century bed changed to a huge, ornamented creation. The frames had large turned posts at each of the four corners, and the headboard was shaped in the style of the day. Basic construction, however, remained the same (see Furniture Construction), with ropes holding the mattress in place. By the middle of the nineteenth century beds changed completely owing to improved construction methods. Screws and slats replaced the earlier mortise-and-tenon joints. The bed was no longer draped; bedposts were eliminated; and new and odd shapes, such as the sleigh bed, were developed. The Industrial Revolution, with its resultant change of style, brought the large Victorian bed into fashion. Huge carved headboards became the center of interest in the Victorian bedroom in much the same manner as the canopied bed previously dominated the eighteenth-century room.

Construction

Before you can satisfactorily determine the age of a a bed, it is necessary to know something about its construction. While styles changed almost every twenty years, the basic bedstead was made in much the same manner from the time of the Pilgrims to about 1825. After that, new power tools made a different type of structure possible.

The bed made from the late eighteenth century to about 1825 had a frame made of four posts, two sides, and two end rails. It usually had a headboard. The actual bed was from 6 feet 4 inches to 6 feet 8 inches long and was 4 feet to 4 feet 6 inches wide. The side and end rails that held the mattress were from 18 inches to 30 inches from the floor. If the bed had a high feather mattress, it was necessary to use a small step stool to climb into bed.

The headboard, from 12 inches to 24 inches wide, was usually made of one piece of pine stained to match the posts. The headboards were fitted into the upright bedposts with a mortise-and-tenon joint and 3- to 4-inch square lumber was used to make each bedpost, which was turned and carved. The rail of the bed that held the mattress fitted into a square section of the post. The mortise-and-tenon construction usually was used, although many beds also had screws and nuts for extra support.

The rail at the side and ends of the bed held the mattress on ropes. Holes or small knobs were placed from 6 inches to 10 inches apart in the rail, and a rope was either placed through the hole or wound around the knob.

One of the best indications of a completely original old bed is the marking used by most markers. The posts and rails were usually marked with Roman numerals from I through VIII, chiseled into the matching parts. To be authentic, all the numbers should have been written by one man. Different handwriting characteristics will indicate to you when a number was written at a later time. If the numbers are the work of one man, it is fairly good indication that the posts and rails are all original.

Styles

The two basic shapes for a bed are high post and low post, with most of the country beds being low post.

High-post beds do not always have four identical posts. Sometimes the two posts at the foot of the bed are carved, while the two at the head remain smooth (Picture 2).

The formal Queen Anne high-post bed in America is very rare. It was the Chippendale-style bed that was extremely popular after the middle of the eighteenth century. The post of this Chippendale bed was fluted and from 7 feet to 8 feet high. In England the post was the same diameter from the top to the bottom, but in America the post was often tapered. The turned design on a post usually began above the rail of the bed. The leg of the bed was a cabriole shape with a claw-and-ball foot *or* straight, square, and untapered. The cabriole leg had carving on the top of the curve called the knee.

The headboard was not over 24 inches wide, slightly arched at the top, or, in some beds, straight across the top.

The Hepplewhite bed (Picture 3), which was popular near the end of the eighteenth century, had reeded posts ranging from 6 feet to 8½ feet high. Because most modern-day rooms have 8-foot ceilings, many of the early beds have been shortened to fit into them. The post of the Hepplewhite bed is tapered from the top to the shape of a vase at the lower part of the post. Below the rail is a square leg with a spade foot. A metal cover, apparently a decoration, hides a bolt that holds the post and sides together where the rail joins the post. It can easily be slid to the side. Such metal bolt covers were used in America, but seldom in England.

The Sheraton bed (Picture 2) is similar to a Hepplewhite bed, but the posts at the foot of the bed are less tapered, and usually with more carving on them and on the legs. In addition, Sheraton beds often had casters, or wheels, at the bottom of the leg so the bed could be moved.

A special style of bed, which was popular near Philadelphia and which was made during the Hepplewhite and Sheraton period, was called the "field bed" (Pictures 33, 34). This bed (circa 1780) had a top, or tester, that was not rectangular in shape but arched like the top of a tent. Originally, this name meant a folding type of bed that could be used near the field of battle by the officers, but eventually it came to mean a small bed with a tent-shaped canopy. Still later, the term "field bed" came to mean any small bed that could be folded and moved. Beds with no tester, but with posts only, were called "field" beds.

The beds of the Empire (1840) period (Picture 8), which followed Sheraton, began to show a heavier and much darker influence. Their posts were heavier, thicker, and more elaborately carved. Spiral carvings were the most popular. At this time the high-post bed lost favor, since the canopy was no longer needed. Thus, beds made during the Victorian era (about 1860) were without posts, even though the headboards were often as tall as the post would have been.

Beds made prior to the Empire period were usually made from mahogany, while the beds made after 1825 were often made from a local wood. Maple was very popular. One of the few formal furniture styles commonly used with country furniture was the heavy-post maple bed made in the Sheraton style. Often an Empire-style high headboard in maple is seen on these traditional beds, with curly maple being the most desired.

The high-post style that is usually classed as "country" is the pencil-post bed (See Picture 6) made in the late eighteenth century (1750–1780). The bed had thin six-sided posts often made of maple and shaped to resemble a pencil. The thinner the post, the better the bed.

Low-Post Styles

Most country furniture beds were of the low-post design because it was easier for a craftsman to make a simple low-post bed, and few country homes had the high ceilings necessary for a high-post bed.

The "under the eaves" bed was in use from 1690 to 1775. It was a bed with a short headpost and a low headboard. The plain, unornamented headboard occasionally had a slight arch or a double arch at the top. The headboard was formed from pine, and the posts were usually made of maple or birch. In a few rare cases the bed was made of oak.

The true low-post bed (Picture 10), with legs in the Chippendale style, was developed about 1760. It resembled the high-post bed of the same period with the exception of the short corner posts. This type is extremely rare.

The Empire low-post beds made from 1820 to 1850 have remained the most popular. They had a headboard with carved decorations, similar to the headboard of the high-post bed of the 1800's. The posts were turned, carved, or reeded, and as high as the headboard. All four posts were the same height, ranging from about 3 feet 6 inches to 4 feet 2 inches, with the base made into a vaselike shape. Many of these beds had footboards as well.

These beds were made from mahogany, cherry, maple, or birch in most areas of the United States, including New England, Ohio, Indiana, Tennessee, and many of the western states.

The sleigh bed (Picture 35) is the 1820 version of a low-post bed. The name was derived from the close resemblance to a horse-drawn sleigh. Most of them were made with mahogany veneer. It was at this time, 1820, that the iron catch was invented for use on a bed.

The "roll-over" style of bed is a Sheraton design dated by some as 1810 to 1820 and by others as 1830 to 1840. The headboard rolled back along the top. Most of the beds had rope lacings, not springs. They were made from local hardwoods such as maple, cherry, or birch.

The Jenny Lind, or spool bed (Pictures 21-24), was made about 1830. This turned spool bed with a headboard and footboard of the same height was one of the most popular styles of country bed ever made. The early beds had straight lines, while those made after 1850 had curved corners on the headboards and footboards. The Jenny Lind was the first bed to use slats and countersunk screws in the construction. (For more information about spool beds, see Chapter 18, "Spool Furniture.")

There are two other important facts to remember about beds. The early beds had lacings or ropes that held the mattress in place. Later beds, made about 1860, used slats to support the mattress, although as late as 1900 lacings were still used.

The twin bed is a style that was popular about 1840. The first twin beds were designed about 1800 by Thomas Sheraton, who pictured a "summer bed" that was really twin beds under one canopy. This style was developed to help keep cool during the hot summer months.

The trundle bed, known as early as the seventeenth century (Picture 38), was made to fit under another bed in the room. It moved on casters, and was about 15 inches high. It was meant for a young child.

1. *High-post bed, eighteenth century* Cherry bed made in 1753 in Connecticut. Note the plain round tapered bedposts. (The Metropolitan Museum of Art)

3. *High-post bed, nineteenth century* Formal Hepplewhite-style bed of carved curly maple, made about 1800. (Taylor and Dull, photography)

2. *High-post bed, nineteenth century* Formal Sheraton-style carved mahogany tester bedpost made about 1800. The posts are turned, reeded, and carved with a scrolled headboard. This is a typical Sheraton-style bedstead. (Taylor and Dull, photography)

4. *High-post bed, eighteenth century* The fluted birch posts and white pine cornice of this New England bed indicate a country maker. The bed was made about 1770 to 1785. (Courtesy Henry Francis du Pont Winterthur Museum)

5. *High-post bed, nineteenth century* Four-poster bed made of butternut wood in Schoharie, New York, about 1800. Note carving of posts and the scrolled headboard. (Index of American Design, Washington, D.C.)

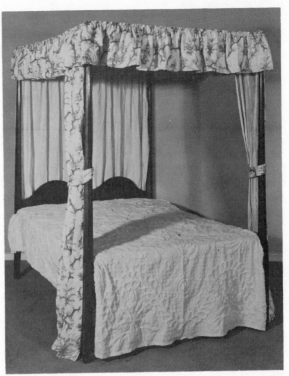

6. *High-post bed, nineteenth century* Pencil-post bed made from cherry and pine about 1810. This piece of country furniture is in the Sheraton style. (Taylor and Dull, photography)

7. *High-post bed, nineteenth century* High-post bed with no tester or top. This is the style between the high- and low-post styles, with thick turned posts and a headboard and footboard made to resemble the low-post beds of the 1800's. (Witte Museum, San Antonio, Texas)

8. *High-post bed, nineteenth century* Formal Empire-period high-post bed with elaborately hand-carved posts of pineapple design. Made about 1820 for use in Vicksburg, Mississippi. (Old Court House Museum, Vicksburg, Mississippi)

9. *High-post bed, nineteenth century* The posts of this bed are turned from maple; the headboard and footboard are of pine, the frame of ash. The bed was found in eastern Ontario, Canada. (Upper Canada Village, Morrisburg, Ontario, Canada)

10. *Low-post bed, eighteenth century* This bed has a walnut headboard. The cabriole legs and the club-shaped rear feet are the type used on the high-post beds of the same period. This formal bed was made about 1750–1760 in Philadelphia, Pennsylvania. It was the type later copied by many country makers. (Courtesy Henry Francis du Pont Winterthur Museum)

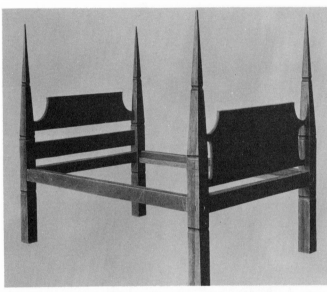

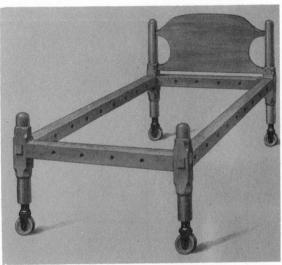

11. *Low-post bed, nineteenth century* Walnut bed made about 1806 in Virginia. Note the adaptation of a pencil post, and the headboard and footboard. (Index of American Design, Washington, D.C.)

12. *Low-post bed, nineteenth century* Shaker bed made in Mount Lebanon, New York, about 1830–1860, from maple and pine woods with a natural finish. The wheels on the bed are characteristic of a Shaker bed. Note the holes for the ropes. (Index of American Design, Washington, D.C.)

13. *Low bed, nineteenth century* Typical Shaker bedstead of maple with rollers (these are not casters, as they do not swivel), made after 1875 at Mount Lebanon, New York. The supporting slats for the mattress went lengthwise. (Shaker Museum, Old Chatham, New York)

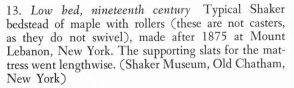

14. *Bed, nineteenth century* This small bed was made of red-painted pine in eastern Ontario, Canada. Notice the slats that held the mattress. (Upper Canada Village, Morrisburg, Ontario, Canada)

15. *Low-post bed, Zoarite, nineteenth century* A child's bed with removable sides made about 1835 in Zoar, Ohio. The Zoarite community produced furniture influenced by German styles. This bed was made of varnished walnut. (Index of American Design, Washington, D.C.)

16. *Low-post bed, nineteenth century* Yellow pine bed made by slaves in Louisiana about 1840. Note the "cannon ball" bedposts and the low footboard. (Index of American Design, Washington, D.C.)

17. *Low-post bed, nineteenth century* The shaped knobs on the headboard and footboard are another variation of the "cannon ball" bed. The headboard and footboard of this maple bed are similar in size and shape. This style was popular in country farmhouses after 1830. (Hale House, Western Reserve Historical Society, Cleveland, Ohio)

18. *Low-post bed, nineteenth century* This low-post bed has maple posts and a butternut headboard and an ash frame. The wood was stained red. It was found in eastern Ontario, Canada. This type of bed is sometimes called a "cannon ball" bed. (Upper Canada Village, Morrisburg, Ontario, Canada)

19. *Low-post bed, nineteenth century* The headposts and footposts of this Canadian bed are identical turned maple posts, stained red. The frame is ash. This type of bed is often split and made into twin beds today. (Upper Canada Village, Morrisburg, Ontario, Canada)

20. *Low-post bed, nineteenth century* Pine bed with holes at the top of the four footposts that could hold an added canopy if desired. This bed was used in Panaca, Nevada, in 1867 and was laced with rawhide on the side knobs. (Nevada Historical Society)

21. *Low-post nineteenth-century spool bed* A dark finished walnut was used in this rope-strung, spool-turned bed about 1836. This type of bed, using factory spool turnings, was made in all parts of the country. (Index of American Design, Washington, D.C.)

22. *Spool bed, nineteenth century* The spool beds with rounded corners on the headboard and footboard were made after 1850. Earlier spool-turned beds with sharp corners are sometimes called "Jenny Lind" beds. (Hale House, Western Reserve Historical Society, Cleveland, Ohio)

23. *Low-post bed, nineteenth century* A child's crib made with spool turnings for use in Mississippi during the mid-nineteenth century. Note top crosspiece. (Old Court House Museum, Vicksburg, Mississippi)

24. *Crib, nineteenth century* Spool turnings were used to make the legs and side spindles of this child's crib made about 1840–1875. Many types of spool furniture were made in the 1815–1880 period. (Hale House, Western Reserve Historical Society, Cleveland Ohio)

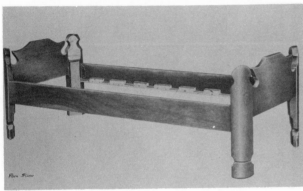

25. *Low-post bed, nineteenth century* This stained reddish-brown Texas-made bed was constructed about 1875. The construction of an inner support shows how the mattress was used and held by the slats rather than by rope. Note the partially rounded posts. (Index of American Design, Washington, D.C.)

26. *Low-post bed, nineteenth century* Yellow pine bed made in Texas about 1875–1880. This small day-bed had unusual head and foot boards. (Index of American Design, Washington, D.C.)

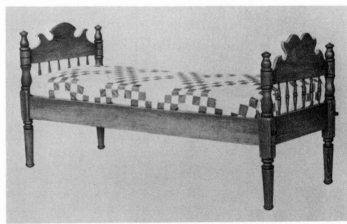

27. *Daybed, seventeenth century* A Pennsylvania-style daybed with an end that resembles the banister-back chairs. The daybed was used for daytime rest, and the back was adjustable so that the user could recline. Most of these early beds were made of walnut. (Courtesy of Henry Francis du Pont Winterthur Museum)

28. *Settee bed, nineteenth century (two views)* Extremely rare curly maple combination settee and double bed made in New York about 1810–1820 in the Sheraton style. (John Walton, New York City)

29. *Settle bed, nineteenth century* The seat, painted gray with black and light-gray decorations, folds forward to form a bed. This settle bed, made before 1850, is believed to be Canadian. (Shelburne Museum, Inc. Photographer, Einars Mengis)

30. *Bench bed, Canadian, nineteenth century* The bench bed, or *banc-lit,* is a style not made in United States areas. This bed was made of pine painted and grained. A stencil design is in the center of the black and yellow stripe of the decorated bed. This style of Canadian bed opens in a special way, by tilting the bench front to the floor. (Upper Canadian Village, Morrisburg, Ontario, Canada)

31. *Bench bed, Canadian, nineteenth century* The bench bed, or *banc-lit,* is a Canadian form. This pine bed was painted black with yellow and green stencil decorations. It was made in eastern Ontario, Canada, before 1840. (Upper Canada Village, Morrisburg, Ontario, Canada)

32. *Child's bed, eighteenth century* Turned birch and poplar child's bed made in Connecticut during the late eighteenth century. Note side of bed and frame for canopy. (Taylor and Dull, photography)

33. *Field bed, eighteenth century* Folding bed made from maple about 1725–1750. Note the plain posts and frame. (Metropolitan Museum of Art, New York; gift of Mrs. Russell Sage, 1909)

34. *Field bed, eighteenth century* This type of easily assembled bed was called a camp bed or tent bed. The entire bed could be taken apart for use in wartime at camps. Notice the square posts and legs. (Courtesy of Henry Francis du Pont Winterthur Museum)

14

35. *Formal sleigh bed, nineteenth century* The Empire bed was made to be placed along the wall in this position with a hanging above it. The country makers were familiar with this formal style, and adapted it to the country sleigh bed. (Courtesy Henry Francis du Pont Winterthur Museum)

15

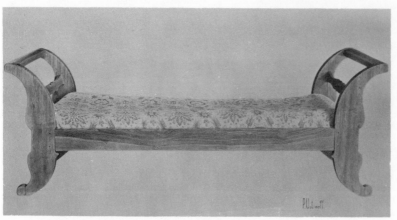

36. *Sleigh bed, nineteenth century* Lightly varnished pine daybed said to be made by a German carpenter in Bastrop, Texas, about 1845. Note the edge of the curved leg. (Index of American Design, Washington, D.C.)

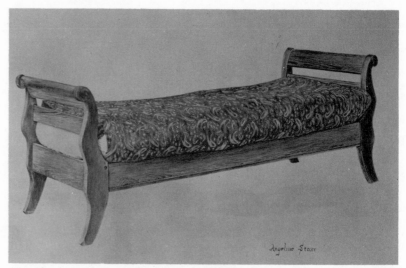

37. *Sleigh bed, nineteenth century* Yellow pine daybed made in Texas about 1879 in the sleigh-bed style. (Index of American Design, Washington, D.C.)

38. *Trundle bed, nineteenth century* The posts of this trundle bed are finished to resemble the low-post bed. Most trundle beds are merely frames for a mattress. (Witte Museum, San Antonio, Texas)

2

Candlestands

ONE OF THE best examples of the many forms of furniture that have remained virtually unchanged for hundreds of years is the candlestand. Any small table that was made to hold a candle, or any of the many frames that hold a candle in the best position for light, is called a candlestand. It is impossible to date many of the candlestands because the styles have been in continuous use for over three hundred years.

Although the candle, as the main source of light, went out of style after the development of the electric-light bulb, the candlestand was still used as a small table. Reproductions of all types are still being made.

The most common candlestand is a small table held by a post and supported by crossbars as feet (Pictures 39, 40). The contoured foot was made during the eighteenth century; the flat foot was the most popular during the nineteenth century.

When a T-bar foot (Picture 41) was used on a candlestand, it was called a "weaver's stand." The flat side of the T was placed next to the weaver so that the candlestand's feet did not interfere with the loom. These were first used during the eighteenth century.

The screw type of candlestand (Pictures 42–44) was made from 1725 to the mid-nineteenth century. The height of the table and candle arm could be adjusted by the screw. The screw and arm were made of wood, with maple the most popular because it was hard enough for use as a screw and did not split or crack.

The candlestand with a tripod foot (Pictures 46–50) was created by formal makers between 1730 and 1790, with the foot generally carved in the style of the day, either Chippendale or Queen Anne. One rare type of tripod stand even had feet carved like shoes but was considered to be European in origin. The tripod candlestand was also made after 1790 in many outlying country areas, but its basic shape was incompatible with the straight lines of the early 1800 styles. Most of the furniture designers in the large cities no longer used this out-of-date styling.

Victorian candlestands had a slightly larger table area because the stand was used to hold either a candle or a lamp.

The cobbler's light (Picture 44) is a screw type of candlestand made with three or four feet. As the name indicates, it was originally used by a shoemaker.

The ratchet stand (Pictures 58, 59, 60) is a very early form that could be adjusted to many heights. It usually had no tabletop, but just held a candle on an arm of the stand.

The tilt-top candlestand is a smaller version of a tilt-top table, with the Chippendale style of tilt-top stands ranging from 22 inches to 26 inches in height. The shaft of the table was turned or carved, and the tripod foot had the usual claw-and-ball or other animal foot found on formal furniture of the day. It was made of all native woods from 1750 to 1790, but the more formal versions always called for mahogany.

The tilt-top tripod stand of the 1790 to 1800 period had a turned shaft with very plain legs. The earlier tripod stand had legs that curved up at the "ankle" and down at the foot. The later Hepplewhite table leg turned down at the ankle and ran into a tiny foot that appeared more like a stump of the leg.

Formal tilt-top stands often were inlaid, while the country pieces were usually plain.

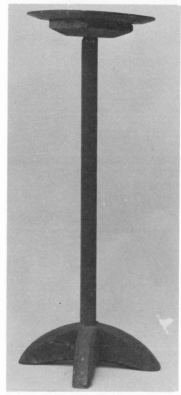

FROM LEFT TO RIGHT

39. *Candlestand, American, mid-eighteenth century* This is an excellent example of a typically shaped candlestand with a supporting post and crossbar feet. The turned base of the post, the well-shaped feet, and the octagonal top all indicate superior workmanship. (Metropolitan Museum of Art, Sylmaris Collection; gift of George Coe Graves, 1930)

40. *Candlestand, Pennsylvania, 1700–1750* This fine candlestand is painted red with a post support and an unusual X-shaped foot. The small circular top is typical of candlestands made during the eighteenth and nineteenth centuries. The post has been roughly cut, which causes it to appear eight-sided. (Metropolitan Museum of Art; gift of Mrs. Robert W. de Forest, 1933)

41. *T-base candlestand, American, eighteenth century* The T-shaped foot and solid octagonal post give this stand a sturdy, no-nonsense appearance. The stand is made of oak and pine. This type of stand was also called a weaver's stand. Notice the slightly contoured foot. (Taylor and Dull, photography)

42. *Candlestand, screw type, painted, American circa 1800* Gold decorations enhance this black-painted maple candlestand. It is 35 inches high, with a well-shaped tripod leg ending in a formed foot. The turning at the base of the screw post indicates the sophistication of the maker. (Art Institute of Chicago)

43. *Candlestand, screw type, American, eighteenth century* The screw type of stand was made to permit the adjustment of the height of the candle. This early example had plain tripod legs and a simple round top with two candles held above the stand on the arms. (Metropolitan Museum of Art; gift of Mrs. Russell Sage, 1909) TOP LEFT

44. *Candlestand, screw type, American, early nineteenth century* This type of candlestand with the candle arm above the table top is sometimes called a cobbler's table. The legs of this maple example have been turned to resemble the legs of an eighteenth century Windsor chair. (Index of American Design, Washington, D.C.) BOTTOM LEFT

45. *Candlestand, American painted, eighteenth century* The elaborately turned post of the small table-like candlestand and the well-formed tripod leg indicate superior workmanship. This stand is painted black, and dates from the very early eighteenth century (Taylor and Dull, photography) BOTTOM RIGHT

19

46. *Candlestand, nineteenth century* Small candle table or candlestand made in Schoharie, New York, of butternut wood. Note the tripod legs and shaped top. (Index of American Design, Washington, D.C.)

47. *Candlestand, Canadian* This maple-topped candlestand has cherry legs. The design is very similar to candlestands made in the eastern United States (Upper Canada Village, Morrisburg, Ontario, Canada) BOTTOM LEFT

48. *Candlestand, Canadian* The stand is adjustable. It is made with a maple top and ash legs. Notice the "porringer" top. (Upper Canada Village, Morrisburg, Ontario, Canada) BOTTOM RIGHT

49. *Candlestand table, unknown date* Curly maple was used to make this tip table. The top is octagonal; the pedestal has a tripod base and snake feet. It was found in Connecticut. (Old Sturbridge Village, Sturbridge, Massachusetts) TOP LEFT

50. *Candlestand, nineteenth century* Shaker-made candlestand with maple legs and cherry top. It has traditionally shaped tripod legs. (Shaker Museum, Old Chatham, New York) TOP RIGHT

51. *Candlestand, American trestle, early eighteenth century* This pine and ash candlestand has the general appearance of a small table. The turned legs and stretcher indicate the excellence of the stand. (Metropolitan Museum of Art, Sylmaris Collection; gift of George Coe Graves, 1930)

52. *Candlestand, Pennsylvania, circa 1850* This large table-like candlestand has an enlarged post and heavy base with ball feet that indicate a Pennsylvania maker. The pine and maple stand was painted off-white with black graining. (Henry Ford Museum, Dearborn, Michigan)

53. *Candlestand, American, eighteenth century* This slender stand has an arm to hold a single candle. The square base is heavy enough to support the weight of the candle high on the post. This form of candlestand was made during the nineteenth century, with little variation in design. (Metropolitan Museum of Art; gift of Mrs. Russell Sage, 1909) LEFT

54. *Iron candlestand, Pennsylvania, eighteenth century* The penny feet and the well-shaped leg indicate a desirable metal candlestand. Notice the wooden box to catch the candle drippings. Many types of metal stands were made. (Taylor and Dull, photography) RIGHT

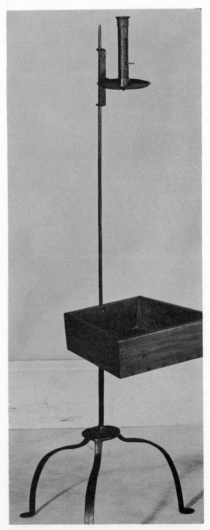

55. *Peg-foot candlestand, Pennsylvania, circa 1815*
The peg feet on this well-made stand are an unusual feature for a nineteenth-century stand. Made from turned maple and with an oval pine top, the stand is 27 inches high and 24 inches wide. (Taylor and Dull, photography)

56. *Adjustable candlestand, eighteenth century* This maple screw-top stand was stained to appear walnut. The turnings, leg shape, and eight knobs on the edge of the center platform are typical of this unusual type of stand. The large top of this stand is interesting. (Taylor and Dull, photography)

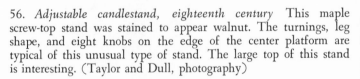

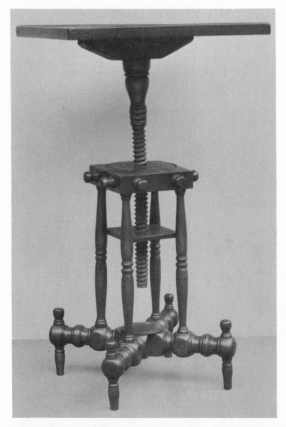

57. *Adjustable candlestand, Connecticut, circa 1750–1800* The elaborate screw mechanism and well-turned posts and feet indicate the quality of this cherry candlestand. It is a very unusual example. (Metropolitand Museum of Art, Sylmaris Collection; gift of George Coe Graves, 1930)

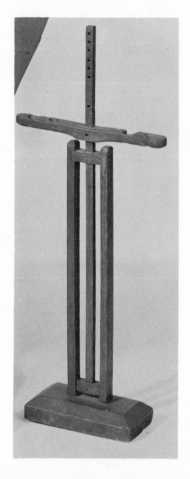

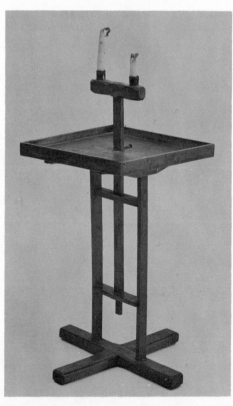

58. *Ratchet candlestand, American, eighteenth century* The adjustable mechanism of the ratchet stand and the crossbar foot are typical of the ratchet candlestand of the eighteenth and nineteenth centuries. It is unusual to have a tabletop instead of a candle holder at the top of the ratchet. The foot is held together with an iron screw, and the stand is of pine. (Taylor and Dull, photography) TOP LEFT

59. *Adjustable candlestand, American, circa 1750* A wrought-iron hasp fits into the grooves on the post of this candlestand, which adjusts the height of the candle arm. The stand is made of oak, and it is 31 inches high, while the candle arm is 13¼ inches long. (Shelburne Museum, Inc.) TOP CENTER

60. *Adjustable candlestand, New England, seventeenth and eighteenth centuries* Black paint covered the ash wood that formed this early candlestand. The candle arm is adjustable, with a peg that fits into the holes of the upright post. (Taylor and Dull, photography) TOP RIGHT

61. *Candlestand, American, adjustable traytop, eighteenth century* A metal pin holds the candle post at the proper height by wedging it against the tabletop. This is an unusual adjusting device. The feet and supporting columns resemble those used by more conventional ratchet-type stands. (Hagley Museum, Wilmington, Delaware) BOTTOM RIGHT

24

3

Chairs—Banister-Back

History

THE BANISTER-BACK CHAIR was named for the turned wooden back supports that look like a stair-rail banister. The chair was sometimes called a baluster-back.

The earliest American chairs that were named are the famous Carver (Picture 62) and the Brewster chairs, which were named for the early Pilgrims who owned the prototype. They were based on English furniture styles of the seventeenth century. One type of English chair that was the father of the Carver and the Brewster type had elaborate turnings and some vertical and horizontal supports on the back. Another type of English chair that influenced American styles was the cane-back chair made during the era of Charles the Second. The seat and a portion of the back were made from caning, and elaborate turnings and carvings were used for the other parts of the chair. Cane chairs were popular in England until about 1700, and in America to about 1720. (There were three separate styles of cane chairs at this time; while the styles are interesting historically, they are too early to be considered part of the scope of this book.)

Some of the English cane-back chairs gradually changed into the Queen Anne style of furniture. Some of the cane-back chairs lost their caning and became banister-backs. The caning was replaced on the back by banisters, and the cane seats were replaced by rush seats. These changes created a style that was more simple in appearance, and easy to make. The banister-back was at its height in America from 1700 to 1725.

The three-legged chair and the Wainscot chair were the two other styles made in America during the seventeenth century. Neither of them directly influenced any style of country furniture.

Construction—The Carver and the Brewster Chairs

A knowledgeable collector should be able to identify a Carver or a Brewster chair, even though it is almost impossible to see one outside a museum.

The Carver chair was made from about 1620 to 1700. The earlier chairs had much heavier but more simple turnings than the late ones. The back of the chair had three horizontal rows with three vertical spindles. Most of the Carver chairs had arms and rush seats (Pictures 62, 63, 64, 65).

The Brewster chair had several rows of vertical spindles on the back and several more rows on each side and the front, with as many as forty or more spindles on a chair. The Brewster chair (Pictures 66, 67, 68) was made about the same time as the Carver chair.

Construction—Banister

Although the English banister-back was usually made from walnut, the American banister-back of 1700 was usually made from maple (Pictures 69, 70, 71). A few of the early chairs were made from beech, hickory, pine, or other local woods.

The banisters that formed the back of the chair were round or split. When the banister was split, the half-banister was placed with the flat side forward so that the back of the person seated on the chair would rest against a row of flat banisters. This was a more comfortable method, but a chair was occasionally made with the rounded side forward. It was called a "reverse banister-back."

Most banister chairs had four split banisters, but they ranged from three to five on a chair. The top had an ornamental crest that was much less elaborate than the crest of the earlier chairs. The top has been one of the areas where there is some regional variation.

Some banister chairs had other features, such as Spanish feet or a large bulbous turning in the center of the stretcher at the front of the chair. Mushroom-shaped knobs were sometimes used at the end of the front post where the arm joined. The mushroom knobs were the inspiration for a similar arm made by the Shakers about one hundred to one hundred and fifty years later.

Daybeds and children's chairs were also constructed in the style of the banister-back.

The style began to simplify about 1730. The top of the chairback was straight or curved, but no carved crest was added. The early chairs had a curved crossrail that was placed a few inches above the seat and across the bottom at the back of the chair. Early chairs had a curved rail that looked like an upside-down cupid's-bow, while the later chairs were made with a straight crossrail.

The fat, turned banisters were gradually replaced by narrow strips of wood. A special group of chairs made in New Jersey had spiral turnings on the vertical pieces. The arms were turned, and they either extended beyond the front post or were set into it. The mushroom knob remained on some.

The banister-back chair lost all the carving and turning by the nineteenth century, and only the placement of the vertical strips in the back of the chair indicates its origin.

Judging a banister-back chair is a matter of comparison. Any eighteenth-century example is important, while any well-made nineteenth-century piece is collectable. Good proportion and turnings will help to determine how well it was constructed.

62. *Armchair, Carver type, late seventeenth century*
Turned rows of spindles and the rush seat are typical of the Carver chair. The heavy turning where the seat joins the back is unusual. (Metropolitan Museum of Art; Rogers Fund, 1941)

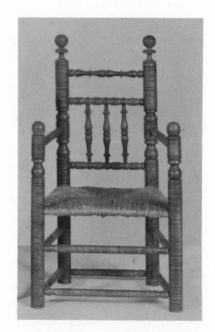

63. *Armchair, Carver type, eighteenth century*
Curly maple chair with rush seat. Origin unknown. (Taylor and Dull, photography)

64. *Armchair, Carver type, seventeenth century*
The posts are maple; the spindles, rings, and stretchers are ash. This is a type of chair that influenced the later country styles. (Metropolitan Museum of Art)

65. *Chair, Carver type, seventeenth century* New-England chair of ash and hickory, made about 1650–1700. Notice the plain legs and stretcher arrangement. (Metropolitan Museum of Art; gift of Mrs. Russell Sage, 1909)

66. *Nineteenth-century chair* This Sheraton-style chair of birch with a rush seat was influenced by the earlier Carver-style chair. (See similar chairs in Chapter 6, "Chairs—Sheraton Fancy, or Painted.") (Mrs. Lilian Umbaugh, Kelso, Washington)

67. *Armchair, Brewster type, seventeenth century* Massachusetts-made hickory and ash armchair of about 1650. Rows of turned spindles in back, sides, and even in the front are characteristic of this style. (Metropolitan Museum of Art; gift of Mrs. J. Insley Blair, 1951)

68. *Armchair, Brewster type, eighteenth century* A simpler Brewster type of chair made about 1700. There are spindles only at the back, not at the sides. Note the sausage turnings. (Morristown National Historical Park, Morristown, New Jersey)

70. *Banister-back armchair, eighteenth century*
Sausage-turned stretchers and fluted banisters are
interesting features of this chair. The straight crossrail and simple crest show that this chair is of a later
date than the one in Picture 69. (Suffolk County
Historical Society, Riverhead, New York)

69. *Banister-back armchair, eighteenth century* This is
a black-painted armchair with sausage-turned stretchers
and rush seat and split banisters, made about 1700. The
mushroom knobs at the end of the arms inspired later
Shaker chairs. The curved crest and crossrail are indications of an early banister-back chair. (Taylor and Dull,
photography)

71. *Banister-back chair, eighteenth century* Five
molded banisters and a shaped crest were used to
form the back of this chair. Restrained bulbous turnings in the center of the stretcher and the rush seat
are typical features of the banister-back chair. This
example was found in Perquimans County, North
Carolina. Note how the crest resembles the fanback Windsor style. (State Department of Archives
and History, Raleigh, North Carolina; Tryon Palace, New Bern, North Carolina)

4

Chairs—Formal

THE CANE-BACK CHAIR (Pictures 72, 73) was a formal furniture style of the 1660 to 1700 period in England, but remained popular in America until about 1720. This chair is sometimes called a "Charles the Second" chair because it was popular in England during the years Charles reigned.

The American version of this chair had carved legs, stretchers, and stiles. Both back and seat were caned, but the back of the chair did not touch the seat. In England these chairs were made of walnut or beech; in America, the furniture makers often used maple or fruitwood, and painted the finished chair black.

The chair in the style of Queen Anne (Pictures 74, 75, 76, 77) was the next form to become popular in America. However, transitional chairs between the Queen Anne and the cane-back chair were made about 1720 to 1750. Its back had the shaped splat popular in Queen Anne designs; but, as in the earlier cane-back chair, the back did not touch the seat. While the crest of this chair had the curve typical of the Queen Anne style, the lower part of the chair, the legs and stretchers, were similar to the earlier cane-chair style.

The true Queen Anne chair was made in America from about 1710 to 1755, although the reign of Queen Anne in England was from 1702 to 1714 (Picture 78). The back of the chair had a vase-shaped splat that touched the seat. The legs were made in the cabriole shape, with stretchers on early chairs; these were removed after about 1725. The curve of the leg made the stretcher unnecessary for structural security. The seat was rectangular or curved, sometimes rush, often covered with a fabric. The foot of the chair was either a club foot, Dutch foot or, on later chairs, a claw-and-ball foot. The top of the chair was curved, usually lower in the center than at the ends. Queen Anne chairs were made of walnut and other native woods. Mahogany became popular with formal makers after about 1750.

The Chippendale style (Picture 79) was the next formal style popular in America. The early Chippendale styles from 1750 to 1755 had the curved leg with no stretcher, popular on Queen Anne chairs, and a pierced or cut-out splat at the back of the chair. The curve at the top of the chair was often higher in the center than at the ends. Later Chippendale chairs had straight legs. These chairs were made from about 1755 to 1785 (Picture 80).

Chippendale style can also refer to several other chairs influenced by the English designs of Thomas Chippendale. The country furniture collector will be especially interested in the formal ladder-back chair (Picture 81). The back of this chair had several vertical pierced splats. The chair seat was straight on all four edges. The legs were usually square and straight, no longer rounded and curved. This Chippendale ladder-back was popular about 1760 to 1775. It was made of mahogany, cherry, and other native woods. The style was similar to the next popular furniture period, the Hepplewhite designs.

All these formal furniture styles, except the cane-back chair, had slip seats. This is a seat that is fitted into a molding. It can be removed and covered with fabric, then replaced. The country versions, however, often had rush seats that were not removable.

It is debatable whether a rustic version of a formal furniture style should be called "country furniture." The formal styles pictured have been chosen both because they are typical of the style and because they are examples of the work of less skilled makers who could not make the elaborately carved and shaped pieces of the Philadelphia and New York makers. These chairs are all probably examples of the work of country furniture makers.

72. *Side chair, seventeenth century* An American chair that shows the elements of design of both England and America. This chair is made of maple and beech, both native American woods, in a basically English style. The English would have used the caning, the ornate carving, and all the proportions. The American maker added the hearts on the stretcher and crest. This chair was made about 1690 in the William and Mary style that influenced all later country furniture. (Metropolitan Museum of Art)

73. *Side chair, early eighteenth century* This Flemish type of chair was probably made in England, although it was used in Hartford, Connecticut, in the early eighteenth century. Notice how it resembles the American-made chair. (Old Sturbridge Village, Sturbridge, Massachusetts)

75. *Queen Anne side chair, eighteenth century* The rush seat, duck foot, shaped splat, turned styles, and stretcher with bulbous turnings are all features that were used in America for years. This chair was made in New York about 1725–1740. Notice its similarity to the next chair made almost fifty years later. (Courtesy, Brooklyn Museum)

74. *Queen Anne chair, eighteenth century* The legs of this maple chair, the stretcher and Spanish foot show its maker still remembered the William and Mary styles of the seventeenth century, although he made the back in the Queen Anne style of the eighteenth century. The rush seat causes some to claim this is a country version of a formal style and should be classed as country furniture. (Taylor and Dull, photography)

76. *Queen Anne side chair, eighteenth century.* Painted chair with duck foot and rush seat was made by Nathaniel Dominy about 1770. This is another transitional chair with features of both William and Mary and Queen Anne styles, formal and country features. (Suffolk County Historical Society, Riverhead, New York)

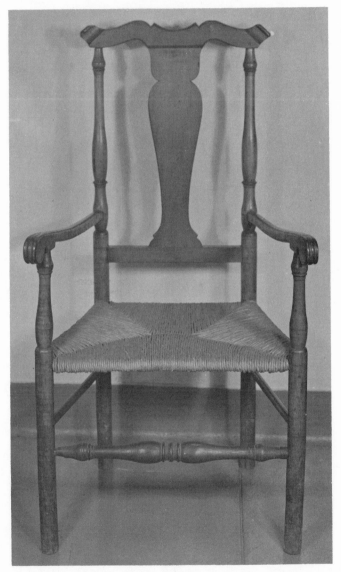

77. *Queen Anne armchair, eighteenth century* This chair, with rush seat and plain legs, has more of the country features, and was made about 1750–1775. It has an excellent crest, and the back of the chair does not touch the seat as it did in the formal Queen Anne style. This style is sometimes called a "fiddleback" chair, but the name "fiddleback" usually refers to a nineteenth century style. (Morristown National Historical Park, Morristown, New Jersey)

78. *Queen Anne chair, eighteenth century*   This walnut chair was branded with the maker's name "J. Langdon." It was used in Massachusetts, although the maker is thought to be from Portsmouth, New Hampshire. Notice the shape of the back, the H-stretcher, and the upholstered seat. (Old Sturbridge Village, Sturbridge, Massachusetts)

80. *Country Chippendale chairs, eighteenth century*   The rush seats and green paint probably make these examples of a country maker. Notice that the chair seat does not touch the back. The crosspiece at the lower back and the stretchers are features of an earlier period. These chairs were made about 1780–1790. (Shelburne Museum, Inc. Photographer, Einars J. Mengis)

79. *Chippendale chair, eighteenth century* The traditional Chippendale shape is seen in this chair. The pierced slat, curved crest, lack of stretcher, and rounded seat are all evident, even though this is not the work of a master cabinetmaker. (Old Sturbridge Village, Sturbridge, Massachusetts)

81. *Country Chippendale chair, eighteenth century* This is a country version of a Chippendale chair in the ladder-back style used by formal makers. Notice the rush seat, square legs, and stretchers. (Old Sturbridge Village, Sturbridge, Massachusetts)

82. *Side chair, nineteenth century* Country-made maple side chair from the Barrington-Strafford, New Hampshire, area. The legs and stretchers are Chippendale style. The base of the shield back has an inlay. (Old Sturbridge Village, Sturbridge, Massachusetts)

83. *Side chair, nineteenth century* A Canadian side chair made from tiger maple about 1840. Notice the Victorian influence in this chair, in the curved legs, and in the back. (Upper Canada Village, Morrisburg, Ontario, Canada)

5

Chairs—Rocking

History

THE ROCKING CHAIR is truly a piece of American country furniture. During the eighteenth or early nineteenth century no formal room ever contained a rocking chair. None of the formal eighteen-century furniture manufacturers ever made a rocking chair unless it was as a special order for a particular customer. It had always been a chair for comfort and use, but never one for formal affairs.

The history of the first rocking chair is blurred in the pages of time. Rockers had been used on cradles for three to four centuries before anyone thought to put a rocker on an adult's chair. We are almost certain that the rocking chair was an American idea. While it has been claimed that Benjamin Franklin invented the rocker, this has never been proved. He did own a rocking chair in 1787, but rockers were made prior to that date. Most rocking chairs made before 1770 were really converted chairs. Two rockers were added to a previously straight chair. It seems that most of the first rocking chairs appeared in the Philadelphia area about 1770. The account book of Eliakim Smith of Hadley, Massachusetts, mentions adding rockers in 1762. The next recorded mention of a rocker was by William Savery, the Philadelphia cabinetmaker. One of his bills mentioned reseating a rocking chair.

There are two basic types of rocking chairs. One was designed and made originally as a rocking chair, while the other was converted from a conventional wooden chair with straight legs. *Most rockers made prior to 1800 were converted.* Even though they were still considered novelties by 1810, rocking chairs were manufactured by many firms. These earlier chairs often did not have arms because most manufacturers patterned them after the converted, handy armless chairs. It soon became apparent, however, that the high-back chairs with rockers appeared more in scale if the chair did have arms; consequently, the majority of the rockers thereafter were made with arms.

Construction

The rocking chairs that were manufactured were made from wood that was most available, convenient, and suited to the structural needs of the chair. The seat was usually made of pine or whitewood, wood that was soft and could be easily shaped. The legs, spindles, stretchers, and arms were made from hardwoods that could be bent, such as maple, oak, hickory, or ash.

The armrest was often made of cherry or applewood. Many of the nineteenth-century chairs had a natural finish on the armrest even though the rest of the chair was painted. The woods used were chosen for their attractive appearance plus the ability to stand wear.

After 1840, some rocking chairs were made entirely of maple, and were often left unpainted. Curly maple was particularly attractive and was frequently chosen for this purpose.

WHAT ROCKERS TELL YOU ABOUT A CHAIR

The shape of a rocker will help determine the age and origin of the chair. Early rockers were short, stubby, and extended an *equal* distance beyond the front and rear legs of the chair. Both ends of the rockers were identical. In other words, the rockers could have been reversed and they would have appeared the same (Picture 94). Some of the early rockers were set into a socket on the chair leg (Picture 84). This type either curved high and was cradle-shaped or had thin knife-blade rockers. Other early rockers were flat, thick, and so wide that the chair leg could be set into the rocker (Picture 93).

From about 1800 to 1815, the back of the rocker extended several inches more in the rear than in the front of the chair. By 1825 the back rocker extended 4, 6, 8, or even 10 inches in the rear. *The greater the distance the rear rockers extended, the later the rocking chair.*

If the side stretcher is very low, near the rocker, the chair has been converted.

THE BACK OF THE CHAIR

The shape of the back of a rocking chair will also help to date the chair. This information can be useful in dating any wooden country chair, but since rockers were made in limited styles after 1800 it is important to tabulate the changes in chairback designs.

1800   The horizontal slat was placed at the top of the back of the chair. This replaced the frame top that had been used in the eighteenth century (Picture 97).

1800   The step top was used on some chairs (Picture 105).

1810–1820   The headpiece is broader than that used earlier, but it is still a rectangular board.

1820   The rectangular piece was steamed and bent to curve into a more comfortable position. The spindles were bent to fit into the curved back (Picture 99).

1825   The Empire styles begin: the rolling crest or chair top, scrolled and molded headpiece, and curved seat and arms. This is the best period of rocking chairs (Picture 112).

1835   The headpiece became plainer until a standard style developed. The headpiece had a rounded top with two semicircles cut out of the bottom (Picture 117).

All dates refer to the city makers of chairs. The country makers used the styles at a slightly later date.

CHAIR SEAT

The wooden seats of the nineteenth-century rock-

ing chair also went through several stages. They closely correspond with the stages of seat development of the painted fancy chairs of the same period.

1800   The chair seat was a flat piece of wood (Pictures 95 and 101).

1825–1840   The seat was either flat or rolling. The rolled seat was shaped like a cyma curve. The front of the seat rolled down and the back of the seat rolled up. The early rolled seats were made of one piece of pine (Picture 109).

1840–on   The rolled seat was preferred. The seat was made in three pieces, the front and back roll separate from the flat center section of the seat (Pictures 112 and 117).

1840–1845   A cane-seated Boston rocker was made (Picture 119).

OTHER CHARACTERISTICS

The arms of rocking chairs made after 1800 were usually curved. The "factory made" chairs had a typical curved arm. From 1865 to 1890 rocking chairs were mass produced and shipped all over the world. The stencil designs used on the chair can be of some help in identifying the area where the chair was made. (See Chapter 6, "Sheraton Fancy, or Painted Chairs.")

It is possible to date a painted rocking chair from the type of painting or stenciling used in the decoration. (See Chapter 6, "Sheraton Fancy, or Painted Chairs.") A Boston rocker can be dated from the shape of the top slat and from the painting at the curved end of the top slat. The earliest Boston rockers had simple rosettes painted at the curved end, and the later rockers had a curled leaf added to the rosette. The leaf became more and more elaborate until about 1835 when the leaf was painted without the rosette. The leaf evolved into an elaborate scroll by 1845, and the later Boston rockers used a scroll or lines that were reminiscent of a scroll.

Regional Types of Rocking Chairs

The Shaker rocking chair remained the same throughout the eighteenth and nineteenth centuries. (See Chapter 17, "Shaker Furniture.")

The tilting chair was developed by the Shakers, and is closely related to the rocking chair. The bottom of the back two legs of the chair was fitted with a ball-and-socket type of arrangement that permitted the chair to swivel to a tilt. The Shakers also made a rocking chair similar to their wooden, tape-seated chairs (Pictures 85, 102).

NEW ENGLAND ROCKING CHAIRS

In New Hampshire and Vermont the rocking chair of the nineteenth century was a variation of the Windsor with broad spindles. Though the rocking chair in northern New York state and northwest Massachusetts was similar to a Boston rocker, it had an extra cross slat and flat spindles (Picture 105). The Pennsylvania rocking chair had broad rockers and was a very solid-looking chair. It was an adaptation of the Windsor. The late Pennsylvania chairs had one-piece arms that bent down to the seat (Picture 120). The arms of the earlier chairs were made in two pieces, one of which was upright and the other horizontal.

Later Types of Rocking Chairs

The Boston rocker is the most famous style of rocker. It was made in New England about 1840. The chair appeared in all parts of the country and was the most popular rocking-chair style except in parts of Pennsylvania, upper New York, and northern New England (Pictures 112–117). Although it was made in many parts of the country, it was always called a Boston rocker. No one is quite sure how its name developed. Some believe the first Boston rocker was made in Connecticut by Lambert Hitchcock at some time between 1826 and 1829.

The true Boston rocker developed from the Windsor. It had a rolled seat, arms, extended rockers, and usually was stenciled. The back of the chair had seven to nine spindles, and the conventional scroll back was used in the 1840's. The chair was painted and stenciled. (See Chapter 6, "Sheraton Fancy, or Painted Chairs.")

The Salem rocker, made about 1840, is similar to the Boston rocker but with a flat seat and a lower back. Around 1845 the seat was caned. It never attained the popularity of the Boston rocker (Picture 118).

The Little Boston was a rocking chair made about 1850. It had no arms, five spindles, and was smaller than the Boston rocker. The Little Boston, also called a "nurse rocker," "nursing chair," or "sewing rocker," was a popular bedroom chair.

The fiddleback Boston rocker is a very late version having a vase-shaped or fiddle-shaped splat. The chair is considered midwestern and was made in Ohio and Indiana, but some have been traced to makers in Maine and New Hampshire. It was made by machine methods after 1845 (Pictures 120–124).

The mammy bench is a very special type of rocker. It was made about 1820 (Pictures 132–134). The long settee with rockers was a variation of a Windsor with a removable fence at one end. The baby was placed on the settee behind the fence, and the chair was rocked from the other end. That way, it permitted a mother to sew or even shell peas while rocking the baby. When the small "fence" was removed, a plain rocking settee remained for family use.

The mammy bench was made in all parts of the country, and was usually painted.

Later forms of rockers were made, but they cannot be considered or judged as country furniture. The later types were mass-produced chairs of the Victorian era. The Lincoln rocker was made in the late Empire style from 1835 to 1855 (Picture 127). It is a heavy scrolled chair that was named for the chair occupied by Abraham Lincoln when he was shot.

The Sleepy Hollow rocker was made in the Midwest from 1850 to about 1870. It was an overstuffed rocker with exaggerated curves, little beauty, but much comfort.

The American Standard rocker was made about 1870 with some of the first changes in the construction of a rocker. It was made so the base remained stationary while the chair rocked on a spring type of mechanism (Picture 130).

84. *Rocking chair, eighteenth century* Child's rocker of maple with ash slats, made in the mid-eighteenth century in Bergen County, New Jersey. Turned posts and shaped slats appear older than the style of post-and-socket rocker used. Perhaps the rocker was a later addition. (Newark Museum, Newark, New Jersey)

85. *Rocking chair, eighteenth century* Shaker chair made at Mount Lebanon, New York, of maple and stained walnut. Typical Shaker construction is seen in the shaped slat, arm support and knob, and plain posts. The seat is not original. (Index of American Design, Washington, D.C.)

86. *Rocking chair, nineteenth century* Rockers were probably added to the ladder-back chair made in Ohio about 1814. The arms and rockers are walnut, the chair hickory, the seat rush. The rockers are almost as short in back as in front. The low stretcher in front makes it appear the rockers were added. (Index of American Design, Washington, D.C.)

87. *Rocking chair, nineteenth century* A midwestern rocking chair made in the early nineteenth century; it has four narrow-shaped slats. Notice the upright part of the chair that supports the arm, and see the small finials. (Hale House, Western Reserve Historical Society, Cleveland, Ohio)

88. *Rocking chair, nineteenth century* An early ladder-back chair with rockers added. Notice how the curved rockers were placed in a socket in the front two legs and outside the post at the rear two legs. The rockers are longer in the rear. (Old Sturbridge Village, Sturbridge, Massachusetts)

89. *Rocking chair, nineteenth century*   This is a three-rung ladder-back rocker with a hide seat. Notice the extension of the rocker in the rear and how the rocker was socketed to the legs. The rockers date after 1825 and were probably added to the chair. (Howard Country Museum, Kokomo, Indiana)

90. *Rocking chair, nineteenth century*   This is an Illinois chair made about 1825. It was taken across country and given a rawhide seat. The posts of the chair were cut by hand, not turned on a lathe. It was made of oak and hard maple. (Cowlitz County Historical Museum, Kelso, Washington)

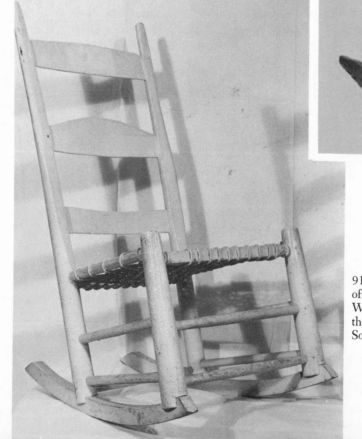

91. *Rocking chair, nineteenth century*   A chair made of soft western maple about 1851 in Cowlitz County, Washington. The seat and rockers were replaced. Note the shaping of the slats. (Cowlitz County Historical Society, Kelso, Washington)

92. *Rocking chair, nineteenth century* This hickory chair, painted gray blue with a split hickory seat, was made in Texas about 1865. The square posts and hickory seat are characteristic of southwestern chairs. The rockers probably were added to a straight chair. (Index of American Design, Washington, D.C.)

93. *Rocking chair, late nineteenth century* Hickory and white oak were used in this Texas-made rocking chair of about 1870. It is a crude handmade chair with heavy legs set into thick rockers. The chairback is that of a "kitchen" chair. (Index of American Design, Washington, D.C.)

94. *Rocking chair, nineteenth century* This Canadian chair was made in western Ontario, Canada. It is made from painted ash with a splint seat. Notice the very unusual proportions of the chairback. (Upper Canada Village, Morrisburg, Ontario, Canada)

95. *Rocking chair, eighteenth century*   This comb-back Windsor rocker was made in New England between 1790 and 1810. It has a comb back and arms. The chair was painted deep red. (Old Sturbridge Village, Sturbridge, Massachusetts)

96. *Rocking chair, nineteenth century*   This comb-back Windsor, made about 1820 in Ohio, was originally painted black. Notice the long extension at the rear of the rocker. (Summit County Historical Society, Akron, Ohio)

98. *Rocking chair, date unknown* A unique rocker found in Delaware. The writing arm is attached to a seat extension. The rockers were probably added to a straight chair. The chair has an unusual back spindle arrangement. It was probably made in the late eighteenth or early nineteenth century. (Index of American Design, Washington, D.C.)

97. *Rocking chair, nineteenth century* This type of Windsor rocker of maple with pine seat is called a "Burlington" or "Shelburne" rocker. It was made by Saxton in Shelburne, Vermont, between 1790 and 1820. (Shelburne Museum, Inc. Photographer, Einars J. Mengis)

99. *Rocking chair, early nineteenth century* A seven-spindle pine rocker painted black. The horizontal slat is the almost rectangular shape bent to fit the curved back popular in 1820. The curved arms, saddle seat, and bent spindles show how the Boston Rocker developed from this type of chair. (Index of American Design, Washington, D.C.)

45

100. *Rocking chair, early nineteenth century* Six fat spindles are curved to fit into the scrolled headpiece. The long extension on the rockers, the turned legs and saddle seat all indicate a chair of the transitional type from Windsor to Boston Rocker made about 1825–1835. (Pensacola Historical Society, Pensacola, Florida)

101. *Rocking chair, nineteenth century* A poplar and hickory chair made about 1830–1840, near Pennsylvania. The six-spindle back and wide crest are typical of that period. (Index of American Design, Washington, D.C.)

102. *Shaker rocker, late nineteenth century* A spindle-back rocker and stool made at Mount Lebanon, New York, by the Shakers in the late nineteenth or twentieth century. Notice the mushroom ends on the arms. (Shaker Museum, Old Chatham, New York)

103. *Rocking chair, nineteenth century* Walnut was used for this chair with a rawhide seat found in Texas. The turned arms and stretchers and general proportion of the chair seem to indicate a chair-maker with skill who produced a complete rocking chair, and did not just add rockers to an already made chair. (Index of American Design, Washington, D.C.)

47

104. *Rocking chair, stenciled, nineteenth century.* A painted and stenciled comb-back Windsor chair made about 1800. Notice the well-shaped comb, the short end at the rear of the rocker, and the typical Windsor spindles. The stiles are flattened and decorated. (Wayne County Division of Archives and History, Lyons, New York)

106. *Rocking chair, early nineteenth century* A comb-back painted rocker of the type made in New Hampshire and northern New England about 1825–1830. The broad flattened arrow spindles, early type of horizontal slat, and shallow saddle seat are all characteristics of this type of rocking chair. (Mr. and Mrs. R. N. Williams II, Philadelphia, Pennsylvania)

105. *Rocking chair, early nineteenth century* A painted and stenciled chair of the type made in New York and western New England about 1830. The flattened arrow-type spindles and extra crosspieces are typical. (Wayne County Division of Archives and History, Lyons, New York)

108. *Arrow-back rocker, nineteenth century*
An Ohio-made black pointed chair of the 1840
period. Notice the height of the back and the
lack of arms. (Summit County Historical Society, Akron, Ohio)

107. *Rocking chair, nineteenth century* A comb-back rocker
with flattened arrow spindles similar to those of the New England rockers but found in Canada. Notice the shaping of the
seat and the generally heavier proportions of the chair. (Upper
Canada Village, Morrisburg, Ontario, Canada)

109. *Arrow-back rocker, nineteenth
century* Another Ohio-made black-
painted armless rocker made about
1825. This chair is said to be the prod-
uct of the Shaker community at Lebanon, Ohio. (Index of American Design, Washington, D.C.)

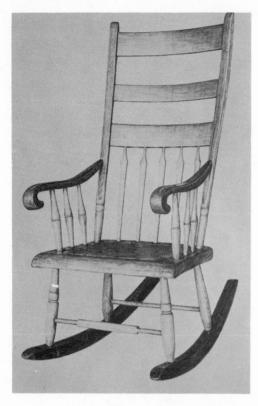

110. *Arrow-back rocking chair, nineteenth century* Hickory back, walnut rockers and oak arms were used in this Iowa-made chair about 1875. Notice that the legs are set into the thick rockers. (Index of American Design, Washington, D.C.)

111. *Rocking chair, nineteenth century* An arrow-back rocker made of soft maple with a basswood seat, made in Canada about 1835. The chair was painted black with free-hand decorations in yellow and green. (Upper Canada Village, Morrisburg, Ontario, Canada) BOTTOM LEFT

112. *Boston rocker, early nineteenth century* A Boston rocker of maple and pine painted, grained, and stenciled. It was made in Boston, Massachusetts, about 1835. Typical rolling crest and headpiece, curved seat, arms and spindles, turned legs and stencil decoration appear on this excellent chair. (Courtesy of the Henry Ford Museum, Dearborn, Michigan) BOTTOM RIGHT

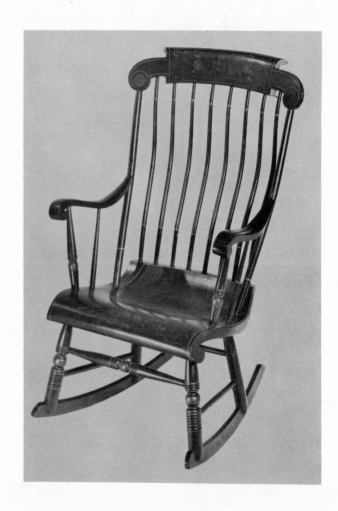

114. *Boston rocker, nineteenth century* A yellow rocker with gold decorations, probably made in Wilmington, Delaware. The style of the chair is of the 1830 period. (Index of American Design, Washington, D.C.)

113. *Boston rocker, nineteenth century* A black-painted rocker decorated with a golden-brown flower basket. The shape of top slat and the rosette-and-leaf design indicate a date of about 1830. (Index of American Design, Washington, D.C.)

115. *Boston rocker, nineteenth century* This black-painted chair with graining has gold and red stenciling of a scene and yellow striping. The seat is stenciled "Siutzen sie sich" in gold. It was brought to Ohio, probably from Pennsylvania, in the 1830's. (Summit County Historical Society, Akron, Ohio)

116. *Boston rocker, nineteenth century* The unusual head-piece, plain legs, and simple stencil decoration date this Boston rocker after 1835. (Bell photo, Lansing, Michigan)

117. *Boston rocker, nineteenth century* This birch rocker has the characteristic rolled seat, curved arms, seven spindles, and simple decorations. The standard headpiece is the type used after 1835. This chair is very narrow; a fat person can not sit on it. The seat is low. It was probably made about 1840. (Mrs. Lilian Umbaugh, Kelso, Washington)

118. *Salem rocker, nineteenth century* This chair may be called either a Boston rocker with a flat seat or a Salem rocker. Characteristic headpiece of the 1825–1835 period and seven spindles show it was made about 1830. Note that the seat curves in front and is neither the rolled seat of the Boston rocker nor the flat seat of the Windsor. (Wayne County Division of Archives and History, Lyons, New York)

119. *Stenciled rocker, nineteenth century* The elaborately stenciled rocker is painted black and has gilt and colored decorations. It was made in New England about 1840–1860. The headpiece with a step top is a design from an earlier period. (Index of American Design, Washington, D.C.)

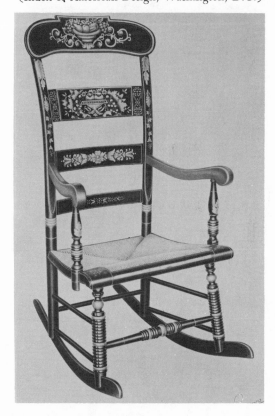

120. *Fiddleback Boston rocker, nineteenth century* A hard maple chair with an oval painting of an outdoor scene. The arms of one piece that bent to the seat are considered Pennsylvania in origin. The chair was made about 1850. (Mrs. Lilian Umbaugh, Kelso, Washington)

53

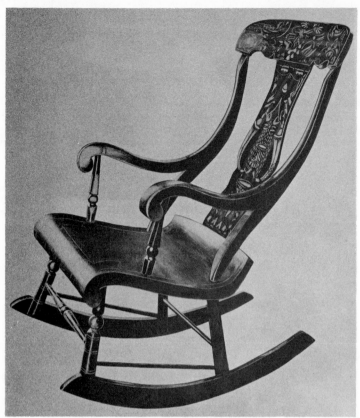

121. *Fiddleback rocker, nineteenth century* A black-painted chair stenciled with gold, red, and white. The chair was purchased in Marine, Minnesota, about 1875. It has the typical fiddleback arms, legs, and extended rocker in rear. (Index of American Design, Washington, D.C.)

123. *Fiddleback Boston rocker, nineteenth century* The center of the rocker is a lyre-shaped piece. This style of rocker was made about 1850. (Howard County Museum, Kokomo, Indiana)

124. *Fiddleback Boston rocker, nineteenth century* A lyre-shaped center splat and two spindles appear on this unusual oak and soft maple chair found in Washington in the 1880's. Note the length of the rocker in the rear and the conventional headpiece. (Cowlitz County Historical Museum, Kelso, Washington)

125. *Victorian caned rocker, nineteenth century*
A mahogany-finished rocker with a deep crowning rail and scalloped edge made about 1860. It has a caned seat and back. (Taylor and Dull, photography)

126. *Rocking chair, nineteenth century* This maple rocker was made about 1845 in eastern Ontario, Canada. One spindle is missing from the center of the back. Notice the very elaborate curve of the arm. (Upper Canada Village, Morrisburg, Ontario, Canada)

127. *Gooseneck rocker, nineteenth century*
This upholstered rocker was called a gooseneck rocker or Lincoln rocker. It was made about 1860. (Old Court House Museum, Vicksburg, Mississippi)

128. *Rocking chair, late nineteenth century*
A red-painted rocker made in Texas about 1895. The square posts are characteristic of the area. Note the footrest and the number of stretchers. This is probably a unique example. (Index of American Design, Washington, D.C.)

129. *Rocking chair, late nineteenth century*
A folding rocking chair made of hard maple with beech rockers. It was made in the 1880's in many factories. This is not an example of country furniture but a part of the history of the rocking chair. (Cowlitz County Historical Museum, Kelso, Washington)

130. *Platform rocker, nineteenth century* An oak chair made in the style of the platform or stationary rocker popular in the 1880's. It was sometimes called a patent or spring rocker. This style was developed to keep the rocker from wearing out the carpet. (Index of American Design, Washington, D.C.)

131. *Rocking chair with headrest, nineteenth century* This black-painted chair was used by Brigham Young. It is a spool-turned chair with unusual "wings" for a headrest. The origin is unknown, but it was used in Salt Lake City, Utah. (Index of American Design, Washington, D.C.)

56

132. *Mammy bench, nineteenth century* This combination rocker and cradle is made in the late "Hitchcock" style, about 1835. It was painted reddish black. The gate is removable. The term "mammy rocker" was probably not used in New England, although today all these combination rocking benches are called by that name. (Old Sturbridge Village, Sturbridge, Massachusetts)

133. *Mammy bench, nineteenth century* Mammy bench, cradle settee, or rocker were all names for this type of bench rocker. It was made about 1830 of painted hardwood. This type of bench was made with the front gate removable. (Index of American Design, Washington, D.C.; Monmouth Historical Society, New Jersey)

134. *Mammy bench, nineteenth century* A maple and pine rocking bench painted black with gold trim. It was made about 1820 to 1840. Notice that there are twelve spindles in the back, not the usual uneven number. (Blount Mansion, Knoxville, Tennessee)

135. *Mammy bench, nineteenth century* A midwestern version of the mammy bench made about 1840. Notice the arrow-shaped spindles. (Hale House, Western Reserve Historical Society, Cleveland, Ohio)

6

Chairs—Sheraton Fancy, or Painted

THE FORMAL furniture styles in England during the late eighteenth century were Sheraton in design and were influential in producing in America the Hitchcock type of chair. Also, because the Adams style of architecture in England was both formal and delicate, designers felt that white and pastel furniture was necessary to avoid overpowering the delicate woodwork of the rooms. Thus the first fancy painted chairs came into prominence.

The first Sheraton fancy chairs in America were brought from England. In 1797 a chairmaker in New York City advertised as a fancy chairmaker from London. His pieces were the painted chairs so popular in England. Because these early chairs were very expensive, only wealthy colonists could afford them. Later, during the nineteenth century, fancy chairs were mass produced, with the result that prices drastically dropped and the painted chair became the favorite of the average man.

Dining room, bedroom, parlor, bar, hotel, and even the river steamboat were furnished with painted chairs. They became so popular in river communities that they were called "steamboat fancies" in some parts of the country. One of the most famous patterns was the "Cleopatra-barge chair," which was made especially for use on a riverboat.

Very few of the early chairs were labeled by the makers. They were first made in the East (especially in New York City and in Massachusetts), then in Pittsburgh, Cincinnati, other Ohio towns, and Hitchcocksville, Connecticut.

Fancy Chairs

The history of the painted fancy chair can be divided into three periods the earliest of which dates from 1800 to 1820, the middle, or the period of stenciling, ranged from 1815 to 1835, and the late, or decadent, period was from 1835 to 1845.

Early period chairs (Pictures 136, 137, 186) resembled the formal chairs from England, with a square seat and a narrow band at the front. The rounded legs were straight up and down, and the banisters and spindles were delicately turned for decoration, with the turnings often decorated with gilt. When the banisters were shaped, they resembled the Adams style of chairs. Some stretchers were also shaped. The back of the fancy chair did *not* touch the seat at any period. Only the uprights ever joined the back to the seat.

The top of the back of the chair (crest) often had a shape called a handgrip (Picture 138), roll top, or pillow. It was larger at the center.

The early period chairs were painted brown, pale yellow, buff, or artificially grained to resemble unpainted wood. Skilled artists applied the decoration with a brush, not by the use of a stencil. The handgrip, sides, and front of the seat were decorated with gold leaf. Gold stripes were painted all around the legs and posts.

A slight change occurred about 1810 to 1815 when the crest rail became wider and some horizontal slats were cut into odd shapes. The upright stiles were flattened on the front, and the stretchers were shaped so that decorations could be applied. By 1815 the legs were no longer straight but had a slight splay at the base (Picture 150).

Many more changes took place during the last half (1810–1820) of the early period of painted chairs. Stencils were used with separate units cut for each piece of fruit or leaf and were used together to form a larger design.

The back of the chair took on a new character. Fretwork and crossbands were used in the backs and stretchers. The cutout shapes in the center back became more elaborate. By the end of the period, chairs with the famous eagle (Pictures 150, 151), shield, and cornucopia (Picture 148) backs were popular in all parts of the country.

The rounded front on a chair seat generally indicates manufacture before 1820. After that date this style gave way to plank seats or roll-front seats. While bamboo turnings had been used on earlier Windsor chairs, it was with the fancy chair that the bamboo look gained great favor (Pictures 141, 162). The front legs were rounded; the back legs were either square or splayed. The seats were rounded, with wider bands appearing at the front edge or apron of the chair.

The rush seat was the first to appear, followed by the cane seat. The top slat became heavier and the main slat remained plain, but the handgrip, pillow, and roll shapes were still popular for the crest. A turned ball was often at the top of the leg where it joined the seat (Picture 156).

Oak leaves, grapes, flowers, shells, or landscapes were stenciled on the chairs. The famous Cleopatra-barge chairs were painted green and gold, with a landscape on the large back panel.

The chairs were made from maple, beech, or curly maple.

Period of Stenciling 1820–1830

The laborsaving devices of this period influenced many of the furniture makers. Eager to turn out a low-cost chair, they began a search for ways to save labor costs. The stencil was an ideal solution. After it was designed and cut by a skilled artist, any trained woman could take over. Thus, only one artist—not many—was needed at a factory. This was a period of heavier furniture designs in Europe and of formal American furnishings. Now shapes of the Empire period became popular with the chairmakers, and the stenciled designs appeared on true Empire-style pieces.

The chair colors became darker as the chairs became heavier. During the Empire period the chairs were painted dark green, brown, vermilion, pumpkin, yellow, or black, with many of them painted with black on red graining that resembled unpainted wood (Pictures 146, 147). Wider gold striping was placed on the front of the post; it did not continue to the back.

All the designs were applied with stencils. Copper and gold were added to the gold and silver that were used during the earlier periods. Red was used in the center of the flowers.

About 1830 transparent oil colors were painted over the stenciled flower designs, with black and green being used for leaves or scrolls on some pieces.

The center slat of the chair was simplified from the ornate eagle and cornucopia and became the turtleback (Picture 149), button back (Picture 153), or plain slat (Picture 154).

The leg of the chair was slightly bent in front, with ring-turned decorations (Picture 153).

It is possible to help date the chairs by the stencil decoration used. If the design shows a grapevine with one or two tendrils, it is said to be an 1825 pattern. Designs with many tendrils appeared about 1830, and those with large and unnatural tendrils would date the design after 1835. Many other technicalities of design, such as the type of paint, placement of border, and colors, will also help to date a chair.

The Late, or Decadent, Period—After 1835

The name "decadent period" would indicate disapproval of the workmanship of the day. This is hardly a fair criticism. It would be better to point out that the chairs were less artistic because they were mass produced. The painting, quickly done by untrained artists, was never intended as great art. The chairs, however, were among the most popular, including the late Hitchcock type, the Boston rocker (see Chapter 5, "Chairs—Rocking"), and the products of the midwestern chairmakers.

The late-period chairs were heavier and less refined than those of the earlier period. True Empire designs were the vogue. The turtleback and button back gave way to the fiddleback or banister-back about 1840. The simple turned chair was made about 1850 to 1860. Early chairs had rush seats; later ones had cane seats. The wooden or plank seat was in style by the 1850's. The latest of the painted chairs with decorations were made about 1840. Most of the chairs were painted with black over red or yellow, which simulated graining. The stenciled patterns of colored overtones, landscapes, or freehand flowers were not of the quality of the early painted chairs.

The striping was done with gold paint, except that the very late chairs were painted with yellow or green stripes. Gold, silver, orange, and other oil paints were used with a minimum of shading.

The chairs were made from maple or hickory wood.

If this type of chair is found without paint, it usually means that a recent owner has stripped it down, making it less interesting to the collector.

Regional Differences in Style

PENNSYLVANIA

The Pennsylvania painted chairs of about 1825 (Pictures 171, 172, 173) were of a highly individual style. The angel-wing top slat had a sturdy, gay appearance with its more curved version of a chair crest.

The balloon-back chair was another unusual Pennsylvania design. The chair was painted dark green, dark red, brown, or other colors, and stenciled with bronze powder, then washed with a bright transparent color. The rounded back is almost exclusively a Pennsylvania design. A few chairs have been found outside Pennsylvania with a similar back, but we believe that they were made near Pennsylvania or by Pennsylvania workmen who migrated.

A variation of the arrow-back chair (Picture 175) is another Pennsylvania style. The arrows were wide and heavy; the plank seat was thicker than those on other chairs. The rocking chairs had rolled front seats.

All the Pennsylvania styles had simpler, more bulbous turnings than those of other areas. The legs were heavier, more splayed, and the striping was wider.

The Pennsylvania furniture was a peasant style with the backgrounds of the painted chairs in pale salmon pink, pale gray, green, yellow, dark red, or brown. Crude, bold flowers, birds, stars, and geometric shapes were brightly painted on the chairs. A few chairs had gold added for decoration. The Pennsylvania Germans sometimes painted chairs that were not made by them.

The unpainted wooden chairs of Pennsylvania origin were made from cherry, walnut, bird's-eye or curly maple.

WINDSOR

When the fancy chair became popular during the 1800's, some Windsor chairmakers decided to start painting their Windsors. (See Chapter 8, "Chairs—Windsor.") As the form gradually changed, it became easier to add decorations to a chair. The top slat became broader. Between 1800 and 1825 the step-down slat was developed. The arrow spindles were made about 1810, with early chairs having many arrows much like the early spindles on a Windsor chair. By the middle of the nineteenth century, only three large arrows remained to remind one of the original form.

Bamboo spindles formed another variation of the Windsor. Five spindles with a wide top and flattened stiles were first used. By 1830 there were four spindles and a plank seat in the traditional form of an arrow-back chair.

REGIONAL SOUTH

During the eighteenth century most of the furniture from Baltimore and other southern cities was formal, elegant, and well made. When the early painted chairs were made in the South (1800 to 1825), the workmen carried on this tradition of fine furniture. The chairs were delicate and formal. By 1825, however, the country feeling invaded the works of the Baltimore maker. The top slat became more sturdy and wide, and extended beyond the side spindles that held it to the seat. This extension of the top slat is a good indication of a southern maker (Picture 178).

As a result of the Directoire influence, the lines at the side of the seat were curved. This is a thickening of the uprights when they touch the seat. This curved bulge levels to the seat. The best indications of a southern chair are straight legs, decorated turnings, and cane seats.

The painting on a southern chair was usually more elaborate than on those of other makers. Gold-leaf and freehand bronze stenciling was popular. The striping was in gold, with the designs often placed to resemble the brass mounts found on formal French chairs.

THE REAL HITCHCOCK CHAIR (Pictures 154, 156)

The name Hitchcock has become a generic term meaning any painted chair of the type made by the Hitchcock factory during the nineteenth century.

There was a Mr. Hitchcock and there was a true Hitchcock chair, so it is wrong to call any chair not labeled or otherwise verified a Hitchcock chair. It is commonly called a Hitchcock-*type* chair.

A Hitchcock chair could be one of several types. The wooden painted chair had turned front legs that were joined by a turned rung. The back of the chair was curved, and the seat was wider at the front than at the back. The front of the seat was rounded. Hitchcock made chairs with several different cutout back slats, Boston rockers, cradle settees or mammy benches, and children's chairs. It has been said that Hitchcock was one of the first to make rocking chairs in a factory.

Lambert Hitchcock was born in 1795 at Cheshire, Connecticut. He moved to Barkhamsted, Connecticut, in 1818, where he established a chair factory. At first he made parts of chairs that were shipped to Charleston, South Carolina, and other southern towns. By 1821 his factory had become so important to the community that the name Hitchcocksville was given to the area near the factory.

Hitchcock began making chairs that he sold in large quantities at a reasonable price. The first chairs had rush seats, but the later ones were made with cane and solid wooden seats. These were marked "L. Hitchcock, Hitchcocks-ville, Connecticut, Warranted."

He built a larger, brick factory in 1826 where one hundred workers made chairs. Children painted the first coat of paint, always red, on the wooden chair frames; then the women decorated them.

After Hitchcock was forced into bankruptcy in 1829 his financial problems were solved by Arba Alford, Jr., who became a partner in the firm. The chairs were then labeled "Hitchcock, Alford & Co., Warranted." Lambert Hitchcock married his partner's sister. Arba Alford ran the production at the chair factory while Lambert Hitchcock traveled extensively selling their painted chairs.

About 1843 Lambert Hitchcock left the company to start a new factory in Unionville, Connecticut. The chairs were the same in construction and decoration as those made before, but now the label read, "Lambert Hitchcock, Unionville, Connecticut." His former partner, Arba Alford, went into business with his brother, Alfred, making the same type of chairs and using the label "Alford & Company." Lambert Hitchcock died in 1852.

Hitchcock chairs are still being made in Riverton (Hitchcocksville), Connecticut. These chairs are marked with the stencil signature first used by the factory, but the N is cut backward as it was on a few of the early chairs. Each new chair is also branded with the letters "H.C. Co." underneath the front seat.

136. *Sheraton fancy chair, Greek revival style, early nineteenth century* A shaped shield-back side chair of painted and gilded wood. (Metropolitan Museum of Art; Rogers Fund, 1954)

137. *Sheraton fancy chair, nineteenth century* A red-brown chair made about 1800–1810 and decorated with gilt decorations. The rush seat is painted white. Notice the cut-out back. (Smithsonian Institution, United States National Museum, Washington, D.C.)

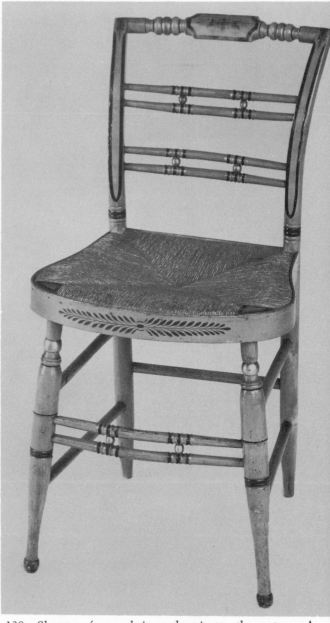

138. *Sheraton fancy chair, early nineteenth century* A maple chair painted yellow and trimmed in green and gilt, made about 1800–1820. Note the rounded chair seat, handle-grip crest, and straight angle of the legs. (Courtesy of the Henry Ford Museum, Dearborn, Michigan)

139. *Sheraton fancy chair, nineteenth century*
A painted chair made with a rush seat. The decorations are stenciled and freehand. Note the back of the chair, the wide top rail, and the slight splay to the leg. (Metropolitan Museum of Art; bequest of Mrs. Maria P. James, 1911)

140. *Sheraton fancy chair, nineteenth century*
This chair is thought to be Canadian because of the Prince of Wales feather and coronet used on the back. It was found in Belleville, Ontario, and is one of a set of eight chairs made about 1830. The painting has been restored on this chair, although another in the set has the original paint. (Upper Canada Village, Morrisburg, Ontario)

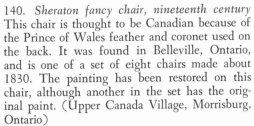

141. *Sheraton fancy chair, early nineteenth century*
A bamboo-turned chair painted and gilded, with a
cane seat. This type of chair was influenced by the
English Sheraton styles. (Metropolitan Museum of
Art; bequest of Maria P. James, 1911)

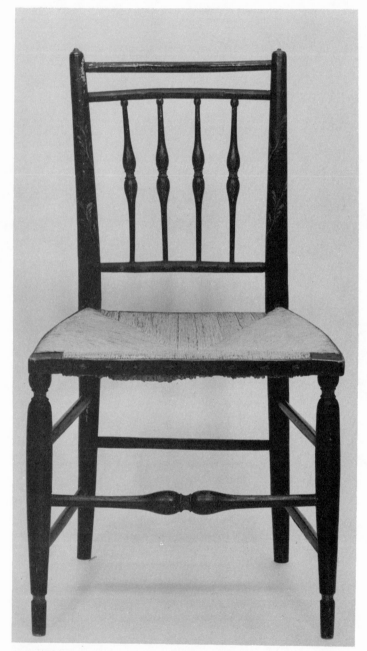

142. *Sheraton fancy chair, early nineteenth century* This black-
painted chair was probably made in New England. It has a simple
leaf decoration in yellow and a rush seat. (Old Sturbridge Village,
Sturbridge, Massachusetts)

143. *Sheraton fancy chairs, early nineteenth century* Yellow-painted chairs with black stripings and a design of grape leaves and tendrils. The plank seat and general shape of chair show both Sheraton and Windsor origins. (Shelburne Museum, Shelburne, Vermont)

144. *Painted chair, nineteenth century* The shaped slat and top slat show the Empire influence on the American chair. This chair is dark green with gold striping, and belonged to E. I. du Pont, who died in 1834. (Hagley Museum, Wilmington, Delaware)

145. *Fancy chair, nineteenth century* A Hudson Valley chair painted black with gold leaf, burnt umber and red decorations. Note the square seat, cutout back, and straight angle of the front legs. The curve where the stile joins the seat is similar to the Baltimore style. (New York State Historical Association, Cooperstown, New York)

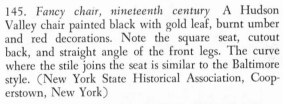

146. *Painted chair, Pennsylvania, nineteenth century*
A maple chair painted red and brown to imitate graining, with olive, yellow, and black trim. It was made in Pennsylvania about 1830–1840. (Courtesy of Henry Ford Museum, Dearborn, Michigan)

148. *Stenciled chair, nineteenth century* A gold-and-black-stenciled chair made in New York City about 1825. The cornucopia main slat, thin slat, roll top, and painted graining are typical. (Courtesy of The New-York Historical Society, New York City)

147. *Detail, Pennsylvania chair* The pillow-shaped handgrip with painted bird decoration of the preceding chair. Notice the painted graining. (Courtesy of Henry Ford Museum, Dearborn, Michigan)

149. *Hitchcock chair, nineteenth century* A crown-top turtleback chair made about 1830, attributed to the Hitchcock factory. (Rhode Island Historical Society)

150. *Hitchcock-style chair, nineteenth century* A cutout eagle-back chair made about 1825–1830. The chair is painted black, with decorations in gold leaf and yellow paint. (Old Sturbridge Village, Sturbridge, Massachusetts)

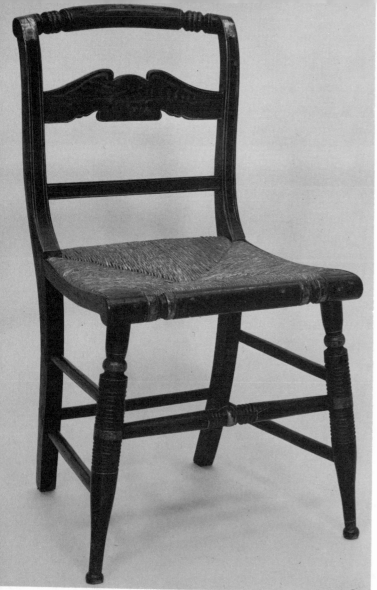

151. *Painted side chair, nineteenth century* The back splat of this chair is cut and decorated and painted black with decorations in gold and yellow. It was made about 1825–1830. (Old Sturbridge Village, Sturbridge, Massachusetts)

153. *Hitchcock-style chair, nineteenth century* The curved back and curved seat made this type of wooden chair comfortable. Notice the angle of the rear legs. The button back and roll top with narrow second slat indicate that this painted, stenciled chair was made about 1830. (Courtesy of the Art Institute of Chicago)

152. *Hitchcock-style side chair, nineteenth century* The diamond-shaped splat of this chair is stenciled with gold-leaf decoration, birds, flowers, and leaves. It was made about 1825–1830. (Old Sturbridge Village, Sturbridge, Massachusetts)

154. *Hitchcock chair, nineteenth century* A painted and stenciled chair made by L. Hitchcock, Hitchcockville, Connecticut, about 1820. The roll top, plain main slat and narrow slat, and arrow designs on stiles are found on other Hitchcock chairs. (Courtesy of the Brooklyn Museum)

155. *Painted chair, nineteenth century* A black-painted chair with stencil decorations made about 1820. Notice the typical pillow-grip crest and turned legs. The seat is rounded. (The Smithsonian Institution, United States National Museum, Washington, D.C.)

156. *Hitchcock chair, nineteenth century* A signed chair, painted black with stencil decorations, made about 1832–1840 in Riverton, Connecticut. On the back it is signed "Hitchcock, Alfred and Co." Note the hand-grip crest and rectangular center slat. (Index of American Design, Washington, D.C.)

157. *Stenciled chairs, nineteenth century* A pair of painted and stenciled chairs made with pillow-shape handgrip top and plain main slat. The border design on the main slat is interesting. (Woodstock Historical Society, Inc., Woodstock, Vermont)

158. *Stenciled chair, nineteenth century* Whitewood and oak were painted green with gold and bronze stenciling in this elaborate chair made in Killingworth, Connecticut, by John Hull in 1829. Fruit and flower designs were cut in separate stencils, then assembled. The rectangular crest and center slat, the skillful stenciling, the plank seat, and simplified legs indicate a chair made near the end of the "period of stenciling." (Index of American Design, Washington, D.C.)

159. *Decorated armchair, nineteenth century* A Canadian chair made of soft maple and basswood, painted black with a stencil design of red bunches of grapes. This chair was made in eastern Ontario, Canada, about 1835. (Upper Canada Village, Morrisburg, Ontario)

161. *Hitchcock-type chair, nineteenth century* A two-slat chair of maple and birch painted black with gold-leaf decorations. It has a rush seat. This two-slat chair dates about 1840–1860. (Index of American Design, Washington, D.C.)

160. *Stenciled chair, nineteenth century* This painted side chair, made about 1830, has a plank seat. It is painted to resemble wood graining. The back splat has a stenciled basket of fruit decoration. (Old Sturbridge Village, Sturbridge, Massachusetts)

162. *Victorian fancy chair, nineteenth century* A black-painted chair made with gold-leaf floral designs on seat, back, and legs, bamboo turnings and birdcage back. This style was popular from 1840–1880. (Index of American Design, Washington, D.C.)

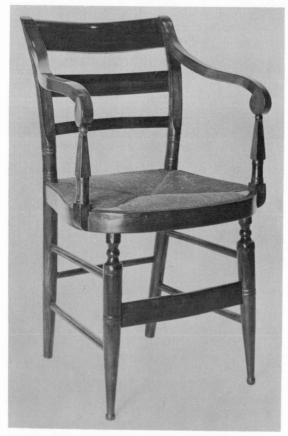

163. *Fancy Sheraton chair, nineteenth century*
This undecorated chair is of the typical shape
of the nineteenth century. Notice the curved
arm. (Rhode Island Historical Society)

164. *Sheraton fancy chairs, early nineteenth
century* This maple and ash chair is painted
and grained. It was probably made in New
England about 1810–1820. The slightly splayed
legs and cutout crossband are unusual. (John
Walton)

165. *Hitchcock side chairs, nineteenth
century* A side chair and armchair
made with cutout slats and unusual roll
top. Notice how the arms are added to
a side chair. (Rhode Island Historical
Society)

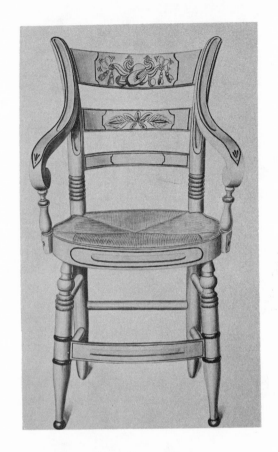

166. *Stenciled chair, nineteenth century* An armchair painted to simulate rosewood, made about 1820. The pillow-shape handgrip top, diamond-shaped slat, and arm style are found on many Pennsylvania chairs. A border design, similar to this one, is usually found on the diamond-shaped slat. (Taylor and Dull, photography) TOP

167. *Sheraton fancy chair, nineteenth century* A yellow-painted chair made with three back slats of graduated sizes. The style and decorations indicate 1815–1820 manufacture. It is attributed to an Ohio maker. (Index of American Design, Washington, D.C.) CENTER

168. *Painted armchair, nineteenth century* A pine and maple chair painted red and black with leaf-and-scroll decoration in yellow and black. It was made and signed (on a paper label) "Joel Pratt, Jun., Sterling, Mass." The style is from 1830–1840. (Courtesy of the Henry Ford Museum, Dearborn, Michigan) BOTTOM

169. *Painted armchair, nineteenth century*
A wooden chair painted red with yellow stripes and cane seat, made in Salt Lake City, Utah, about 1856. It is said it was owned by Brigham Young. Note the square uprights on the back. (Index of American Design, Washington, D.C.)

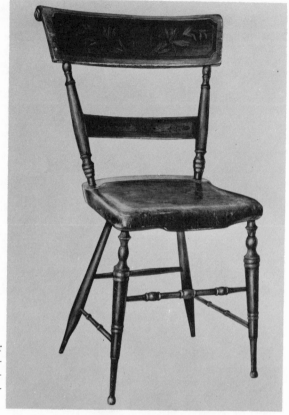

170. *Painted chair, nineteenth century* A poplar-wood chair painted red with gold-leaf and green decorations, made in Lancaster, Ohio. The plank seat and wide top slat indicate manufacture about 1835. It was designed and made by a local cabinetmaker. (Index of American Design, Washington, D.C.)

171. *Stenciled chair, Pennsylvania, nineteenth century* This chair, made in Pennsylvania about 1830–1840, is painted light olive green with gold stenciled morning glories. The typical back has two slats and spindles with knobs. (Courtesy of the New-York Historical Society, New York City)

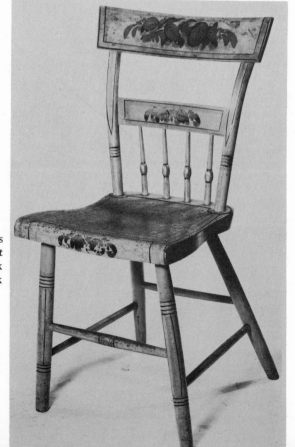

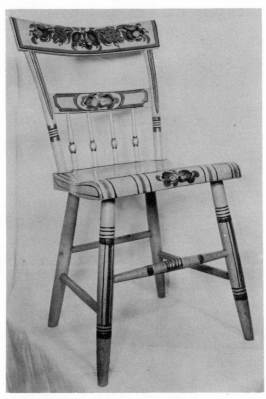

172. *Painted chair, nineteenth century* A Pennsylvania-style chair with typical decorations, of the style used about 1840. Notice that the front of the plank seat is decorated. (Index of American Design, Washington, D.C.)

173. *Painted chair, Pennsylvania, nineteenth century* A maple and pine chair painted green with red and yellow trim. It was made in Pennsylvania about 1810–1835. Note that there are just three large arrows in the back. (Courtesy of the Henry Ford Museum, Dearborn, Michigan)

174. *Painted arrow-back side chair, nineteenth century* This maple chair with a basswood seat was made in eastern Ontario, Canada. Many Canadian chairs used this combination of wood instead of the pine used in the United States. The chair is green with yellow lining and red and gilt stencils. (Upper Canada Village, Morrisburg, Ontario)

175. *Painted arrow-back side chair, nineteenth century* This chair was painted black with a stencil decoration in gilt and silver gilt. It was made in eastern Ontario of the typical soft maple and basswood combination. Notice the rolled seat front. (Upper Canada Village, Morrisburg, Ontario) BOTTOM RIGHT

176. *Stenciled slat-back Windsor chair, nineteenth century* A late chair made about 1825. The arrow-shaped spindles and three slats in the back, shallow saddle seat, simple legs, and simple stencil decoration all indicate the first quarter of the nineteenth century. (Wayne County Division of Archives and History, Lyons, New York)

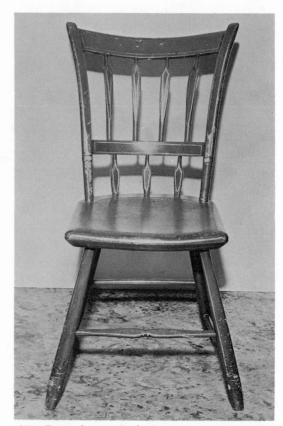

177. *Painted arrow-back chair, nineteenth century* A red-painted chair made about 1830, with striping as the only decoration. The plank seat, two rows of arrow spindles, and plain legs indicate the date of manufacture. The shaped stretcher in front is unusual. (Detroit Historical Society)

178. *Southern chair, nineteenth century* A light mahogany chair made with natural finish and decorations. The back is joined to the chair in typical southern style. This chair belonged to Samuel Chase (signer of the Declaration of Independence) who died in 1811. It was made near Annapolis, Maryland. (Index of American Design, Washington, D.C.)

FROM LEFT TO RIGHT
Painted chairs, Zoar, Ohio. Three painted chairs from the Zoarite Community made
between 1830 and 1870: 179. This side chair is maple painted brownish orange and
stenciled "From/ Geo. Deckman/ Manufacturer/ Bedsteads, Bureaus/ Tables & c./ Mal-
vern, O." 180. A maple chair with pine seat, painted black with off-white and gold trim
and stenciled fruit-and-flower design in rose. It was made by Jule Chalk. (179 and 180
Courtesy of the Henry Ford Museum, Dearborn, Michigan.) 181. A chair similar to 180,
but with different painted decorations. (Index of American Design, Washington, D.C.)

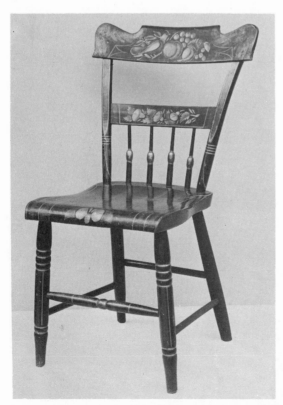

182. *Painted chair, Pennsylvania, nineteenth
century* Made about 1825, with four spindles
and the flattened upright. Notice the angel-wing
slat at the top of the back. (Metropolitan Museum of Art; gift of Mrs. Robert W. de Forest,
1933)

183. *Painted chair, Pennsylvania, nineteenth century* The chair is painted in imitation of rosewood with a tulip design. It was made about 1842 with a modified angel-wing top slat. (Index of American Design, Washington, D.C.)

184. *Painted side chair, nineteenth century* The brand "S. Haskin" appears underneath the seat of this chair. He worked in Lyn, Ontario, Canada. The chair is painted with a light color and shellac glaze to resemble tiger maple. The freehand painted decorations are black. This Canadian chair has many features that resemble Pennsylvania German chairs. (Upper Canada Village, Morrisburg, Ontario)

185. *Painted chair, mid-nineteenth century* The pine seat and oak back of this miniature chair (16½ inches high) are painted with typical Victorian decorations. (Courtesy of Art Institute of Chicago)

187. *Painted settee, nineteenth century* A yellow-painted Windsor settee with black rings and pink roses, painted to imitate bamboo. It was made about 1825. (Taylor and Dull, photography)

186. *Painted settee, early nineteenth century* This settee was made about 1800 in New York City of chestnut wood painted red, cream, pink, white, and green on a black background. It is typical of the formal Adam and Hepplewhite styles. Notice the square leg. (Index of American Design, Washington, D.C.)

188. *Painted settee, nineteenth century*
A gray settee with colored flowers and
geometric designs, made about 1830.
Though the origin is unknown, it is probably the New England area or Pennsylvania. (Index of American Design, Washington, D.C.)

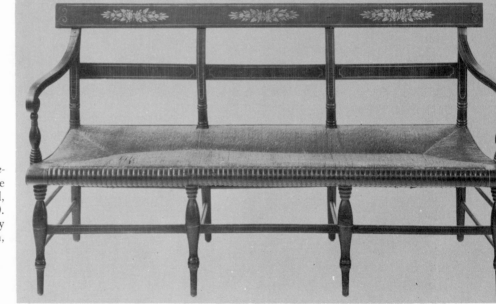

189. *Painted settee, nineteenth century* This maple
settee was painted, grained,
and stenciled about 1820.
Note the seat front. (Courtesy
of the Henry Ford Museum,
Dearborn, Michigan)

190. *Settee, early nineteenth century*
This maple settee with a rush seat was
made in the Sheraton style. Notice the
turned legs and the shaping of the arms.
(Index of American Design, Washington,
D.C.)

7

Chairs—Slat-Back or Ladder-Back

History

THE DESIGN for the ladder-back or slat-back chair originated in England during the 1600's. It may have derived from the cane chair in much the same manner as the banister-back evolved from the earlier types of cane chairs.

English chairs of the 1685 period had high backs that were decorated with carving. The posts and legs were turned, and horizontal slats were placed between the posts. The name "ladder-back" refers to the resemblance of the back of a chair to a stepladder.

The early eighteenth century (1700–1725) in America was the beginning period of the ladder-back chair. The simple early eighteenth-century chair led to several different types of ladder-back chairs in the late eighteenth and nineteenth centuries.

The country furniture makers found that the ladder-back design was ideally suited to their methods of manufacture. The chair became more simple until it reached the design of the Shakers with no ornamentation, just utilitarian beauty. The sophisticated city furniture maker borrowed from the designs of the early ladder-backs and developed a Chippendale and Hepplewhite style with horizontal bars at the back. During the Empire period many of the country makers borrowed ideas or designs from the Hepplewhite versions of the ladder-back, thus developing a country version of the more formal chair. The painted fancy chairs and Hitchcock-type chairs were the informal adaptations of the city design.

Types of Ladder-Back or Slat-Back Chairs

One rare type of seventeenth-century ladder-back chair had square posts with no turnings and a slat back. The back posts above the seat were slightly tilted, with the rungs and seat stretchers set into the posts. Either two or three horizontal, flat, unbent slats were placed at the back of the chair. The chairs were made from oak, maple, hickory, or pine. A variant of an earlier European chair, they were made in Massachusetts and other parts of New England.

The Carver-type chair was another rare chair of the seventeenth-century Pilgrims (see banister-back chair). This was an armchair with large posts two inches or more in diameter. The finials were made from ash or maple. Three slats were placed across the back of the chair. These slats were straight except for the cutout corners.

In New England this chair was generally made from hickory or oak.

The eighteenth-century slat-back chair was lighter in weight even though it had more slats and a higher back. The slats became wider; the finials were decorative additions; and the turnings on the posts were more bold. Posts were usually made from maple, the seat rail of hickory, the slats and rungs from ash, hickory, or oak.

Two types of the chairs were classified by an earlier writer as "northern" and "central" to indicate the state where the chairs were made. (These regional differences are discussed in the next section.)

The Pennsylvania-style chair had been developed by the mid-eighteenth century (Pictures 198, 199). The chair had smaller posts and arms that were about 1¾ of an inch in diameter, with narrower slats.

The chair of the late eighteenth century economized on both material and effort. The slat- or ladder-back chair became a simple two- or three-slat chair with unturned and undecorated posts. Sometimes the slat was shaped, but it was often straight with narrowed corners. The nineteenth-century chairmaker continued the simplification until there were only two slats remaining between the upright and unadorned posts. Some makers made the "rabbit ear" (Picture 227) by flattening the front of the upright posts. It was popular during the early 1800's.

The early chairs (1700–1800) had many slats, high backs, and turned legs, arms, and back posts.

New England or "Northern" (Pictures 194, 195, 196)

The back posts of the eighteenth-century New England chair were ornamented with turned rings and other designs. The chair slat was generally cut straight across the lower edge and curved on the upper edge. It was never bent outward. Five slats were the maximum number used, and this chair is now considered much better than a comparable three-slat example. The finials were well turned, at times almost round. The stretchers on the chair were turned. The best examples had decorative "sausage turnings" that actually looked like chains of "hot dogs."

New England ladder-back chairs were made from maple, cherry, oak, or ash, and were painted black, dark red, or occasionally green.

Pennsylvania or "Central" (including Pennsylvania, southern New Jersey, Maryland, and Delaware) (pictures 198, 199)

The Pennsylvania-type chair had no ornamental turning on the back posts. The slats had curved upper and lower edges, and those with a very high arch in the center are believed to be from the Delaware River Valley area.

Thus two features that quickly help to determine whether a chair was made by a New England or a Pennsylvania maker are the back posts, which were turned on New England chairs, plain on Pennsylvania chairs; and the slat, which was kept straight in New England and curved in Pennsylvania.

The Pennsylvania chairs have five or even six rungs across the ladder back. The rungs are usually graduated in size, with the widest rung at the top. The post tapers to the floor, often ending in a ball foot.

The chairs were made from maple and were painted black, dark red, or green. After 1740 they were painted any color with some decorated with flowers.

French Canadian (Picture 200)

A third type of ladder-back chair should be mentioned. Many northern New England and Canadian makers, influenced by the French designs, made a chair with a serpentine or salamander slat. The Canadian chairs resemble French furniture with the curved arms and even slightly curved posts. These, first made in the eighteenth century, are still made, in a simplified form, in rural Quebec.

Southwestern (Pictures 235–240)

The early settlers in the southwestern part of the United States were influenced by Spanish, Mexican, and French designs familiar to many of them. It must be remembered that the Spanish were among the first to settle in California and the coastal areas and that the Spanish conquest of Mexico has dictated some of the styles popular in the southern regions of the territories. The area known as New Mexico included the states we now call New Mexico, Arizona, Colorado, and Texas. French settlers from the New Orleans area also traveled to the West.

The Spanish colonists, priests, French settlers, and the eastern pioneer traveling West influenced country furniture styles of the nineteenth-century Southwest.

The chairs made in the regional style had square stiles, while all the other country chairs in America were made with round stiles. The squared posts were occasionally curved at the back to accommodate the back of the person using the chair. A notched hook-like finial (Pictures 238, 239) was carved at the top of the post instead of the rounded finial found on eastern chairs. The chair leg was usually squared, although the finest examples were made with curved legs of the French influence, and still others were made with a straight leg. Armchairs repeated the curve of the leg in the lower part of the arm.

The solid wooden rectangular seat extended beyond the legs at the front of the better New Mexican pieces (Picture 235). Many less sophisticated chairs were made with rawhide or rush seats.

Mortise-and-tenon construction was used on the colonial southwestern chairs, while nails and other metals appeared only on later pieces. The Duncan Phyfe styles were apparent in many of the country chairs of the Southwest after 1840.

Western yellow pine, cottonwood, juniper, hickory, oak, pecan wood, and walnut were used to make the chairs.

California Mission–Style Chairs, Nineteenth Century (Pictures 244–249, 253, 254)

The "priest" chair that was made by Indians for use in the mission had the square leg and stile of other southwestern country chairs. The mission chairs were heavy and bulky in appearance. The back of the chair had a very wide top slat with a carved and decorated narrow slat, or wide backpiece covered with leather. The distinctive curved arms and the unusual carved seat apron are Spanish in origin.

Isle d'Orléans Chair, Eighteenth Century (Pictures 251, 252)

An unusual chair design found in many Canadian homes was developed along the lower St. Lawrence region. During the eighteenth and nineteenth centuries the chairs were made from painted pine. The back of the chair was rectangular, without spindles or slats. The chair seat was usually a rectangular wooden plank with a straight apron. The legs were squared and chamfered, with the stretchers needed for added support located near the floor.

This type of chair appears to have been made only in the lower St. Lawrence region. It was named for an island in the St. Lawrence near Quebec City called the Isle d'Orléans.

Nineteenth-Century Chairs, Slat-Back

A slat-back chair with turned posts and oval slat-backs has been made in the Appalachian mountain area since the early 1800's. They were made from maple, hickory, and chestnut with seats of woven cornhusks. The chair was usually constructed from green and seasoned wood, without nails or glue, and held together by shrinkage. Southern slat-back chairs have either no finial or a steeple-shaped finial and heavy slats. These chairs are made by individual families. Their descendants have often continued to use the same design and method used during the last century.

Chair Seats

Most ladder-back chairs were made with rush seats (Picture 208). The eighteenth-century example showed a straight and a checkered type of rush weaving. In straight rushing (Picture 203) each strand overlapped the other. In checkered rushing (Picture 201) four strands overlapped the next four strands, making a checkered diagonal. The two styles of rushing continued into the nineteenth century when splint seats (Picture 206) gained popularity. Western and southern chairmakers often used regional materials for the seat instead of rush. The southern cornhusk seats (Picture 234) and the western and French-Canadian rawhide thong seats (Picture 34) are examples of area design and style making use of available materials.

The Shakers used a special tape seat that was woven on a loom, and sold it by the yard to those living outside the Shaker colony. They also used their tape to make checkered seats for their own chairs (See Chapter 17, "Shaker Furniture.")

Wood

Each section of the country had its own available woods. Most of the ladder-back chairs were originally painted. Maple was popular in Massachusetts; Maine and New Hampshire preferred birch; southern makers used walnut, cypress, cherry, ash, hickory, poplar, or pine; Connecticut chairs were made from poplar. Other areas used cherry, apple, pear, pine, oak, chestnut, walnut, or curly maple. The posts were usually made from partly seasoned wood so that when they dried completely they became oval and not circular in shape, since wood shrinks only in one direction.

The parts were held together with wooden pins or dowels during the eighteenth century, but the nineteenth century nails were used in most of the eastern areas.

When the ladder-back chair became the style of the country maker, the back of the chair gradually became lower. The number of slats diminished until a two-slat chair remained. By mid-nineteenth century the chair had only two slats and no turnings.

High-Back Settle Bench (Pictures 255, 256, 257, 258)

The settle is a seventeenth- and eighteenth-century design that resembles the settles used in English country homes. Since there was no central heating, the high back was developed to keep out a draft. The back was made from several wide boards of rectangular construction. Additional protection from drafts was furnished by a partially hooded top with protruding sides that served as armrests.

Most of the settles were made from painted pine.

The seat often was used as a storage unit, having either drawers or a lift top. A few nineteenth-century high-back settles are known, but most of them date from about 1675 to 1800.

Corner Chair (Pictures 259, 260, 261, 262)

Corner furniture has been popular with designers since the eighteenth century when the formal Queen Anne corner chairs were made. Any corner chair had the seat placed with one corner toward the front. The front of the seat formed a right angle with a leg at each corner and the back was supported by the three back legs.

In dating a corner chair, notice the construction of the legs and back, which were made in all the styles of country furniture from 1725 to 1875.

Wagon Seat (Pictures 263, 264, 265, 266, 267)

The wagon seat was a double seat used in a wagon; it was removed when needed at the meetinghouse. The chair was made in the general style of the other country furniture of its time. It had short legs to accommodate the construction of a wagon. Because the driver and his assistant sat in the seat, it had to be of proper height for easy driving and narrow enough to fit the bed of the wagon.

Most examples resemble slat-back chairs. They were made from pine, maple, or hard native woods about 1780 to 1850.

Novelty Chairs (Pictures 268–276)

Several types of chairs evolved during the nineteenth century that are unrelated to other chair designs discussed.

The hollowed-out log made into a chair (Picture 273) was an inevitable idea that appeared in all parts of the country during the nineteenth century, and possibly as early as the seventeenth and eighteenth centuries. In Texas and other western areas (Picture 274) a chair was made from cow horns joined together to form the legs and back. It was popular during the late nineteenth century, inspired by the curves of the popular Victorian formal furniture.

The Gothic type of chair (Pictures 271, 272) with three legs and a vase-shaped back was a design known for years in Europe and copied by the American settlers in the eighteenth and nineteenth centuries.

Most folding chairs were factory produced, but there were some country versions made. Folding chairs (Picture 275) with cloth seats are a late nineteenth-century idea.

Victorian novelty chairs (Pictures 241, 242, 243) were made by some country makers, but most of them were shipped from eastern or midwestern chair factories to all parts of the country.

191. *Slat-back chair, eighteenth century* Maple and ash chair with turned posts and shaped slats, made about 1725–1750. (Metropolitan Museum of Art; gift of Mrs. Russell Sage, 1909)

192. *Slat-back armchair, eighteenth century* Ash and maple were used to make this chair with turned posts and legs, sausage-turned stretchers, and four shaped splats. (Metropolitan Museum of Art; gift of Mrs. Russell Sage, 1909)

193. *Slat-back armchair, eighteenth century* Four-slat back and simple stretcher and legs are seen on this chair made about 1700. Notice the arms. (Courtesy of the Brooklyn Museum)

194. *Slat-back armchair, eighteenth century* A maple and hickory chair, probably made in New England or New York. The leg is plain below the seat, turned above the seat where it supports the arm. The shaped slats are flat on the bottom edge. (Sleepy Hollow Restorations, Inc., on the Tappan Zee, Tarrytown, New York)

195. *Slat-back armchair, eighteenth century* Maple chair with mushroom ends on arms. The mushroom was part of the turned post and was never added as a separate part. (Metropolitan Museum of Art; gift of Mrs. Russell Sage, 1909)

196. *Slat-back armchair, early eighteenth century* Hickory and ash chair with turned posts and mushroom knobs. The three-slat back has a decorative shape at the top edge of each slat. (Metropolitan Museum of Art; gift of Mrs. J. Insley Blair, 1949)

197. *Slat-back chair, eighteenth century* Three slats form the back of this chair made about 1750–1775, in New England. Notice the well-made finials and stretchers. The slats are graduated in size. (Courtesy of National Park Service, Morristown National Historical Park, Morristown, New Jersey)

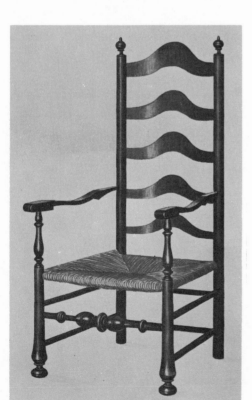

198. *Slat-back armchair, eighteenth century* Pennsylvania chair made of maple about 1725. The posts are plain and the six curved splats are shaped top and bottom and graduated in size. Notice the intermediate spindle below the curved arm. Ball feet and ball turnings on spindle show early origins. (Courtesy of the Henry Ford Museum, Dearborn, Michigan)

199. *Slat-back armchair, eighteenth century* Maple, pine and ash were used for this Philadelphia, Pennsylvania, chair made about 1725–1750. The five arched slats are graduated from top to bottom. The rush seat is typical. (Index of American Design, Washington, D.C.; Brooklyn Museum)

200. *Slat-back armchair, nineteenth century* Birch chair made with salamander slats and turned posts and legs. It was made in the late eighteenth or early nineteenth century, probably in Canada. (Metropolitan Museum of Art, Sylmaris Collection; gift of George Coe Graves, 1930)

201. *Slat-back chair, eighteenth century* A three-slat chair with plain posts and plain back. The seat is made with diagonal rushing. (Metropolitan Museum of Art; gift of Mrs. Russell Sage, 1909)

202. *Slat-back chair, nineteenth century* This New England four-slat ladder-back chair with rush seat was made about 1800. Notice the finials. (Old Sturbridge Village, Sturbridge, Massachusetts)

203. *Slat-back armchair, late nineteenth century* A very wide four-slat-back armchair made about 1860. Notice the splint seat. (Shelburne Museum, Inc. Photographer, Einars J. Mengis)

204. *Slat-back chair, late eighteenth century* Side chair with a split ash seat. Notice the finials and the plain legs and stretchers. (Detroit Historical Commission)

205. *Slat-back chair, late eighteenth century* This hickory and Virginia walnut chair was made in Pennsylvania. Notice the fly whisk, which tradition says was invented by Benjamin Franklin. On each post are the marks made when the maker measured to place the slats and stretchers. These ring marks are often found on nineteenth century chairs. (Taylor and Dull, photography)

206. *Slat-back chair, nineteenth century* This child's chair, probably made in Florida, has unusual finials (compare with Canadian chairs), shaped slats, and unturned uprights. (Pensacola Historical Society. Photograph by Lew Ashley)

207. *Slat-back chair, nineteenth century, Canadian* The slender shaped slats and finials are unusual on this Canadian chair found in Dickenson's Landing, a town on the St. Lawrence River. The posts and legs are maple; the rungs and slats are ash. The seat is made of the hide off a cow's head. (Upper Canada Village, Morrisburg, Ontario)

208. *Slat-back chair, nineteenth century*
Maple chair made by the Shakers at Mount Lebanon, New York. The finials and construction with square pegs are typical of the Shaker chairs. Notice the rush seat. (Shelburne Museum, Inc. Photographer, Einars J. Mengis)

209. *Slat-back ironing chair, nineteenth century*
Shaker chair made by the South Union Shakers in Logan County, Kentucky. Notice flattened back stiles. (Shaker Museum, Inc., Auburn, Kentucky)

210. *Canadian chair, nineteenth century* The shaped slats in this chair are characteristic of the French-Canadian type of chair made in Stormont and Dundas County from 1830 to 1850. The chairs were originally painted red, gray, or blue. This one is made of ash with a woven splint seat. (Upper Canada Village, Morrisburg, Ontario, Canada)

211. *Slat-back chair, nineteenth century*
Three graduated slats form the back of this nineteenth century chair made of oak. The seat is split bottom or splint bottom. The back supports are partly flattened. Notice the shaped post that forms the foot, a style often found in the Midwest. (Cowlitz County Historical Society, Kelso, Washington)

212. *Slat-back chair, nineteenth century*
A three-slat back, plain posts, and stretchers were used on this chair which was made about 1825 in Illinois. The chair is oak; the original seat was rawhide, now replaced by rope. Notice the shaping of the back slats with the graduated slats, largest at the bottom. (Cowlitz County Historical Society, Kelso, Washington)

213. *Ladder-back chair, nineteenth century* The "rabbit ear" back stile and the shaped foot on the leg indicate a midwestern chair. This chair was used in Ohio. Notice the shaping of the arms and the double stretcher. (Hale House, Western Reserve Historical Society, Cleveland, Ohio)

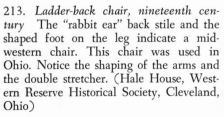

216. *Slat-back chair, date unknown*
This is an unusual chair, probably made in Texas. Notice the leg shape. The four slats and finials indicate an early nineteenth-century date. The seat is missing. (Index of American Design, Washington, D.C.)

214. *Slat-back armchair, nineteenth century* A midwestern chair of the 1830 period. The finials still remain on this chair, but soon after this date finials were omitted. Notice the arms and the narrowing of the leg to form a foot. (Howard County Museum, Kokomo, Indiana)

215. *Slat-back chair, nineteenth century* This child's chair, with a two-slat back and rawhide bottom, was made of oak and hard maple and painted black with gilt trim. The rockers have been added. Although found in Washington, it was not made in the West. Notice that the arms are like those on the preceding midwestern chair. (Cowlitz County Historical Museum, Kelso, Washington)

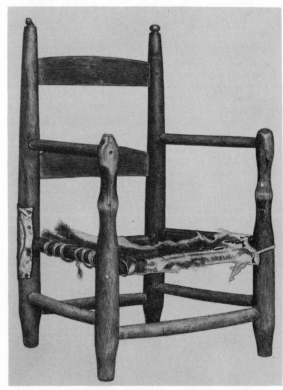

217. *Slat-back chair, nineteenth century* A child's chair made about 1868 in Austin, Texas, of brown painted hickory. Notice the shaping of the armrest supports. (Index of American Design, Washington, D.C.)

94

218. *Slat-back chair, nineteenth century* High chair made in Texas about 1870 of painted hickory. Finials and arm support are shaped like those of other chairs found in the area. (Index of American Design, Washington, D.C.)

219. *Slat-back chair, nineteenth century* A pine chair with rush seat made in Mascot, Florida, about 1830. The slats are of a refined shape that resembles the Sheraton chairs of the nineteenth century. Notice the finials and turnings at the top of the leg post. (Index of American Design, Washington, D.C.)

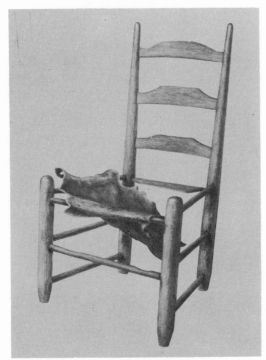

220. *Slat-back chair, nineteenth century* A white oak chair with cowhide seat made about 1821 near Pensacola, Florida. The shaped splats are graduated in size. There are no finials or turnings. (Index of American Design, Washington, D.C.)

221. *Slat-back child's chair, nineteenth century*
A painted hickory chair with cowhide seat made in Fernandina, Florida, about 1810. The finials remain, even though the chair was built in an amateurish manner. (Index of American Design, Washington, D.C.)

222. *Slat-back high chair, nineteenth century*
An oak chair made about 1860 in Florida. Note the shape of the slats. (Index of American Design, Washington, D.C.)

223. *Slat-back chair, nineteenth century* Three slat back and rawhide seats are seen on this Texas-made chair. The finials remained on the Southwest chair long after they had disappeared in the Midwest. Notice that the leg is the same width at the top and bottom. (Index of American Design, Witte Museum, San Antonio, Texas)

224. Slat-back chair, nineteenth century
This low chair, with cowhide seat, was used for churning. This type of chair was made in the East about 1830, but the style was used in other parts of the country for many years. This chair was found in Florida. (Pensacola Historical Society. Photo by Lew Ashley)

225. Slat-back chair, late nineteenth century
A typical three-slat chair of the nineteenth century. This hickory chair, with a high rawhide seat, was made in Fredericksburg, Texas, about 1875. (Index of American Design, Washington, D.C.)

226. Slat-back chair, nineteenth century
Graduated slats and flattened uprights are seen on this hickory chair with a laced rawhide seat. The chair was made near Huntsville, Texas, about 1860. (Index of American Design, Washington, D.C.) LEFT

227. Slat-back chair, nineteenth century
A hickory chair, painted yellow brown, with laced rawhide seat made about 1860. Notice the flattened posts, the narrowing of the leg to form a foot, and the shaped top of the slats. Although these are midwestern features, the chair was found in Texas. (Index of American Design, Washington, D.C.; Witte Memorial Museum) RIGHT

228. *Slat-back chair, nineteenth century* A child's chair of midwestern origin, made about 1840. The legs have been shortened. Note the graduated slats and flattened uprights. This style of upright is called a "rabbit ear" or "donkey ear." (Cowlitz County Historical Museum, Kelso, Washington)

229. *Slat-back chair, nineteenth century* This child's armchair, made about 1820, has freehand painted decorations. (Old Sturbridge Village, Sturbridge, Massachusetts)

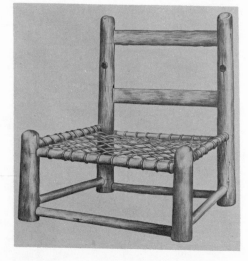

230. *Slat-back chair, nineteenth century* A hickory child's chair made in Arkansas about 1833. Note that all uprights are round. (Index of American Design, Washington, D.C.)

231. *Slat-back chair, nineteenth century*
This chair, made in Utah in 1867, has a three-slat back and a rush seat. It is painted red brown with white lines. Note the shape of the slats. (Index of American Design, Washington, D.C.)

233. *Slat-back variation, nineteenth century* This wooden chair, painted green, was made about 1859. This odd-style chair, found in Utah, is an offspring of the ladder-back design. (Index of American Design, Washington, D.C.)

234. *Slat-back chair, nineteenth century* A "Creole" chair made about 1830 with woven corn-shuck seat. The frame is of solid oak, pegged together. Notice that the stretchers go through the leg, although in most nineteenth-century chairs the stretchers go into the posts, not through them. (Cole County Historical Society Museum, Jefferson, Missouri)

232. *Slat-back chair, eighteenth century* A child's chair made of pine painted red. It has shaped board sides with a low wing for the armrest. (Hagley Museum, Wilmington, Delaware)

235. *Slat-back chair, nineteenth century* Southwestern-style chair of pine with mortise-and-tenon construction. The Duncan Phyfe styles and the Spanish influence are seen in this chair made in New Mexico about 1825. Notice the curve of the legs and the back posts, the rectangular seat that extends over the legs, and the apron, all features of this style. (From the Collection of the Museum of New Mexico. Photograph by Laura Gilpin)

236. *Slat-back chair, nineteenth century* Southwestern-style high chair with typical curved uprights supporting the arms. (Witte Museum, San Antonio, Texas)

237. *Slat-back chair, nineteenth century* A laced chair, made in Texas about 1865, in the southwestern style, of hickory and oak painted brown. The curved back support and shaped lower slat are characteristic. (Index of American Design, Washington, D.C.)

238. *Slat-back armchair, nineteenth century* Varnished pecan wood and a rawhide seat were used to make this chair, about 1846 to 1850, in Quihi, Texas. The southwestern style characteristics can be seen in the shape of the front supports for the arms and the unusual finials. (Index of American Design, Washington, D.C.)

240. *Slat-back chair, late nineteenth century* This walnut chair, with rawhide seat, was made about 1885 in Fredericksburg, Texas. The square posts are found on southwestern chairs. (Index of American Design, Washington, D.C.)

239. *Slat-back armchair, nineteenth century* Pecan-wood chair, painted dark brown, made in Quihi, Texas, about 1846 to 1850. Note square upright and curve of front support for arms in southwestern style. (Index of American Design, Washington, D.C.)

241. *Slat-back variation, nineteenth century* A Victorian chair with shaped slats and a cane seat made in Indiana about 1845. Although this is not a true slat-back chair, the relationship can be seen. (Cowlitz County Historical Museum)

242. *Victorian side chair, mid-nineteenth century* This factory-made chair, of oak and maple, is of the Victorian period. Note how this chair has some of the features of the early country furniture. (Mrs. Lilian Umbaugh, Kelso, Washington)

243. *Victorian side chair, mid-nineteenth century* Another factory-made chair, of maple with a cane seat, from about 1850. This should not be considered country furniture; it is a factory chair made at the time the country pieces were used. (Mrs. Lilian Umbaugh, Kelso, Washington)

244. *California mission chair, nineteenth century* Sometimes called a "priest's chair," this hand-carved pine chair with leather seat and back was made by Indians directed by a padre at the Mission San Miguel Arcangel about 1820. The square posts, stretchers, and apron are characteristic of this style. (Index of American Design, Washington, D.C.)

245. *California mission chair, nineteenth century* Judge Witherby's chair from California. Note the shaping of the chair crest, the finials, and the apron. (Junipero Serra Museum, San Diego, California)

247. *California mission chair, eighteenth century* This hand-carved pine chair was probably made in California in the late eighteenth century. Note the Spanish-influenced designs in the carvings and the special notched type finial found on many southwestern chairs. (Index of American Design, Washington, D.C.)

246. *California mission chair, nineteenth century* Native pine chair made at the Santa Barbara Mission in California by Indian neophytes about 1820. (Index of American Design, Washington, D.C.)

248. *California mission-type chair, nineteenth century* This pine chair, joined by pegs, was made near Trampas, New Mexico, about 1860. Note the square post, apron, carvings, and overhanging seat. (Index of American Design, Washington, D.C.)

249. *California mission-type chair, nineteenth century* A chair of unknown origins found in New Mexico. The style is similar to other chairs found in this area. (Index of American Design, Washington, D.C.)

250. *Oak chair, seventeenth century* An oak chair with a seat and back upholstered in Turkey work, possibly English. Compare this style with the "Ile d'Orléans" type. (Shelburne Museum, Inc. Photographer, Einars J. Mengis)

251. *Ile d'Orléans chair, eighteenth century* This red-painted chair, probably Canadian, was made in the eighteenth century. The rectangular back with no spindles resembles an earlier French style. This style is sometimes called "Côte de Beaupré" because it is found in the lower St. Lawrence region (Shelburne Museum, Inc. Photographer, Einars J. Mengis)

252. *Ile d'Orléans chair, eighteenth century* Originally painted green, this wooden chair was probably made in Canada. Note the characteristic back and the turned legs and stretchers. (Shelburne Museum, Inc. Photographer, Einars J. Mengis)

253. *California mission bench, nineteenth century*   A native pine bench, with hand-carved mortised joints, made by Indian neophytes at the Mission Purísima Concepción de María Santissima, California. Notice how the crest of the bench, square posts and arms resemble chairs of the same style. (Index of American Design, Washington, D.C.)

254. *Bench, eighteenth century*   A hand-carved pine bench made by New Mexican craftsman in the eighteenth century. Note the decorative carving. (Index of American Design, Washington, D.C.)

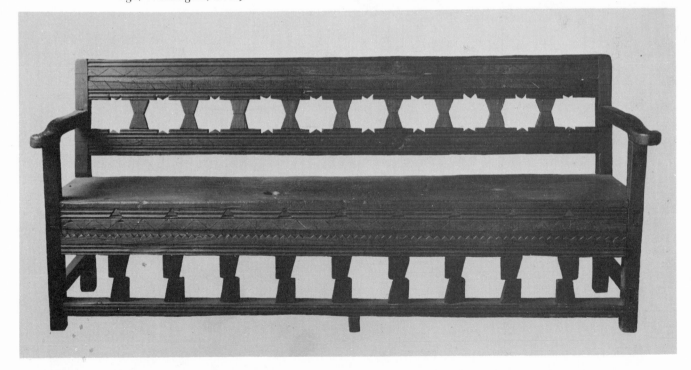

255. *Settle, late seventeenth century* A pine settle of plain design. The high back kept the drafts off. The hood is found on many fine settles. (The Metropolitan Museum of Art; gift of Mrs. Russell Sage, 1909)

256. *Settle, early eighteenth century* A pine settle with well-shaped arms and small hood. This type of settle has often been copied. Note construction of the back. (Courtesy of National Park Service, Morristown National Historical Park, Morristown, New Jersey)

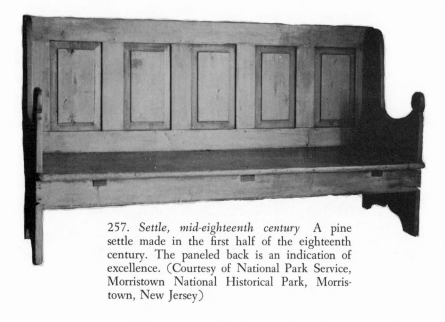

257. *Settle, mid-eighteenth century* A pine settle made in the first half of the eighteenth century. The paneled back is an indication of excellence. (Courtesy of National Park Service, Morristown National Historical Park, Morristown, New Jersey)

258. *Settle, late eighteenth century* A red-painted pine settle made in New England about 1775–1800. The seat of a settle often opened into a wood box. The settle seems to have developed from the chest. (Courtesy of the Henry Ford Museum, Dearborn, Michigan)

260. *Corner chair, eighteenth century* This chair is made of maple and ash. Note the center slat and turned legs. (Metropolitan Museum of Art; gift of Mrs. Russell Sage, 1909)

259. *Corner chair, eighteenth century* A maple chair made about 1720–1730. This type of chair is sometimes called a roundabout chair. The Spanish foot at the front leg and the turned legs indicate the early origin. (Metropolitan Museum of Art; gift of Mrs. Russell Sage, 1909)

261. *Corner chair, nineteenth century* A hickory chair, painted yellow and red, made in Austin, Texas, about 1868. It was made in the slat-back style of the area. (Index of American Design, Washington, D.C.)

262. *Corner chair, nineteenth century* This midwestern corner chair resembles the designs of the Shakers. It has a rush seat. The entire chair was painted black. It is probably a unique example; corner chairs of nineteenth-century furniture are very rare. (Kovel collection)

107

263. *Wagon seat, eighteenth century*   This poplar seat, made in Pennsylvania about 1780, was used on a wagon, then removed and used at the destination. Notice the heart cutout and the turnings. (Metropolitan Museum of Art; gift of Mrs. Robert W. de Forest, 1933)

264. *Wagon seat, eighteenth century*   Pine wagon seat made about 1795 in Connecticut. Note the finials. (Index of American Design, Washington, D.C.) TOP

265. *Wagon seat, eighteenth century*   Seat made of maple and hickory. Notice the large center posts. (Metropolitan Museum of Art; gift of Mrs. Russell Sage, 1909) BOTTOM

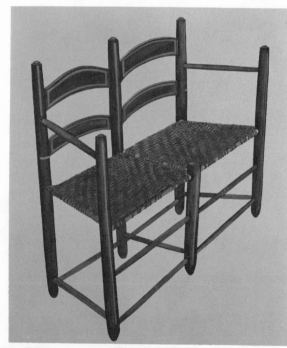

266. *Wagon seat, mid-nineteenth century*   This double seat, used on a wagon about 1847, is in the ladder-back style of the period. Found in Minnesota, it was probably made in Connecticut. (Index of American Design, Washington, D.C.)

267. *Child's wagon seat, nineteenth century* Notice the cutout designs at the back of this Pennsylvania seat made about 1800–1810. (Courtesy of the Art Institute of Chicago)

268. *School seat, nineteenth century* A pine seat made in Allenhurst, Florida, about 1865. The sides are notched to form legs in the same way as in early eastern chests. (Index of American Design, Washington, D.C.)

269. *Chair, nineteenth century* This southern chair was handmade, with woven corn shucks on the back and seat. The legs and stretchers are cut to a rough shape. (Historic Mobile Preservation Society, Mobile, Alabama)

270. *Armchair, eighteenth century* This armchair, with turned stretchers and unusual back, was made about 1750-1775. The chair is not a true slat-back, but has the same construction features. (Courtesy of National Park Service, Morristown National Historical Park, Morristown, New Jersey)

109

271. *Wooden chair, eighteenth century* This three-legged chair with a solid back was made in the late eighteenth century. This style was made in Europe and has continued, almost unchanged, through the years. (Courtesy of National Park Service, Morristown National Historial Park, Morristown, New Jersey)

273. *Wooden log chair, nineteenth century* The chair was made of a basswood log with a pine board seat. It was made in Racine, Wisconsin, about 1840. (Index of American Design, Washington, D.C.)

272. *Wooden chair, nineteenth century* This German-style chair was made of pine, near Bellville, Texas, about 1864. Note the crude seat. (Index of American Design, Washington, D.C.)

274. *Horned chair, nineteenth century* Chairs of steer horns were made in all the ranching areas in the late nineteenth century. These chairs were upholstered with hides. (Witte Museum, San Antonio, Texas)

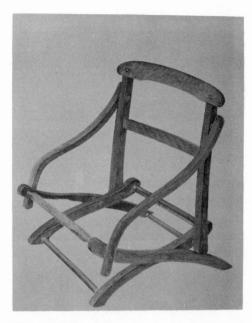

275. *Folding chair, nineteenth century* A Victorian chair of oak, painted red, made about 1870 in Fitzgerald, Georgia. The seat is missing. This type of folding chair is still made in factories. (Index of American Design, Washington, D.C.)

276. *Bootjack chair, nineteenth century* A wooden chair with leather seat, probably made in New Orleans, Louisiana, in the mid-nineteenth century. (Index of American Design, Washington, D.C.)

8

Chairs—Windsor

History

THE FIRST WINDSOR chairs were made in the Berkshire district of England during the sixteenth century. Windsor was an important city, and its name was soon given to all wooden chairs made locally.

Wheelwrights or wagon-wheel makers made the first Windsors. The legs and spindles of the chair were shaped by the same tools used to make a wheel spoke. The chair arms were bent in the same manner as the felly of the wheel. The chair made by the wheelwright and the chair made in Gothic times for royalty were the inspirations for the eighteenth-century Windsor. The Windsor as we know it was popular in England by the last quarter of the seventeenth century. It is a sturdy provincial piece of furniture, probably the best-known type of "country" furniture.

The Windsor was first mentioned in America about 1708, when John Jones listed an English Windsor in his inventory of possessions. The first Windsor made in America was crafted about 1725. Philadelphia furniture makers who had seen English Windsors made by English workmen living near Philadelphia made a few of the stick construction chairs. By 1740, there were furniture makers who specialized in Windsors, with some makers offering either all wooden or rush-bottomed chairs.

The earliest example of a comb-back American Windsor that we know of was pictured in an advertisement by Andrew Gautier in 1765.

It is believed that the Windsor chair was known throughout the colonies before the Revolution, and was shipped from city to city. Some are known to have been shipped to the West Indies.

As the chairmakers from Philadelphia moved to other areas, their designs and manufacturing skills moved with them. By 1770 the manufacture of Windsors was a trade in Philadelphia, Massachusetts, Connecticut, and Rhode Island. The craft spread quickly, and by 1810 there were Windsor chairmakers listed in Lexington, Kentucky.

The styles in America became more elaborate with the Empire and Victorian era, and the country furniture designs reflected the trend for fancy carvings and scrolled lines. The new styles brought many new types of country furniture. The Sheraton fancy chair replaced the Windsor in popularity, and by 1850 the handmade Windsor was out of style. The Victorian captain's chair was a nineteenth-century adaptation of the eighteenth-century low-back Windsor.

The Windsor chair was made of four basic parts. Each part was constructed from wood that was suited to the shape and use of the part. A fine Windsor chair was made with the right piece in the right place with the proper proportions.

THE SEAT

The seat of a well-made Windsor was constructed from pine or other soft woods without knots. It was usually made from a two-inch plank with the top surface hollowed out to fit the anatomy. The soft wood was easy to model and did not warp. A well-made Windsor always had a well-shaped seat that was and still is comfortable for sitting.

THE SPINDLES

The spindles of a well-made Windsor were of hickory, white oak, ash, or maple, woods that would not split or splinter. The spindles of a Windsor chair were shaped by hand. Holding a slim straight rod in his hand, the maker shaped it with a sharp tool, removing bits of wood from the ends of the stick and leaving a slight hump where his hand held the stick. The hump was never in the same place; thus, a careful examination of any Windsor will show whether the spindles were turned by hand or machine; if by machine, the spindles would be identical in size and shape. On an early type of lathe it was impossible to turn a spindle. The end of the flexible thin wood would wave about like the end of a whip. Some of the early spindles, however, were polished on a lathe. The very thin spindles were made on a special type of lathe that is still being used, but because of the limited market for the fine Windsors almost no factory reproductions are being made in this manner. Thicker spindles, or the bamboo-turned spindle, appear on almost all reproduction Windsors.

Spindles of special types appearing on later Windsors were made from different wood. The arrow-back flat spindle or splat (Picture 311) was usually made from maple.

THE LEGS

The chair legs were made from maple, birch, ash, or chestnut. The stretcher and arm stumps were often made from maple or other woods that could be cut on a lathe. The chair legs were turned on a lathe in the design peculiar to the area where the chair was made. It is possible to identify the origin of the eighteenth-century Windsor from the turnings. Craftsmen traveled from state to state as migration began toward the West. The workmen tended to make a chair in the style they first learned in their native state, making it difficult to attribute location to many of the nineteenth-century Windsors. Many makers labeled their furniture under the seat.

THE BACK

The back of the Windsor chair was usually made from the same type of wood as the spindles. Hickory, ash, white oak, and maple were used because they could be steamed and bent. Many other woods do not have the flexibility necessary for the 60-degree back curve. If the arm rail of the chair was bent (not

shaped by carving), the wood was one of the flexible types that could also be used for the back.

Special types of Windsors had other parts made from the most suitable woods. The comb-back chair had combs made from hickory or white oak, as most of the other woods splintered too easily when they were cut. When wedges or wooden pins were needed, seasoned wood was always used.

Each part of a fine Windsor was of the necessary size and strength. To understand the purpose of each piece it is necessary to know exactly how the Windsor and all later styles of wooden chairs were constructed. The method of joining and the use of each part determined the design of the chair. Many modern designers claim that a piece of furniture can be beautiful only if it is useful. The Windsor chair was one of the first designs with economy of structure dictated by use.

The Making of a Well-Designed Windsor Chair

The actual order of construction varied with the maker, but he usually began with the seat. The seat was shaped with hand tools, and the legs and stretchers were then attached through holes in the seat. The legs were wedged and/or glued into the seat of the chair. If the legs were wedged, a hole was made three-fourths of the way into the bottom of the seat. The leg could not be seen from the top of the chair. A small hole was also bored into the leg, and a wedge was forced into the hole to hold the leg in place. Nineteenth-century Windsors often used glue plus a wedge.

If the seat and the legs were made from green wood, the legs would remain in place as the wood shrank. Other parts of the chair were usually made from seasoned woods, and the chair became rigid as the parts that shrank were forced closer together.

The early chairs had holes on the bottom of the seat for the legs, placed from three to four inches from the edge. The angle of the hole determined the angle, or splay, of the leg. The legs of most Windsors were at a 75- to 80-degree angle to the floor. The seat of the chair was about 18 inches from the floor during the eighteenth century and from 16½ to 17 inches from the floor in the nineteenth century. Chair legs were often shortened to accommodate rockers. Such shortened legs lower the value and beauty of the chair. A chair that has obviously been made for a child or a small lady would have dimensions that are smaller in every detail. The back would also be lower to remain in proportion with the height of the seat.

The stretcher of the chair was made from dry, seasoned wood. It was the shrinking of the green chair leg that held the seasoned stretcher and gave much strength to the Windsor chair.

The legs and stretcher of the chair were first turned on foot-treadle lathes and later on power lathes. There were regional differences in the turnings of eighteenth-century chairs. The nineteenth-century chairs were made with bobbin-shaped or simulated-bamboo turnings.

The stretcher of the chair was made so that the thickest part of the side stretcher held the end of the cross stretcher. The finished stretchers looked like an **H** with the fattest part where the lines of the **H** crossed. This was the only practical way to construct the chair. If you find a chair on which the stretcher is wider at any other place, it is probable that the chair has been altered or repaired.

The back and arms were then joined to the rest of the chair. The lower end of the arm and the lower end of the back were placed into sockets bored in the seat and held by wedges and glue. The style of some chairs required certain pieces to be bent. This was accomplished by steaming the wood and bending it into position until the piece dried into shape.

The comb-back and bow-back chair had spindles that went through the shaped arm. This required that the arm be of sufficient thickness to remain sturdy after being pierced by from seven to twelve holes.

Next, it was necessary for the craftsman to butt the upper ends of the spindles into the back of the seat and force all the pieces into their proper holes, using more glue and wedges if necessary. The joinings were often the strongest part of the chair, and it is interesting to note that a break appeared between the holes and not at them.

The finished chair was painted dark green, Indian red, brown, black, yellow, or white. It had to be painted because so many types of wood were used.

The early chairmaker produced a spindle that was about three-fourths of an inch in diameter. It was made with a knife and a special sharp tool called a drawshave. Later, the spindles were partially turned on a lathe, with some of them 44 inches in length. It required an expert to be able to turn a spindle without its whipping.

An interesting feature of the Windsor unrelated to its use is the number of spindles used in the back. All Windsors had an odd number of spindles unless the chair had arms. The more spindles, the earlier the chair. There are examples of eighteenth-century chairs with eleven spindles. A nine-spindle Windsor is considered very desirable.

The Windsor was made for comfort, easy handling, and low cost. The fine saddle seat, comfortable and durable; the turned legs set at an angle that made tipping impossible; the well-shaped arms with knuckles that are smooth and eager to be held—all are characteristics of a fine Windsor chair. The many-spindled back and well-shaped crown with attractive "ears" at each end have given it added beauty. Each part was as thin as possible, making the chair light in weight. At the same time each part was made as large as necessary to enable the chair to remain structurally sound. A Windsor was shaped to best fit the human anatomy.

Although the Windsor is an eighteenth-century form, many nineteenth-century Windsors have some of the same qualities of the earlier chairs. The later chairs were heavier and clumsier. The turnings remind one of the restrained eighteenth-century regional turnings but without their distinctive quality. Many talented nineteenth-century chairmakers produced fine examples of Windsors. They might have been made with fewer spindles and turnings, but it still was a chair of comfort and fine style.

Styles

All stick-construction furniture is called Windsor furniture, but special names have been given to the different styles of Windsor furniture throughout the years. Most of these names refer to the shape of the piece. A high-back or a low-back Windsor is easy to identify, but a little thought and effort are required to realize when you are looking at a "brace-back, comb-back, writing-arm Windsor."

Windsors have been divided into many classifications.

Low Back (Pictures 277, 278)

The low-back Windsor had short spindles and a semicircular rail at the top and arms of the chair. The style began in Philadelphia about 1740 and spread to New Jersey and New York by 1780. Some of the early low backs had up to seventeen spindles. The "firehouse" Windsor and captain's chair are later examples of stick furniture based on the low-back design.

Comb Back (Pictures 279–282)

The low-back Windsor was expanded to the comb back. The spindles in the center of the chair extended through the low back to form a top addition to the chair. The comb, or a cupid's-bow piece of wood, was at the top of the spindles. The chair was more comfortable than a low back because the comb-back section could be used as a headrest. The chairs originated in the Philadelphia area about 1750 to 1780, with the design spreading to New Jersey, New York, and New England.

Fanback (Pictures 283–287)

The back spindles of the fanback Windsor were placed like the ribs of an opened fan. This style of Windsor had spindles that went from the seat to the top of the back with no crosspiece. The top of the back had a rail that was shaped like a cupid's bow. It is easy to distinguish the comb back from the fanback even though top pieces are of the same shape. The comb back appeared to have an extra piece added to the chair. The fanback cannot be made without its top piece. These Windsors were popular from 1760 to 1800. Late chairmakers used the fanback as the inspiration for the rod-back, arrow-back, and other nineteenth-century wooden "kitchen" chairs. (See the nineteenth-century Windsors at the end of this chapter.)

Hoop Back (Pictures 288, 289)

The most confusing Windsors to identify are the hoop back and loop back. The hoop back has also been called a bow back. It is a low-backed chair with an added top piece, which is curved. This chair originated in Philadelphia, and was first made about 1750 or 1760. It remained the most popular type of Windsor for about seventy-five years, and there were many late variations of the hoop-back chair.

Loop Back, or Bow Back (Pictures 290–297)

The loop back is a chair with a silhouette similar to the hoop back. One exception is that there was no bar across the center of the spindles. Each spindle goes from the seat to the curved top. This style was first made about 1780. A late nineteenth-century version is often seen today.

New England Armchair (Pictures 299, 300)

This famous Windsor style was regional in design. The New England armchair is a hoop-back chair with arms. The arms were formed by the curved piece that formed the top of the back. This chair had a structural weakness. The double curve at the back of the arm was often strained and was easily broken. Many of the New England armchairs are found with a repair at this point. This style was made in New England from 1785 to 1810. The difficulties of manufacture and the lack of sturdiness made the style unpopular.

Added Features

Any of the six basic Windsor shapes could have added features and special names. The writing-arm Windsor (Picture 278) had an extended arm with a flat surface made for writing. It was first made in 1760. It has been copied by many schools in their armchairs. A left-handed writing arm is especially rare. Writing arms appear on all the later types of Windsors and wooden chairs.

The brace back (Pictures 287, 298) was a Windsor with an added support at the back of the seat. The wooden plank seat was shaped like a ping-pong paddle. Several long spindles went from the seat to the top of the back, and gave the chair strength. These supports are most easily seen from the side of the chair.

The eighteenth-century Windsor was a well-made, sturdy, and inexpensive piece of furniture. It was only natural that the chairmakers would continue to make Windsor-like chairs. Some of the nineteenth-century chairs that are related to the Windsor are the result of an adaptation of the eighteenth-century Windsor and the late eighteenth-century Sheraton fancy chair. They used features of each style, and the pieces are classed either as a Windsor or as a fancy chair. The ones with spindles perpendicular to the floor appear most like the Windsor. Those with many crosspieces cutting the back are more like the chairs commonly called banister- or ladder-backs.

Rod Back (Pictures 303–306)

The rod back was the most popular of the nineteenth-century Windsor-type chairs. The chair had a straight top that was often several inches wide. Some chairs had bamboo-like turnings, and were light in weight. They were made from 1800 to 1830. The chair may have been painted or left with the natural finish. The step-down crest rail (Picture 309) came into style about 1825. The crest is the very top of the chairback. A step-down crest rail has a shaped top, not the straight top of the earlier chairs or the bow-shaped curve used on the early Windsor. This type of chair was often painted, and has some of the same characteristics as the famous Hitchcock-style chair, the most important painted chair of the nineteenth century. (See Chapter 6, "Chairs—Sheraton Fancy, or Painted.")

An interesting change took place in the stick-construction chair about 1810. Each spindle was made wider, and the bottom was cut to resemble an arrow. The chair was called an arrow-back (Pictures 310, 311, 312) and was made from 1810 to about 1835. It was often painted and stenciled. (See Chapter 6.)

The "firehouse" Windsor (Pictures 313, 314) closely resembled the shape of the low back. It was a production-made chair produced in a factory from about 1850 to 1870. The stretchers were not so crude in shape, and the spindles were much larger than those of the eighteenth-century chairs. The captain's chair (Picture 316) is a later version of the low-back Windsor, and was made from 1875 to 1900. The arms are socketed into the seat. The captain's chair often has a double stretcher.

The loop-back chair was adapted to a special nineteenth-century style from about 1880 to 1920, which we commonly call a "kitchen" Windsor. It is often seen covered with many layers of paint. The back of the chair has a few fat spindles that have been turned on a lathe. They are made from oak, ash, maple, or other hardwoods. The seat is not saddled but is a flat plank. The chair was originally varnished or painted.

Windsor furniture of the eighteenth and nineteenth centuries included settees, rockers, children's chairs, high chairs, cradles, and a few tables (Pictures 319–327). The eighteenth-century examples are handmade with shaped seats and thin spindles. Most of the pieces had turned stretchers and carefully carved knuckles on the arms and crests of the chairbacks. The nineteenth-century examples gradually lost all the detail. The spindles were fatter, the seats were usually flat, and by the end of the century they were made entirely by machine. The legs and arms lost more and more curves until no turned designs were apparent. The

nineteenth-century piece is often painted and decorated with stencils and striping. Many of the eighteenth-century pieces were painted, but always in a solid color. The arms were occasionally left in the natural wood.

There were regional variations in the design and turning during the eighteenth century, but by 1840 the difference had disappeared and chairs of all types appeared in all sections of the country. Hundreds of chairmakers worked in each of the states east of the Mississippi, and each one made a slightly different type of chair. Very few of the wooden chairs were labeled by the maker.

Regional Differences in Eighteenth-Century Turnings

During the eighteenth century the carvings that appeared on the legs and stretchers of chairs and tables were different in each area of the country. The variations continued into the early nineteenth century, and often a small part of the turnings will show the area that influenced the furniture maker. As the population moved west, the chairmakers moved with it, and a New England maker may have been working in Ohio, using the designs he learned in his youth. The turnings became less and less elaborate during the nineteenth century until by 1860 most chair legs had no turnings.

PHILADELPHIA (Picture 282)

The Windsor chair made in Philadelphia during the eighteenth century had a blunt arrow design. This was a ball foot, a narrow ring, and then a bun. The main leg was a straight cylinder topped by a narrowing vase-shaped section. This type of leg was made in Philadelphia, and occasionally in New York.

CONNECTICUT

The stretcher had a large ball in the center, and ring turnings. The spindle was evenly tapered. The seat was straight across the front. It had a deep, cutout saddle. The chair seat was often U-shaped.

NEW ENGLAND (Picture 279)

The New England Windsor had no foot, and the lower part of the leg was cone shaped. A ring was placed above the long cone; then vase-shaped turnings were made up to the ball that joined the seat. The stretchers had a bulge in the center, *not* a ball. The spindles of the New England chair had the enlargement, which the maker held while whittling, about one-third of the way up from the seat. The oval-shaped chair seat had a curved front and a very shallow saddle.

BAMBOO (Pictures 292, 302)

Bamboo turnings were found on eighteenth-century Philadelphia chairs. The style most common during the nineteenth century spread through Pennsylvania and other states (Picture 291).

277. *Low-back Windsor, eighteenth century* Tulip, poplar, maple, and oak were used to make this 28-inch-high chair. Continuous arm with applied crest, outward curve of arm ends, turned spindles supporting arms, saddle seat, played, turned legs, and stretcher with bulbous turnings are all indications of a good chair. (Metropolitan Museum of Art; gift of Mrs. J. Insley Blair, 1947)

279. *Comb-back Windsor, eighteenth century* This seven-spindle Windsor has the typical New England turned legs, fine saddle seat, and shaped crest. (Taylor and Dull, photography)

278. *Low-back writing-arm Windsor, nineteenth century* Oak was painted black with red trim to make this Windsor chair with the drawer and writing arm. The turned legs, spindles, back construction, and stretchers are in the style used in the late eighteenth century. The painted decorations are nineteenth-century in style. (Index of American Design, Washington, D.C.)

281. *Comb-back Windsor, eighteenth century* A six-spindle chair that has turned stretcher, shallow saddle seat, unusual proportions. Most Windsor chairs have an odd number of spindles. This is probably a chair made in New England. (Taylor and Dull, photography)

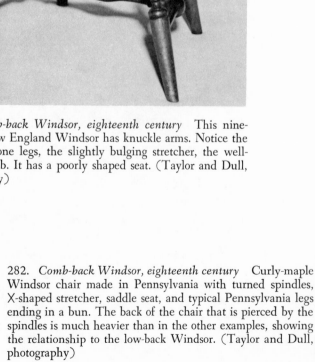

280. *Comb-back Windsor, eighteenth century* This nine-spindle New England Windsor has knuckle arms. Notice the vase and cone legs, the slightly bulging stretcher, the well-shaped comb. It has a poorly shaped seat. (Taylor and Dull, photography)

282. *Comb-back Windsor, eighteenth century* Curly-maple Windsor chair made in Pennsylvania with turned spindles, X-shaped stretcher, saddle seat, and typical Pennsylvania legs ending in a bun. The back of the chair that is pierced by the spindles is much heavier than in the other examples, showing the relationship to the low-back Windsor. (Taylor and Dull, photography)

283. *Fanback Windsor, nineteenth century* A five-spindle Windsor side chair painted brown with yellow floral sprays, made about 1790–1820. Note the well-shaped crest, turned stiles, and saddle seat. (Shelburne Museum, Inc. Staff photographer, Einars J. Mengis)

284. *Fanback Windsor, eighteenth century* New England–style legs, turned stiles, and seven-spindle back are seen on this fanback Windsor. This style of chair is sometimes misnamed a comb back because the top crest is called a comb. (Taylor and Dull, photography)

285. *Fanback Windsor, eighteenth century* Oak, maple, and spruce were used in this chair made about 1775–1800. The scrolled ears on the crest are well carved. The seven-spindle back and turned legs indicate the eighteenth century. (Metropolitan Museum of Art; gift of Mrs. Russell Sage, 1909)

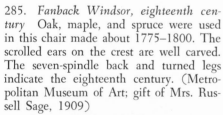

286. *Fanback Windsor, nineteenth century* This pine and ash side chair was made in New England about 1800. Six spindles were made to fit into the scroll-eared top crest. Notice the simple turnings of the legs. (Courtesy Museum of Fine Arts, Boston)

287. *Fanback Windsor, brace back, eighteenth century*
The two spindles that form a V at the back of the chair seat are the braces. Any shape of Windsor can have a brace back. The small seat on this chair is called a stool seat. Note the simple crest, the turned, thick stiles, and the angle of the legs. It is probably of New England origin. (Taylor and Dull, photography)

288. *Hoop-back Windsor, eighteenth century* Hickory, pine, and maple were used in this chair, which was made about 1770 in New York or Connecticut. It has a seven-spindle back. Only the spindles that go through the low back armpiece are counted when determining whether it is a seven- or nine-spindle chair. (Sleepy Hollow Restorations, Inc., on the Tappan Zee, Tarrytown, New York)

289. *Hoop-back Windsor high chair, eighteenth century* Windsor chairs of all types were used to make high chairs. This chair was made in Philadelphia, about 1750, of oak and hickory stained dark brown. The well-turned legs are set at a sharp angle to give more stability to the chair. (Index of American Design, Washington, D.C.; Brooklyn Museum)

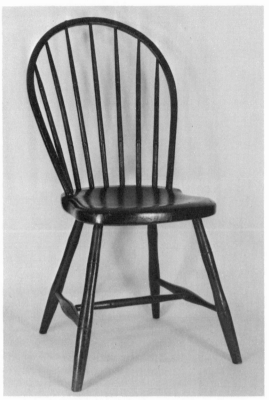

291. *Loop-back Windsor, nineteenth century*
A New England side chair made about 1800 from hickory and pine painted apple green. The concave stretchers are most unusual. It has well-shaped spindles and back but a shallow seat. (Courtesy of the Henry Ford Museum, Dearborn, Michigan)

290. *Loop-back Windsor chair, eighteenth century*   One of the original Windsor chairs used at Mount Vernon. Martha Washington made yellow and brown needlepoint cushions for these chairs. This chair has seven spindles and the simplest of legs and seat. This style is also called a bow-back Windsor. (Mount Vernon Ladies' Association, Mount Vernon, Virginia)

292. *Loop-back Windsor, nineteenth century*
Hickory, oak, and pine were painted black to make this nine-spindle New England chair about 1800. The X stretcher is rare. The legs and spindles are bamboo turned. The extra curve in the loop that forms the back of this chair makes a style that sometimes is mistakenly called a balloon back. The true balloon-back chair is not a Windsor. (Courtesy of the Henry Ford Museum, Dearborn, Michigan)

293. *Bow-back Windsor, nineteenth century* A child's high chair that has cross stretchers with bent wood reinforcements. It is made of pine painted green, in the late eighteenth or early nineteenth century. (Shelburne Museum, Inc. Photographer, Einars J. Mengis)

294. *Loop-back Windsor, nineteenth century* Hickory spindles, maple legs, and poplar seat used in this chair are the most usual woods for a Windsor because of the structural advantages of each wood. This is probably an early nineteenth-century New England chair. The seven-spindle back and simplified vase turnings of the legs and thick seat suggest a date of about 1820. (Index of American Design, Washington, D.C.)

295. *Loop-back Windsor, nineteenth century* The bamboo turnings used on this chair were popular about 1820. The seat of the chair is made of poplar, a wood often used in the Midwest. Notice the narrowing of the leg to the end, another midwestern trait. (Hale House, Western Reserve Historical Society, Cleveland, Ohio)

296. *Loop-back Windsor, date unknown* This is a hickory chair of simplest possible Windsor construction. The spindles are uneven; the legs and stretcher crudely shaped. This chair was found in Delaware. (Index of American Design, Washington, D.C.)

298. *Loop-back armchair, brace back, eighteenth century* This Windsor chair was made in Hartford, Connecticut, of curly maple and mahogany. The spindles and legs are gracefully turned. The added arms and braced back add to this fine example of Windsor form. (Taylor and Dull, photography)

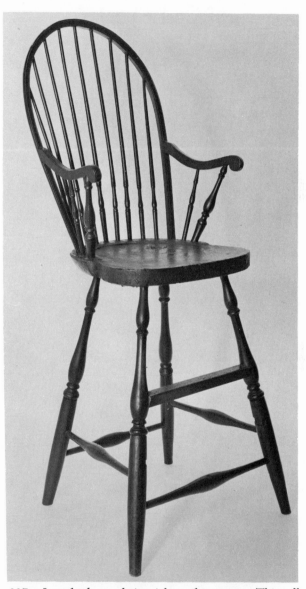

297. *Loop-back armchair, eighteenth century* This tall Windsor chair is of loop-back style with added arms. It was probably a child's chair with an added footrest. Notice how the arms have been joined to the back of the chair; also notice the box stretcher arrangement that gives added stability. (Rhode Island Historical Society)

299. *New England Windsor armchair, eighteenth century* This Rhode Island chair has a curved back that forms the arms. The nine-spindle chair has well-turned legs and arm supports. (Taylor and Dull, photography)

301. *Fanback Windsor, eighteenth century* An unusual ash and pine chair made in Pennsylvania about 1780. The rectangular shape is a forerunner of the rod-back chair. (Metropolitan Museum of Art; gift of Mrs. Robert W. de Forest, 1933)

300. *New England armchair, eighteenth century* A pine, maple, and hickory chair painted buff with black trim at the turnings. The thumbprint design on the bowed rail was burned in. The chair was made about 1760. (Courtesy of the Henry Ford Museum, Dearborn, Michigan)

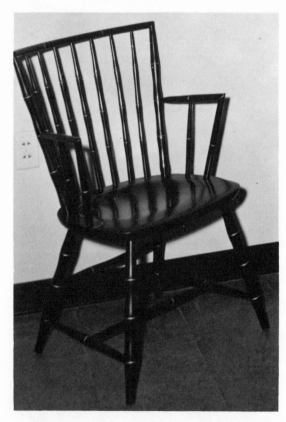

302. *Rod-back armchair, nineteenth century* A bamboo-turned painted rod-back chair of the style popular about 1825. The Sheraton influence is apparent. (Valley Forge Historical Society, Valley Forge, Pennsylvania)

303. *Rod-back chair, early nineteenth century* This maple and hickory chair with five spindles, bamboo turnings, and typical straight top was made in Economy, Pennsylvania, by Economites between 1826 and 1868. (Index of American Design, Washington, D.C.)

305. *Rod-back chair, late nineteenth century* Tradition says this huge chair was used in a sugar house when the maple syrup was being boiled on an Ohio farm. It has features of a late (circa 1880) chair; notice the bent arms and the front stretchers. (Hale House, Western Reserve Historical Society, Cleveland, Ohio)

304. *Rod-back chair, early nineteenth century* The bamboo decorations of the stiles and the legs and the thick seat are interesting in this refinished rod-back chair. It was made in Cuyahoga County, Ohio (near Cleveland), and is marked by the maker with a black stamp. (Kovel collection)

306. *Rod-back chair, nineteenth century* This four-spindle chair was made of pine in Des Moines, Iowa, about 1875. It is often called a "kitchen chair." This chair had hard use and has been braced at the back with metal, and the legs appear to have been shortened because of the low seat and the low placement of the stretchers. Sit on this type of chair. If the seat is too near the ground to be comfortable, the chair has lost part of its legs. (Index of American Design, Washington, D.C.) TOP LEFT

307. *Painted chair, late nineteenth century* A Victorian chair made of soft maple and oak about 1860, probably in the West. It was originally painted black and trimmed with flowers. Notice the three very thick turned spindles and the chair crest of the type used on a Boston rocker. (Cowlitz County Historical Museum, Kelso, Washington) CENTER TOP

308. *Victorian chair, nineteenth century* A black lacquer chair, painted with fruit design, that has thick turned spindles and shaped top typical of the late Victorian styles. This is the final form of the rod-back chairs. Notice the thick seat and plain legs. (Howard County Museum, Kokomo, Indiana) TOP RIGHT

309. *Step-down arrow-back chair, nineteenth century* The step-down back of the chair came into style about 1825. This chair was probably painted but is now in refinished condition. Notice the thick plank seat and the narrowing of the legs. This chair was made in Ohio. (Kovel collection) CENTER RIGHT

310. *Arrow-back painted chair, mid-nineteenth century* Victor Wallace of Oregon City, Oregon, made this chair in 1848 of western soft maple. It was painted. Note the rectangular shape of the seat, the plain legs, and box stretcher. (Cowlitz County Historical Museum, Kelso, Washington) BOTTOM RIGHT

311. *Arrow-back chair, nineteenth century* An arrow-back or kitchen chair made about 1860 of painted wood. It is a style used in all parts of the country. The name "kitchen chair" refers to several styles: the rod-back, arrow-back and loop-back wooden chairs with plank seats and straight legs of the 1860's. The flattened style is sometimes called a "rabbit ear." (Index of American Design, Washington, D.C.)

312. *Armchair, nineteenth century* The arrow-back walnut armchair was made by Economites at Economy, Pennsylvania, about 1826–1868. Notice the curled arms of Pennsylvania style, and the unusual flattened arrow spindles in the back. (One arrow spindle is missing.) (Index of American Design, Washington, D.C.)

313. *"Firehouse" Windsor, nineteenth century* Aspen wood, stained red, was used in this 1860 "firehouse" Windsor chair from Willard, Utah. The eight large spindles with ring turnings, the shallow seat, the plain turned legs, and the armrest construction show this to be a typical example. These chairs were made from New England to the Midwest in factories about 1850–1870. Some chairs from the West were handmade versions. (Index of American Design, Washington, D.C.)

314. *"Firehouse" Windsor high chair, nine-teenth century* The "firehouse" style was pop-ular from 1850–1870. Not only the adults' chairs, but high chairs and children's chairs were made in this style. (Michigan Historical Society)

315. *"Firehouse" Windsor, nineteenth century* Because the old firehouse often used a chair of this type, the name "firehouse" Windsor has re-mained. The eight spindles and turned legs are typical. (Hale House, Western Reserve Histori-cal Society, Cleveland, Ohio)

316. *Captain's chair, nineteenth century* The machine-made thick spindles and the wide back are indications that this chair was factory made. The term "captain's chair" means this type of late-nineteenth-century chair or a similar chair with arms that are a continuation of the back. (From the collection of William Pinney, Cleve-land, Ohio)

317. *Captain's chair, nineteenth century* Ma-chined spindles and back and arms bent to the seat are typical of the late-nineteenth-century captain's chair. Many had the wire support seen here running from the side rung to the arm. (Kovel collection)

319. *Windsor settee, eighteenth century* Whitewood (tulip or poplar), maple, and ash were used to make this settee in Pennsylvania. Notice how the back resembles the low-back Windsor. The legs had typical Pennsylvania turnings. (Metropolitan Museum of Art; gift of Mrs. J. Insley Blair, 1947)

318. *Victorian armchair, nineteenth century* This maple and ash chair with curved top crest and thick turned stiles of mid-nineteenth century is a distant relative of the low-back Windsor. (Cowlitz County Historical Museum, Kelso, Washington)

320. *Windsor settee, nineteenth century* "A. Steel" made and signed this brown-painted settee in Philadelphia about 1800. Note the bamboo turnings and thin crest rail. (Taylor and Dull, photography)

321. *Windsor settee, eighteenth century* The center shaped splat is typical of the English Windsor, but not the United States chairs. This Canadian settee was made about 1780 in eastern Ontario. It has a basswood seat, elm back, and maple legs. (Upper Canada Village, Morrisburg, Ontario)

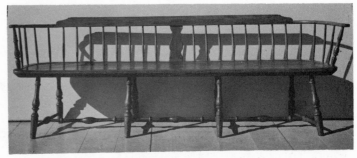

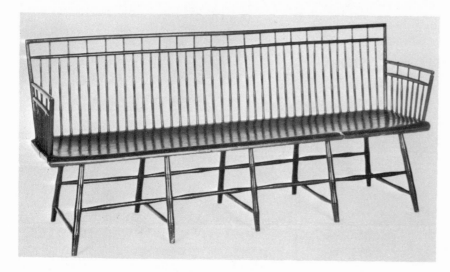

322. *Windsor settee, nineteenth century* This pine, maple, and hickory settee has a birdcage top at back and arms. It was painted black when made about 1800–1810. (Courtesy of the Henry Ford Museum, Dearborn, Michigan)

323. *Windsor settee, nineteenth century* A bamboo-turned settee that was made about 1810. The birdcage top shows the Sheraton influence. (Art Institute of Chicago)

324. *Settle, nineteenth century* This pine settle was made by the Shaker community of Canterbury, New Hampshire. The Shaker designs are their own, but the inspiration of the Windsor chair is apparent. (Shaker Museum, Old Chatham, New York)

325. *Windsor-like chair, nineteenth century*
Some country furniture makers were inventive, and a chair like this might be the result. Made of oak, this is a unique chair. (Shelburne Museum, Inc. Staff photographer, Einars J. Mengis)

326. *Children's Windsor chairs, eighteenth century* Windsor furniture came in all sizes. This is a group of chairs showing the small sizes used for children as early as 1760. (Old Sturbridge Village, Sturbridge, Massachusetts)

327. *Windsor cradle, nineteenth century* Maple and pine painted green were used to make this New England cradle about 1800. Notice the birdcage top and bamboo turnings. (Courtesy of the Henry Ford Museum, Dearborn, Michigan)

9

Chests

History

CHESTS, KNOWN FOR YEARS in Europe, were made by the first cabinetmakers in America. Originally they were just rectangular boxes joined together with mortise-and-tenon joints. (See Chapter 19, "Furniture Construction.") The very earliest seventeenth-century chests were held together with white oak pegs. Early pine chests that were nailed together are not considered as fine.

Many types of furniture, such as the dower chest, chest-on-frame, and even the cupboard, can be called chests. The earliest were large boxes, without drawers, but with a lid that lifted open. Later, one drawer was added, then two, three, and so on, until the chest was all drawers and the top could no longer be raised.

The very early seventeenth-century chests were mainly oak, but Pennsylvania chests were walnut or painted tulipwood. Most of the later chests were made of pine.

CHEST-ON-FRAME

Each era has its own forms that are evolved because of the needs of the times. The seventeenth century saw the development of a furniture form called a chest-on-frame. In earlier centuries a box with a drawer for storing special papers had been used. It was set on a frame with tripod legs, stretchers, and a shelf at the bottom of the frame. The chest-on-frame was small, with one drawer and a lid that could be lifted. This type of chest is very rare.

Seventeenth and Early Eighteenth Centuries

Several rare chests were made during the seven- teenth and eighteenth centuries. Even though they are seldom seen for sale, it is important to learn how the shape and style of the chests changed so the newer examples can be dated. There will always be the chance that one of these very rare early examples is still waiting unrecognized in some attic or barn.

The seventeenth-century chests were made from oak or pine. The Ipswich chest, or the Connecticut sunflower chest (Picture 329), was made from 1660 to 1680. The Hadley chest (Picture 328) was made from 1675 to 1700 (see section "Dower Chests" in this chapter), and there are about 150 known examples. Other types of chests with paneled front moldings and not carvings were made in the seventeenth century. The Guilford painted chests were made from 1690 to 1720.

All styles finally led to the William and Mary three-drawer chest, which was the first set of drawers. All the earlier styles influenced the Pennsylvania dower chest and those that followed in the eighteenth and nineteenth centuries.

WILLIAM AND MARY CHEST OF DRAWERS, 1690–1720

The first true chest of drawers was developed during the late seventeenth century (Picture 330) when the times showed a need for drawers to be used for storage.

The easiest characteristic to remember about William and Mary furniture is the ball foot. A large round wooden ball was used as the foot for chairs, tables, and chests of drawers.

Early Pilgrim furniture of the seventeenth century was made by a method called rectangular construction. Four boards were put together in the same manner as a picture frame. A single panel of wood was used to fill the inside completely. The units were then joined together to make chests and boxes. The early eighteenth-century chests looked like the older type, but instead they had large panels of wood divided by strips of molding.

The early chests that were made from mahogany have split through the years, but the chests made from oak have remained whole.

The chest of drawers with large ball feet had tiny teardrop-shaped drawer handles that were characteristic of the formal furniture of the period.

The style of William and Mary was very short lived, and the styles of Queen Anne soon came in with larger and higher chests.

Chest-on-Frame—Queen Anne, 1720–1750

The Queen Anne period was very "leggy." Many pieces of furniture were made with long graceful legs that almost seemed too frail to support the heavy wood above. The Queen Anne chest-on-frame is a good example of thin legs being used with a bulky top. A chest was made in two sections: a top that was shaped like a box with five or six drawers, and a bottom section having four typical Queen Anne cabriole (curved) legs (Picture 335).

The drawers of the chest were made in graduated sizes, with the smallest at the top. The front piece of the drawer always overlapped the edge of the drawer opening.

The finished chest-on-frame ranged from 4 feet to 6 feet high and was made of walnut, cherry, or maple (Picture 336). This style led to the highboy, or chest-on-chest, which was the magnificent formal furniture style of the late eighteenth century.

Chest of Drawers—Chippendale or Late Queen Anne, 1750–1785

The most common style of chest of drawers copied by the country furniture makers was the style of Thomas Chippendale. Because fashions traveled more slowly during the early nineteenth century, the furniture of the country furniture makers appeared in a style popular years earlier.

The chests had three or four drawers, with the edges of the drawers protruding beyond the section that held them. The handles were the ball type popular on the formal furniture of the same period, but more simple in design. Each drawer usually had a keyhole. The bracket feet were curved and low. (The chest in picture 338 is unusual because the keyholes are missing.)

The low country chest was made from maple, cherry, walnut, or mahogany. Many were painted red.

Hepplewhite Chest, 1785–1820

Many country furniture makers worked in the Hepplewhite style. Their chest of drawers had a straight front with an overhanging top with drawer fronts flush with the front of the chest. The foot was an outcurved French foot (Picture 340), and on better pieces it was joined by a valanced skirt. The decorative shaping of the bottom front of a chest is one of the signs of a good furniture maker.

The Hepplewhite low chests were made from mahogany, cherry, birch, maple, or the fancy grained maple such as curly or bird's-eye.

It is very rare to find a country piece made with the serpentine or curved front so often used on formal furniture.

Dower Chest or Blanket Chest (Pennsylvania Type)

The earliest Pennsylvania dower chests were made of carved oak during the eighteenth century. The carving was very flat. This style has become associated with the name "Hadley type chest." It is rare, and all of the known examples have been listed and pictured. Each newly discovered Hadley chest is carefully added to the list (Picture 328).

The Pennsylvania chest of the type most often found by the collector is the more common painted dower chest made from about 1760 to 1830, and in limited quantities after that time. Even recent brides have been given a modern chest decorated with the initials of the bride and groom and copied from a handmade eighteenth-century chest.

The lid that overhangs the top on the painted Pennsylvania chest is usually attached by a wrought-iron hinge. The edges of the chest are molded (rounded in a special way). The sides of the chest are made from a single large board joined at the corners by a dovetail joint (see Chapter 19, "Furniture

Construction"). The keyhole was placed at the center of the chest, requiring a metal or ivory inset.

The early chests had no drawers, but on the inside was a "till" that could be moved from side to side. In some of the Pennsylvania dower chests the sliding tray or "till" at the top of a chest is still used.

The base of this chest was plain or simply scalloped. The early ones made in the William and Mary style had ball feet (Picture 357) and the later ones in Chippendale style had bracket feet (Picture 354). At the bottom of the later chests one long drawer or two shorter drawers next to each other were used.

Dower chests were always painted with the name or initial of the bride and the date of the wedding. The decorations were often made to resemble a three-paneled chest, with initials in the center (Picture 351). (See Chapter 16, "Pennsylvania Furniture.")

BLANKET CHEST—SURVIVAL EXAMPLE, 1800–1830

The early blanket chests of the eighteenth century were modeled after the earlier Pennsylvania styles, which had a lid on the top and a chest of drawers at the bottom. Often the side of the chest went to the floor, and was notched to form the foot (Picture 373).

By the nineteenth century many of these chests had more than one drawer, some having only one real drawer and several that were false and could not be opened. When the lid was raised, the space concealed by the false drawers was available for blanket storage (Picture 380). This chest was made to resemble a four-drawer chest of drawers and not a blanket chest. These survival examples were made

from soft woods, and painted, but most of them are now found in a stripped-down and refinished condition.

The country blanket chest changed during the Empire period and became more in keeping with the formal styles. Posts were added to the corners, the legs became more like animal feet, and the chests became heavier in appearance and construction.

VICTORIAN CHESTS, 1860–1880

The Empire styles gradually changed into the typical chest of the Victorian period (Picture 348). The country chests were often made from pine, with rounded corners and rounded edges on the top of the chest. There were usually four drawers in a Victorian chest, with the smallest at the top. Wooden knobs with cast-iron keyholes were used. The back of the chest was made from three or four narrow boards that had been grooved so the boards could be joined in much the same manner as tongue-in-groove paneling. This type of back is an indication of a chest made during the last half of the nineteenth century. The back of earlier chests was formed by one or two very large boards.

The base of the chest had a curved valance, and wheels or casters were frequently put on the legs.

These Victorian country chests were made from pine or other soft wood, and many were originally grained or painted. Some of the examples were "factory made" in much the same manner as the Hitchcock-type chairs.

328. *Hadley type of chest, eighteenth century* Oak chest, carved, made in 1706. The box in the picture is a seventeenth-century Bible box. (Courtesy of the Brooklyn Museum, New York)

329. *Sunflower chest, seventeenth century* Rare Connecticut tulip and sunflower chest of quartered oak, pine, and maple, made about 1680. It is carved, and painted black and red. (Courtesy of Henry Ford Museum, Dearborn, Michigan)

330. *William and Mary blanket chest, sixteenth century* New England chest with ball feet and rectangular construction. (Art Institute of Chicago, Chicago, Illinois)

331. *Chest-on-frame, nineteenth century* Virginia-made chest-on-frame, about 1800. Note the stretcher, turned legs, and shaped apron. (Courtesy of Art Institute of Chicago)

332. *Chest-on-frame, Queen Anne, eighteenth century* This New England pine chest on stand with thin curved legs has graduated-sized drawers. (Taylor and Dull, photography)

333. *Chest-on-frame, Queen Anne, eighteenth century* A curly-maple chest made in England. It has four drawers, graduated sizes, and cabriole legs. Note the small ball finials on the apron front. These two finials are all that is left of the extra legs used in the William and Mary period. (Taylor and Dull, photography)

334. *Chest-on-frame, Queen Anne, eighteenth century* A painted maple and poplar piece made in Guilford, Connecticut, about 1760. The painted graining is unusual. (New Haven Colony Historical Society)

335. *Chest-on-frame, eighteenth century* This maple chest on a low frame was made in New England. The proportion of this piece is typical of the tall chest-on-frame style. (Taylor and Dull, photography)

336. *Chest-on-chest, eighteenth century* The chest-on-chest was another popular form of formal cabinetmakers. This piece was made in New England of maple in the late 1700's. (Taylor and Dull, photography)

337. *Chest-on-chest, nineteenth century* This chest was made in Santa Barbara, California, about 1880, of California redwood. It has typical Victorian carved wooden drawer pulls. Note the scalloping at the edge of the drawers and cabinet doors. (Index of American Design, Washington, D.C.)

338. *Chest of drawers, Chippendale, eighteenth century* This curly-maple chest of drawers has an unusual scalloped decoration on top. (Taylor and Dull, photography)

339. *Chest of drawers, nineteenth century* A painted pine chest marked "Made by E Morse, Livermore (Maine) June 7th, 1814." It is painted to imitate graining. (Courtesy of Henry Ford Museum, Dearborn, Michigan)

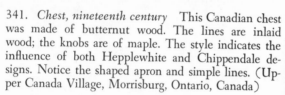

341. *Chest, nineteenth century* This Canadian chest was made of butternut wood. The lines are inlaid wood; the knobs are of maple. The style indicates the influence of both Hepplewhite and Chippendale designs. Notice the shaped apron and simple lines. (Upper Canada Village, Morrisburg, Ontario, Canada)

340. *Chest of drawers, Hepplewhite, nineteenth century* This unique marble-topped chest of drawers was made in Connecticut about 1800. The family record of Deacon Thomas Giddings is carved into the top. Note the graceful valanced skirt and outcurved legs found on many better Hepplewhite chests. (Shelburne Museum, Inc.)

342. *Chest of drawers, Hepplewhite, nineteenth century* Curly-maple bureau made about 1815. This typical plain chest has four drawers, brass mushroom handles, and a valanced skirt. (Taylor and Dull, photography)

343. *Chest of drawers, Pennsylvania, nineteenth century* A painted pine and poplar chest made in the second half of the nineteenth century. Note the feet and the panel at the side and the dentil molding at top. (Metropolitan Museum of Art; gift of Mrs. Robert W. de Forest, 1933)

344. *Chest of drawers, Pennsylvania, nineteenth century* Chest of drawers made of painted pine about 1830. The dark blue-green background is decorated with flowers in red and buff. Note the feet. (Courtesy of the Henry Ford Museum, Dearborn, Michigan)

345. *Chest of drawers, nineteenth century* The plain wooden knobs and the simple lines of this chest indicate a country maker. Notice the graining of the cherry wood used to make the chest, and the elaborately cutout apron. (Hale House, Western Reserve Historical Society, Cleveland, Ohio)

346. *Chest of drawers, nineteenth century* Texas-made chest of cypress wood. It has spool-turned decorations and was made in the Hepplewhite style. (Index of American Design, Washington, D.C.)

347. *Chest of drawers, nineteenth century* Mahogany, painted dark brown, made about 1845 in Indianola, Texas. Notice the lack of feet and the turned knobs. (Index of American Design, Washington, D.C.)

348. *Chest of drawers, nineteenth century* Black chest, painted with gold decorations, made about 1849. Only a trace of a foot was made. It has turned mushroom knobs. (Detroit Historical Commission)

349. *Chest of drawers, nineteenth century* A waxed mahogany chest made near Huntsville, Texas, before 1860. It has Chippendale-style bracket feet. The side of the chest and the side of the legs were made from one piece in the manner of the blanket chests. The four-drawer arrangement indicates Victorian origin. (Index of American Design, Washington, D.C.)

350. *Dower chest, Pennsylvania, eighteenth century* A pine chest with painted decorations made in 1784. Note the rail feet, molding on the edge of the bottom, decorated top, and three-panel painting on front of chest. (Index of American Design, Washington, D.C.)

351. *Dower chest, nineteenth century* A pine chest painted brown with tulips, carnations, and lilies. It was made in Pennsylvania in 1814, a fine example of a panel-painted chest. (Taylor and Dull, photography)

352. *Lift-top chest, Pennsylvania, eighteenth century* A painted yellow pine chest made in Lancaster County, Pennsylvania, about 1780. Three panel-painted decorations, Chippendale-style bracket feet, and shaped apron are features of interest. (Index of American Design, Washington, D.C.; Metropolitan Museum of Art)

353. *Lift-top chest, Pennsylvania, nineteenth century* This painted chest was signed "John Seltzer 1808." The typical urn of flowers is used in the decorative painted panels. Note the simple Chippendale-style foot and wood-grained painting covering the chest. (John Walton)

354. *Blanket chest, eighteenth century* A painted pine chest signed by the maker, Christian Seltzer, Jonestown, Pennsylvania, dated 1784. It is painted red with off-white panels containing jugs, flowers, and leaves in red, green, tan, and brown. Note the simple bracket feet. (Courtesy of Henry Ford Museum, Dearborn, Michigan)

355. *Dower chest, Pennsylvania, nineteenth century* This chest is dated 1804 and was probably made by Johann Rank, Jonestown, Pennsylvania. It has simple bracket feet and wood-grained painting with three panel decoration of urns of flowers. Note the keyhole escutcheon and painted top. (Courtesy of the New-York Historical Society, New York City)

356. *Dower chest, Pennsylvania, nineteenth century* The pine chest is painted blue and gray on a stippled brown background. It was made about 1800. Note the lack of feet. (Courtesy of the New-York Historical Society, New York City)

357. *Blanket chest, eighteenth century* This chest, inscribed "Anna Katrina, 1772," was made of North Carolina pine and painted red with decorations of blue and orange. The wrought-iron strap hinges and turnip or ball feet are important. (State Department of Archives and History, Raleigh, North Carolina; in Tryon Palace, New Bern, North Carolina)

358. *Blanket chest, eighteenth century* A Chippendale-style chest with black "graining" on white. A nineteenth-century owner applied paint to the eighteenth-century chest. (Old Sturbridge Village, Sturbridge, Massachusetts)

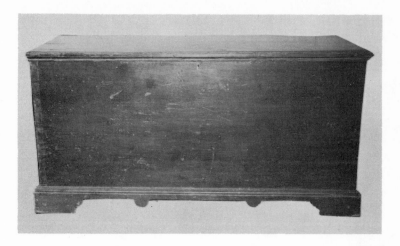

359. *Blanket chest, nineteenth century* A pine chest made about 1830 in the earlier style of the Chippendale chest. Note the simple bracket feet and scallop of the apron. (Olmsted County Historical Society, Rochester, Minnesota)

360. *Blanket chest, nineteenth century* A simple chest with an adaptation of the Chippendale foot, made about 1855 in Houston County, Texas, of spruce painted white. (Index of American Design, Washington, D.C.)

361. *Blanket chest, nineteenth century* A pine chest painted with flags, flowers, and leaves of red, white, and blue, made in Ohio about 1830. Notice the thickness of the wood used to make the base and feet. (Courtesy of the Henry Ford Museum, Dearborn, Michigan)

144

362. *Blanket chest, nineteenth century* A decorated chest labeled, "N R Stephens Chair Factory 1832." Some chair-design stencils decorate the inside of the top. (New York State Historical Association, Cooperstown, New York)

363. *Chest, mid-nineteenth century* This chest has a painted feathered decoration of shell-like patterns in vivid green, brown, red, and yellow. The chest was used for clothing storage and was probably kept under the bed. Since houses prior to 1840 were poorly equipped with closets, these chests were essential. (The Smithsonian Institution, United States National Museum, Washington, D.C.)

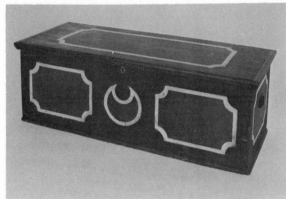

364. *Blanket chest, nineteenth century* A box of painted pine constructed with no feet. It is dark red and green with cream-color decoration. The chest was made in New York State about 1800. (Shelburne Museum, Inc.)

365. *Sea chest, nineteenth century* A carved and painted pine chest made at sea or in Gloucester, Massachusetts, about 1840. It has rope handles and no feet. (Index of American Design, Washington, D.C.)

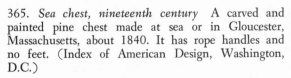

366. *Blanket chest, one drawer, eighteenth century* A painted pine chest made in Guilford, Connecticut. Note the molding around the bottom of the chest even though the legs are extensions of the sides. It has teardrop handles. (Metropolitan Museum of Art; gift of Mrs. J. Insley Blair, 1945)

368. *Dower chest, Pennsylvania, nineteenth century* A painted poplar chest made about 1800. The two drawers have wooden handles. Note the design at the center of apron. (Metropolitan Museum of Art; gift of Mrs. Robert W. de Forest, 1933)

369. *Dower chest, Pennsylvania, eighteenth century* A lift-top chest with two drawers at the bottom. Note the elaborate painted decoration, including the girl's name and the date, 1788. It has bracket feet, a shaped apron, and hardware in the Chippendale style. (Index of American Design, Washington, D.C.; Metropolitan Museum of Art)

367. *Chest, one drawer, eighteenth century* This unusual pine chest was made in Marlborough, Massachusetts, about 1702. The top, feet, and moldings are painted black, and the front and sides are painted with parallel wavy lines in black. Notice the ball feet. (The Smithsonian Institution, United States National Museum, Washington, D.C.)

370. *Chest, one drawer, eighteenth century*
This painted chest has the notched side to serve as a foot, and flush bottom drawer. The hardware is the teardrop shape of the early eighteenth century. (The Smithsonian Institution, United States National Museum, Washington, D.C.)

371. *Blanket chest, one drawer, nineteenth century* A red-stained pine chest made by the Shakers in Canaan, New York, about 1836. The bracket foot is inspired by the designs of other craftsmen. The wooden knobs are typical of the Shakers. (Index of American Design, Washington, D.C.)

372. *Blanket chest, nineteenth century* A walnut chest made about 1835 in Tennessee. The apron and foot are in the style of Chippendale chests of an earlier period. It has Hepplewhite hardware. (Index of American Design, Washington, D.C.)

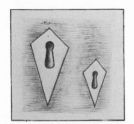

373. *Blanket chest, one drawer, nineteenth century*
This painted pine chest was made in Pennsylvania about 1830. The red and black swags and tassel are painted decorations. The notched extension of the side serves as a foot. Wooden knobs were used on the single drawer. It has a scalloped apron. (Courtesy of the Henry Ford Museum, Dearborn, Michigan)

374. *Blanket chest, one drawer, nineteenth century*
This pine chest was made in Cape Cod, Massachusetts. It has a straight front and is painted red with punch decorations. The notched side serves as a foot. (Shelburne Museum, Inc. Photographer, Einars J. Mengis)

375. *Blanket chest, one drawer, nineteenth century*
This brown and yellow painted, grained chest, made in New Hampshire, has brass drawer pulls and escutcheon. Note the Chippendale shape of the foot and the notching at the side. (Shelburne Museum, Inc. Photographer, Einars J. Mengis)

377. *Blanket chest, two drawers, eighteenth century* This well-proportioned chest was made of pine. It has wooden knobs. (Taylor and Dull, photography)

376. *Blanket chest, two drawers, eighteenth century* A pine blanket chest made in Long Island, New York, in the Hepplewhite style. (Taylor and Dull, photography)

378. *Blanket chest, Canadian, nineteenth century* The top of the chest opens for storage. Both drawers open in this painted grained chest of the mid-nineteenth century. Notice the shaped skirt. (Upper Canada Village, Morrisburg, Ontario, Canada)

149

379. *Blanket chest, two drawers, nineteenth century* This Shaker-made chest, made of pine stained red, has two drawers of different sizes. The Shakers used the typical notched side as a foot. (Index of American Design, Washington, D.C.)

381. *Blanket chest, many drawers, nineteenth century* The top three drawers are a false front; the bottom drawer is real. The top opens. The red-painted chest has brass hardware. (Detroit Historical Commission)

380. *Blanket chest, many drawers, nineteenth century* This pine blanket chest is painted red. The lower section has two drawers that are real. The top drawers are false, and the top opens for blanket storage. (Taylor and Dull, photography)

382. *Chest, nineteenth century* This early Victorian chest (c. 1850) has two top drawers and doors with a gothic arch that hide two shelves. The chest is stained red and yellow to simulate cherry and maple. It was made in North Lancaster, Ontario, Canada. (Upper Canada Village, Morrisburg, Ontario, Canada)

383. *Cabinet, nineteenth century* This mahogany and redwood cabinet was made in California about 1850–1870. (Index of American Design, Washington, D.C.)

150

10

Cradles

THE BABY'S BED known as a cradle is an ancient form of furniture with its earliest beginnings well recorded. Pictures of rocking cradles from the fourteenth and fifteenth centuries show that the basic design has changed very little through the years.

The oldest cradles were shaped like a box with rockers added. Prior to the eighteenth century a hood or cover was added.

The first American cradles were made with the rectangular panel construction typical of all Pilgrim furniture. Turned spindles served as decorations.

The sides of the later cradles were made with spindles. Often a canopy was placed above the bed.

Because the same design was used for centuries, it is difficult to date cradles. Cradles and all baby furniture were seldom disposed of, making it possible for several generations to use the same cradle.

The sleigh cradle (Picture 392) was developed about 1830. It was styled after the sleigh bed used during the same time. This special type of cradle was popular only for about twenty years.

384. *Cradle, seventeenth century* One of the earliest American cradles used in the original Pilgrim settlement. The turned spindles and paneled sides were like those used on chests of that period. (Pilgrim Society, Plymouth, Massachusetts)

385. *Cradle, nineteenth century* This canopied bed was probably originally a crib, with the rockers being added later. (The Woodstock Historical Society, Woodstock, Vermont)

386. *Cradle, nineteenth century* This maple cradle was made in Clarksville, Texas, about 1845. Rockers may have been added. (Index of American Design, Washington, D.C.)

387. *Cradle, nineteenth century* Walnut cradle made near Marshall, Texas, between 1834 and 1840. The posts supported a top canopy. (Index of American Design, Washington, D.C.)

388. *Cradle, nineteenth century* Pine, ash, and maple cradle made in Kalamazoo, Michigan, about 1830. Note how the style resembles the spindle-back chairs of the period. (Index of American Design, Washington, D.C.)

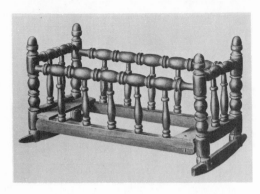

389. *Cradle, late nineteenth century*
A pine cradle, varnished red, made about 1870 in Texas. This is a doll cradle with unusual turned spindles. (Index of American Design, Washington, D.C.)

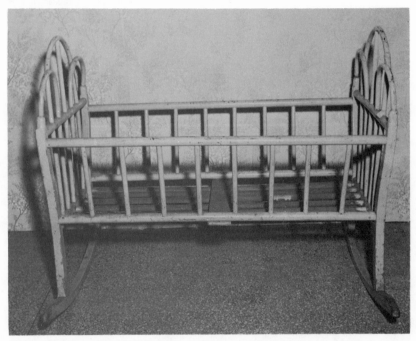

390. *Cradle, nineteenth century* An elm soaked in water was bent into shape to form the head and foot of this cradle made about 1859. (Howard County Museum, Kokomo, Indiana)

391. *Cradle, eighteenth century*
Hooded cradle made from walnut during the late eighteenth century. The scalloping is excellent. Note the shape of the rocker. (Shelburne Museum, Inc. Photographer, Einars J. Mengis)

153

392. *Cradle, nineteenth century* A sleigh cradle, painted mahogany, with date marked in gold: on headboard, 1834; on the footboard, 1888. The cradle was found in Maine. (Shelburne Museum, Inc. Photographer, Einars J. Mengis)

394. *Cradle, mid-nineteenth century* A cottonwood cradle made by a Pennsylvania maker about 1850. Note well-shaped side and openings that served as handles. (Cowlitz County Historical Museum, Kelso, Washington)

393. *Cradle, nineteenth century* A midwestern cradle made about 1850. (Olmsted County Historical Society, Rochester, Minnesota)

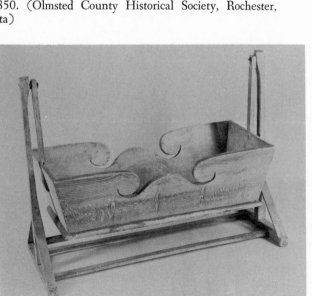

396. *Cradle, nineteenth century* A box cradle made of pine in Fredericksburg, Texas, about 1876. Note the corner posts. (Index of American Design, Washington, D.C.)

395. *Cradle, nineteenth century* A hanging cradle made of pine, painted with grained pattern. It was made in 1875 in Braintree, Vermont. (Shelburne Museum, Inc. Photographer, Einars J. Mengis)

11

Cupboards

History

A CUPBOARD could be any piece of furniture used for storage, including the press cupboard, open cupboard, or hutch; corner cabinet, china cabinet, and the closed dresser. Cupboards of the same design and construction are often called by different names even though they are the same basic piece of furniture.

Cupboards have been, and are, used as storage places for dishes, pewter, and other eating utensils. Clothes were placed in a different type of cupboard, called a "kas cupboard" (see Chapter 16, "Pennsylvania Furniture"), by the Dutch.

The first American cupboards were made about 1660.

There are two types of cupboards and dressers: those built in one piece, usually as a part of the architecture of the house, and those built in two sections that could be moved around the room. The built-in cupboard rarely had feet, and was made so that the room molding continued at the base and often at the top of the cupboard.

PRESS CUPBOARD AND COURT CUPBOARD

The court cupboard is a low cupboard, made during the seventeenth century, with an open shelf near the floor and a boxed-in area at the top for storage. These cupboards are rarities, and are mentioned here only because they are part of the ancestry of the cupboard.

The press cupboard was also a seventeenth-century furniture design. It resembled the court cupboard except that the bottom shelf was closed by doors. Of rectangular construction, it had turned decorations popular at the time. It was used as we use a sideboard today. Press cupboards were made of oak, pine, or maple. They were the first pieces of furniture to re-

semble the cupboard of the country maker of the eighteenth and nineteenth centuries.

THE OPEN CUPBOARD, HUTCH, OR DRESSER

The open cupboard (Pictures 398–405) is also called an open dresser or a hutch cupboard. Most of the furniture makers now producing reproductions of country furniture call their pieces hutch cupboards.

They were first made during the early 1700's. The sides, top, and shelves were all scalloped or otherwise notched and decorated. Double doors were hung on exposed hinges at the bottom. The same style of hutch cupboard was made from 1730 to 1840, but they can be dated from the construction of the drawers, the type of lumber used on the back of the piece, the hardware, and other details. The furniture makers of the nineteenth century continued to make open cupboards, but with less elaborate scalloping and molding.

Spoon notches were rare in New England. The New England cupboard was usually made with a plain cornice and small knobs for the drawers and doors. Pieces made in Pennsylvania had elaborately scalloped cornices.

According to some definitions, a true hutch must have two doors on the bottom with the top and the bottom of the piece the same width. There may or may not be a drawer in the center.

The pewter cupboard is defined in much the same manner as a hutch cupboard except that the front of the piece is narrower at the top than at the lowest shelf (Picture 402). Because these definitions are technical, they have been ignored by most dealers and writers. The terms "hutch cupboard" and "pewter cupboard" are used interchangeably. In this book we have used whichever name is given by the museum or owner of the piece pictured.

Closed Cupboard

The closed front cupboard (Pictures 406–414) was usually made in two parts, the upper section with wooden or glass doors and the bottom section with wooden cupboard doors. The general appearance of the closed cupboard resembled the open cupboard because it was made during the same general period, from 1730 through all the following periods of furniture making. The country cupboard was made from walnut, maple, cherry, mahogany, or painted pine.

Corner Cabinets

The corner cabinet (Pictures 415–422) is any three-sided cabinet made to fit into the corner. Because it took little space it was a popular style, with some actually built into the house as a permanent architectural feature. Many of the architectural corner cabinets have been removed from old houses and sold separately.

Eighteenth-century examples of the early cabinets were made with a diagonal front and molded cornices. The cabinet went straight to the floor, with no molded base, and the top half or two-thirds of the piece had cabinet doors or shelves. Some of the most desirable corner cabinets were made with shell-like domes and scalloped shelves, but these were not pieces of country furniture. Pillars or trim that resembled pillars were placed at the edge of the cabinet by the more careful craftsmen. The doors at the bottom of the cabinet hid several shelves.

One of the best methods to date a corner cupboard is through the hinges, hardware, and moldings. The butt hinge was used after 1800. The **H** hinge was used during the eighteenth and early nineteenth centuries. If the cupboard was made for use in the kitchen, it was usually made from pine, then painted. Unpainted pine, considered formal, was used in the dining room. The **H** hinge was either left black or painted white, whichever made it the least conspicuous. Formal cabinets had the brass hardware of the style for the period.

The molding used on the corner cabinet before 1790 was usually a simple half round that was worked into the design. After 1790 the moldings were made in many different elaborate shapes.

The nineteenth-century corner cupboard was similar to the earlier examples, with less elaborate trim and molding after 1825. Pine was frequently used.

Sideboards and Other Dining-Room Storage Units

The sideboard was a Sheraton design first developed in England about 1780. Many English dining rooms had a long table that was flanked by two boxlike storage units for dishes or wine. Sheraton combined the end units and the table into one large piece of furniture that he called a sideboard. Many variations of this design in the Sheraton, Hepplewhite, and Empire styles were made in America, although few country examples of the eighteenth-century sideboard were made (Pictures 433, 434).

A shorter version of the sideboard was made in New England. South of the Mason-Dixon Line, particularly in Virginia, the hunt table developed (Pictures 436–439).

The formal sideboard went through many changes in shape; the center bowed in or out, the number of drawers increased, and the general appearance became bulkier and heavier. Some of the Empire-style sideboards had so many drawers they were almost cabinets made with drawers to the floor.

The sideboard is not a country style and is not described in detail; however, the hunt table is definitely a part of the country furniture of America.

Sugar Chest

The sugar chest was a popular southern form that was in use until about 1870 when it became easier to obtain sugar from a store.

A chest on legs, it had a bin for sugar and often one for coffee and another for spices. All the drawers and bins were locked. The sugar chest was usually kept in the dining room for use during dinner. Examples were made by fine formal cabinetmakers and less skilled country makers. Walnut, cherry, and other native southern woods were used (Pictures 441, 442).

Huntboard, 1800–1850 (Pictures 40–43)

The huntboard is another southern piece of furniture. Like the sideboard, it was popular, with formal cabinetmakers working in the style of Sheraton, as well as the country furniture maker. It was about 40 inches to 48 inches high. Its central cupboard was surrounded by drawers. These huntboards had no added carving or inlay. The legs were plain, often rectangular, with no foot. The huntboard was made of pine, walnut, cherry, or maple.

397. *Press cupboard, seventeenth century*
Painted oak and pine were used to make this cupboard in New England. This style of cupboard was the forerunner of the cupboard used in the eighteenth and nineteenth centuries. (Courtesy of Henry Ford Museum, Dearborn, Michigan)

398. *Open cupboard, eighteenth century* This Pennsylvania German style of dresser was made of walnut. Decorative molding, notched shelves for spoons, brass hardware on drawers, and rattail hinges are all features of the best cupboards of this type. Note the feet. (Metropolitan Museum of Art; Rogers Fund, 1945)

399. *Open cupboard, seventeenth century* Chestnut wood was used in this early country cupboard. Simple construction methods are apparent in the door and in the lack of feet. (Old Sturbridge Village, Sturbridge, Massachusetts)

400. *Open cupboard, seventeenth or eighteenth century* This unpainted pine cupboard with scalloped trim, H hinges, and well-constructed doors shows the skill of the maker. (Index of American Design, Washington, D.C.)

157

401. *Open cupboard, eighteenth century*
Extending rail feet support this green-painted pine cupboard. The rattail hinges and scalloped trim show that the country maker had skill, but the small wooden door latch and construction of the front reveal less talent. (Index of American Design, Washington, D.C.)

402. *Open cupboard, nineteenth century* This New England cupboard is sometimes called a pewter cupboard. It was made of pine early in the nineteenth century. Notice the scalloped edges, the panel door, and the feet. (Courtesy of the Henry Ford Museum, Dearborn, Michigan)

403. *Open cupboard, nineteenth century* This walnut dresser with well-formed bracket feet has scalloped trim. The plate guardrail is an interesting feature. (Taylor and Dull, photography)

404. *Open cupboard, nineteenth century* This brown-painted pine open-front dresser was made about 1820. The lack of trim and the hidden hinges for the doors indicate the nineteenth century. (Taylor and Dull, photography)

405. *Open cupboard, nineteenth century* This poplar and pine cupboard was called a "tower" in Nashville, Tennessee, where it was made about 1810. The wooden latch for the doors is located at an unusual spot above the two doors. (Index of American Design, Washington, D.C.)

406. *Closed cupboard, eighteenth century* Pine was used in this well-constructed cupboard. The curve of the leg is repeated at the open shelf. The bottom cupboard doors have panels. It is probably a piece made in New England. (Taylor and Dull, photography)

407. *Closed cupboard, nineteenth century* A craftsman from Pennsylvania, probably Berks County, made this pine "dresser" about 1828. The curved bracket feet, trim at the edge of the sides, the panel doors, and the top molding show that this is the work of a skilled cabinetmaker. (Index of American Design, Washington, D.C.)

408. *Closed cupboard, nineteenth century* This pine cupboard, or dresser, is painted dark green, with moldings and details painted red. It was made in Pennsylvania about 1820. The turned applied decorations are similar to those used on "spool" furniture. Notice the well-shaped glazed doors. (Taylor and Dull, photography)

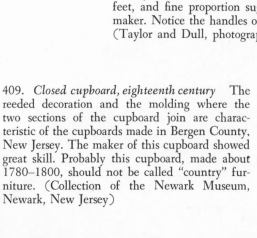

410. *Corner cupboard, late eighteenth century* This inlaid cherry corner cabinet with a white-painted interior was made in Pennsylvania. The bail handles, bracket feet, and fine proportion suggest a skilled maker. Notice the handles on the drawers. (Taylor and Dull, photography)

409. *Closed cupboard, eighteenth century* The reeded decoration and the molding where the two sections of the cupboard join are characteristic of the cupboards made in Bergen County, New Jersey. The maker of this cupboard showed great skill. Probably this cupboard, made about 1780–1800, should not be called "country" furniture. (Collection of the Newark Museum, Newark, New Jersey)

411. *Closed cupboard, eighteenth century* A skilled cabinetmaker from North Carolina made this cupboard of cypress and pine. A slide shelf is between the top and bottom sections. The stopped fluting on the decorative pillars in front is a sophisticated design, probaby too well made to be classed as "country" furniture. (Collection of Mr. and Mrs. R. N. Williams II, Philadelphia, Pennsylvania)

412. *Cupboard, nineteenth century* A southern cupboard made of cypress and other woods. The door hinges are exposed. This is a simple cupboard of the type made in the mid 1800's. (Historic Mobile Preservation Society)

413. *Closed cupboard, china cabinet, nineteenth century* This pine cupboard with mahogany veneer was made in Bastrop, Texas. The scalloped edging at the top looks like a later addition. The lower cupboard doors were made in the manner of many Spanish-influenced pieces of the Southwest. (Index of American Design, Washington, D.C.)

414. *Closed cupboard, nineteenth century* This walnut china cabinet with spool-turned decorations was made in 1854, in San Antonio, Texas. Notice how the cupboard door and drawer arrangement remains from the eighteenth-century styles. (Index of American Design, Washington, D.C.)

161

'415. *Corner cabinet, eighteenth century* This curly-maple corner cabinet was made in the Hepplewhite style. The shaped cornice top is the work of a skilled maker. This is probably not a "country" piece. (Taylor and Dull, photography)

416. *Corner cupboard, eighteenth century* This pine corner cupboard was made in the late eighteenth century. The interior is painted blue. It was made to blend with the baseboard of the room. Notice the fluting. (Taylor and Dull, photography)

417. *Corner cupboard, eighteenth century* This cupboard, made of Virginia walnut, is attributed to a Pennsylvania workman. The Chippendale-style legs show that this was not a built-in cabinet. H hinges and panel doors are features of the eighteenth century. (Taylor and Dull, photography)

418. Corner cupboard, nineteenth century This is an unusual carved pine corner cupboard that was made about 1800. The ropelike trim at the top, the side fluting, and the diamond-and-shield decorations at the side are indications of a skilled workman.

420. Corner cupboard, nineteenth century This walnut cupboard was made in eastern Ohio. The fluted trim and curved apron and feet are well designed. (Courtesy of Art Institute of Chicago)

419. Corner closed cupboard, or china cabinet, nineteenth century A unique Pennsylvania painted pine cabinet made about 1820. The panels are painted to simulate graining. The carved decorations, fluting, and shaping of glass panes are remarkable. Glass handles are used on the drawers. (Taylor and Dull, photography)

421. Corner cupboard, nineteenth century This pine cabinet with H hinges was made in two pieces. The wooden mushroom knobs and drawer arrangement are typical of the nineteenth century. (Collection of Mr. and Mrs. R. N. Williams II, Philadelphia)

163

424. *Chest, nineteenth century* A small chest made of white pine in Michigan about 1850. The scalloped apron and backboard are an earlier style than the leg construction and hardware indicate. Note the thickness of the lumber used for the drawer fronts. (Index of American Design, Washington, D.C.)

422. *Corner cupboard, nineteenth century* This pine cupboard is of southern origin. Notice the replacement locks on the doors. (Old Court House Museum, Vicksburg, Mississippi)

423. *Hanging corner cupboard, nineteenth century* A small cupboard with a scrolled open shelf below, made in Dobbs Ferry, New York, about 1810. (Index of American Design, Washington, D.C.)

425. *Cabinet, Zoarite, nineteenth century* The bonnet cabinet was called a "Haube-Kaeschtle" in Zoar, Ohio, where it was made in 1836. The black walnut was painted. Notice the rattail hinges. (Index of American Design, Washington, D.C.)

426. *Cabinet, Zoarite, nineteenth century*   A cherry bonnet cabinet made about 1835 in Zoar, Ohio. The panels are decorated with painted flowers. (Index of American Design, Washington, D.C.)

428. *Closed corner cupboard, nineteenth century*   This is a mahogany built-in called a "three-cornered safe." It was made near Laredo, Texas. The scalloped panel of the door shows Spanish influence. Notice the concealed hinges and porcelain knobs. (Index of American Design, Washington, D.C.) LEFT

429. *Narrow closed cupboard, nineteenth century*   Brown-stained pine was used in this cupboard made at Mount Lebanon, New York, about 1820. Note the unusual catch on the lower door. (Index of American Design, Washington, D.C.) RIGHT

427. *Corner cupboard, nineteenth century*   This cupboard, made in 1845, is probably the top half of a large built-in cabinet. Notice the porcelain knobs. (Olmsted County Historical Society, Rochester, Minnesota)

430. *Corner cupboard with open shelves, nineteenth century*   This is an unusual pine shelf made about 1810. (Lawrence Romaine, Weathercock House, Middleboro, Massachusetts)

431. *Wardrobe, nineteenth century* A cabinet of pine, painted yellow, made in San Augustine, Texas. This was used as a clothes closet. Notice the unusual pin-type hinge and the legs that are extensions of the sides. (Index of American Design, Washington, D.C.) LEFT

432. *Wardrobe, nineteenth century* A natural pine cabinet made in Nacogdoches, Texas, about 1845. The simplest type of construction and hardware were used. (Index of American Design, Washington, D.C.) RIGHT

433. *Sideboard, eighteenth century* This is a Hepplewhite-style curly-maple sideboard with a serpentine (curved) front that was made in Pennsylvania. The undecorated surfaces place this in the "country" furniture category although the sideboard is a "formal" furniture shape. (Taylor and Dull, photography)

434. *Sideboard, nineteenth century* This curly-maple Hepplewhite sideboard was made between 1800 and 1810 in Springfield, Massachusetts, by William Lloyd. The original paper label states, "Country produce taken in payment or approved credit if desired—Feb 16 1813." Notice the hardware and the straight leg. Most English sideboards have spade feet; American ones have the straight leg with no foot. (John S. Walton)

435. *Sideboard table, eighteenth century*   Pine and oak were used in this New England piece that is sometimes called a sideboard table, although the formal sideboard was designed after this was made in the early eighteenth century. Notice the stretchers on the legs, and compare the general form with tables of this period. (Taylor and Dull, photography)

436. *Sideboard table, side table, or hunt table, eighteenth century* The southern areas call this a hunt table. It was made, of pine, in Virginia. Notice the cabriole legs in front and profiled legs in rear. (State Department of Archives and History, Raleigh, North Carolina; in Tryon Palace, New Bern, North Carolina)

437. *Sideboard or hunt table, nineteenth century*   Honey-colored pine hunt board made in Virginia about 1800. This is a furniture form found only in the South. (Taylor and Dull, photography)

438. *Hunt board, nineteenth century*   A Hepplewhite hunt board made of yellow pine about 1800–1810. The scalloped apron is unusual. This piece is now being reproduced. (Courtesy Henry Ford Museum, Dearborn, Michigan)

167

439. *Hunt board, nineteenth century* This is a Hepplewhite hunt board of southern origin made of dark-brown-stained pine about 1810. Note the unusual decorative grooving of the drawers and the sides. (Courtesy of Henry Ford Museum, Dearborn, Michigan)

440. *Cellarette, nineteenth century* The cellarette held wine bottles. This example, made of pine and poplar, is of unknown origin. Drawer construction, plain legs, and simple hardware date it in the first half of the nineteenth century. (Index of American Design, Washington, D.C.)

441. *Cellarette (sugar chest?), eighteenth century* Mahogany chest with pullout shelf made in the style of 1750–1775. The scalloped apron and curved legs show the skill of the maker. (Index of American Design, Washington, D.C.)

442. *Sugar chest, nineteenth century* Sugar, tea, and spices were stored in the bins of the sugar chest. This cherry chest was made about 1830 in Tennessee. Turned legs and wooden knobs are on the drawer. (Index of American Design, Washington, D.C.)

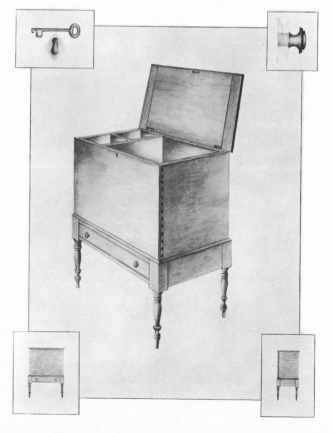

12

Desks

THE DESK was originally a Bible box on a stand. The idea of a one-piece bureau desk developed because the Bible box needed a table stand. By 1770, a desk with three or four drawers and a slanted front was popular. This slanted top was also called a "falling front." The front could be opened, exposing a convenient writing area on the inside. The eighteenth century also saw the development of the secretary, a combination desk and bookcase. During the nineteenth century the flat-top desk became popular, and the famous schoolmaster's desks were developed.

There are several features that may or may not appear on a desk. A kneehole desk had drawers on each side and a space for the knees in the center. The pullout writing shelf was an eighteenth-century adaptation that added to the usefulness of a desk. A wooden shelf slid out and gave extra work surface. A roll-top or a tambour front was occasionally used to conceal the many compartments inside the top of the desk. Doors could also hide the cubbyholes.

The eighteenth-century desk fascinates many of the collectors because it was the period of the secret compartment and hidden drawers.

CHIPPENDALE-TYPE SLANT-FRONT DESKS, 1750–1775 (Picture 446)

The formal furniture makers produced many examples of the eighteenth-century Chippendale desk. The slanted front flipped down and was held by two slide-out supports. There were many compartments and three or four small drawers inside the desk. The desks were elaborately put together, with scrolls above the compartments, curved sunbursts, reeding, and other decorative cabinetwork. Each tiny drawer in a well-made desk could be replaced upside down and would

still slide freely. Later, less precise workmen rarely made truly square small drawers like these.

The desk had bracket feet that were typical of the other furniture of the period; its hardware was in the style of Thomas Chippendale.

The desk was about 3 feet to 4 feet wide and 3½ feet high. It was made from curly maple, maple, walnut, cherry, birch, or mahogany.

SLANT-FRONT HEPPLEWHITE, 1785–1800 (Pictures 447, 448, 449)

The general shape and construction of the desk continued into the Hepplewhite period, with the hardware changing to the oval or round type, the feet curving out in a shape known as a French foot, and a curved skirt added. The desks were made of cherry, maple, birch, or mahogany.

NINETEENTH-CENTURY SLANT-FRONT DESK (Pictures 450, 451, 452)

The nineteenth-century desk continued in the same general style, except that the inside became plainer and the small drawers and dividers were made without the decorative carpentry. The skirt was straight, and the feet were plain bracket style or plain rectangular. The nineteenth-century slant-front desk was popular in all parts of the country. Examples have been found in maple, cherry, birch, walnut, pine, and many in red-painted pine.

DROP-LID DESK, OR FALL FRONT (Picture 453)

The drop-lid desk was made in the same general style as the slant front, but the writing surface was not slanted. The desk resembled a bureau or chest of drawers, but the top section, instead of being a drawer, was a fall front that opened as a writing surface. The Chippendale-style fall front was made from 1750 to about 1780, and the Hepplewhite style from 1790 to 1800. Less elaborate versions of the fall front continued to be made by the nineteenth-century country cabinetmaker.

Another type of drop-lid desk, made about 1840 and most often seen in country furniture, appeared to be a box on a table, and in some instances the top and bottom sections actually were made separately. There was one large drawer in the top section. The table-like part had round Sheraton legs, heavier Empire legs, or spool-turned legs, depending on the age. These were made of cherry, pine, poplar and, later, of walnut.

SECRETARY DESK (Pictures 454–457)

A special type of desk appeared in country furniture about 1810. The formal cabinetmakers were producing masterpieces of cabinetry called tambour desks. Because the country furniture maker could not attempt the tricky style of joining thin pieces of wood, he made a cupboard desk. It resembled the city maker's tambour desk but with cupboard doors instead of tambour doors. The finished piece resembled a table with one drawer and a top section that was narrower than the table and had two cupboard doors that concealed

the shelves. Such desks were made from mahogany, maple, cherry, or birch.

SECRETARY DESK, BOOKCASE TYPE (Pictures 455, 456, 457)

The true secretary desk was really a bookcase and a desk. Many types of secretaries were made by the formal furniture makers. The writing surface was a fall-front, fold-over, cylinder front, or pullout type. Each secretary was made in the style popular for other furniture of the same period. Most secretaries were made by skilled cabinetmakers and had glass doors and arched tops with other formal design elements. The country makers made secretaries with large heavy legs and added carvings in the Empire style (about 1840).

SCHOOLMASTER'S DESK, 1820–1870 (Picture 463)

The schoolmaster's desk, never made by the city cabinetmaker, is a true piece of country furniture. It was used in schools and many small business offices. The lid could be raised, uncovering a large compartment for the storage of books. It had square or turned legs with no feet or very small feet.

Occasionally there was one drawer in the desk. Inkwells, pencil trays, and special grooves indicate that the desk was used at school. It had taller legs than the child's desk still in use. The schoolmaster's desk was almost always made from pine or other soft wood.

443. *Slant-front desk, American, eighteenth century* This very early (1700–1710) desk is made of Virginia walnut. The feet are of the William and Mary design. The general shape of the desk remained through the eighteenth century with only a change in the shape of the leg. (Metropolitan Museum of Art; gift of Mrs. Russell Sage, 1909)

444. *William and Mary slant-front desk, Pennsylvania, eighteenth century* This Pennsylvania desk is similar to the preceding example. It is made of pine and maple. Notice the difference in drawer placement. (Taylor and Dull, photography)

446. *Chippendale desk, eighteenth century* A typical Chippendale-style desk with the legs and hardware associated with the style. (Garth's Auction Barn)

445. *Queen Anne slant-front desk, eighteenth century* The typical Queen Anne leg is seen on this curly-maple desk. It is placed on a lowboy frame. The curved skirt is of interest. (Taylor and Dull, photography)

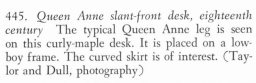

449. *Pine slant-front desk, date unknown* The stretcher and leg arrangement on this desk and the thick lumber used indicate a country maker of some ability. Notice how much of the hardware is wood, not the expensive metal used by city makers. (Collection of Mr. and Mrs. R. N. Williams II, Philadelphia, Pennsylvania)

447. *Hepplewhite slant-front desk, eighteenth century* This is the formal mahogany cabinetmakers' desk that inspired the country furniture makers of the late eighteenth and early nineteenth centuries. The shaped skirt, oval brasses, drawer arrangement, and compartment details were all adapted by less skilled makers. (Taylor and Dull, photography)

448. *Hepplewhite slant-front desk, late eighteenth century* This country-furniture cherry desk, shown open and shut, was made about 1800 in Connecticut. (Summit County Historical Society, Akron, Ohio)

450. *Slant-front desk, nineteenth century*
This pine desk was made with walnut pillars about 1835. It was influenced by the Norwegian settlers of Minnesota. Notice the plain bracket feet. (Olmsted County Historical Society, Rochester, Minnesota)

452. *Painted slant-lid desk, nineteenth century* This painted-pine desk was made in Albany, New York, about 1840. It is yellow with red, green, and black leaf and line trim. The slant lid has a scene of horses and soldiers. (Courtesy of the Henry Ford Museum, Dearborn, Michigan)

451. *Slant-front desk on frame* (open and shut) The turned legs and wooden hardware on this curly-maple desk indicate a country origin. This slant front reminds one of the fall-front desk of the nineteenth century. (Shelburne Museum, Inc.)

453. *Fall-front desk, nineteenth century* This walnut desk was made about 1855 for a schoolteacher, and is sometimes called a schoolmaster's desk. The turned legs and drawer arrangement are typical of this type of desk. (Index of American Design, Washington, D.C.)

454. *Secretary desk, nineteenth century* The curved legs and heavy lines of this walnut desk indicate the southwestern origin of this Texas-made desk of 1820. The arrangement of cabinet drawers and writing surface is that of a nineteenth-century country secretary desk. It was probably made by slaves. (Index of American Design, Washington, D.C.)

455. *Secretary desk, nineteenth century* This walnut desk has no drawers in the base and all wooden doors on the bookcase. It was probably made in San Augustine, Texas. (Index of American Design, Washington, D.C.)

456. *Secretary desk, late nineteenth century* The heavy legs and bulky top indicate the 1875 date of this walnut desk and bookcase or secretary desk. It was made in Missouri. (Index of American Design, Washington, D.C.)

458. *Trustees' desk, nineteenth century* Shaker-made desk of stained pine made about 1830–1840 at Mount Lebanon, New York. The desk was to be used by two men at once. This is probably a unique example. (Hancock Shaker Village, Hancock, Massachusetts)

457. *Secretary desk, nineteenth century* Mahogany, cherry, and pine were all used in this 1840 desk. The legs and cathedral windows in the bookcase are unusual. It was made in Michigan. (Index of American Design, Washington, D.C.)

459. *Empire secretary desk* The curly-maple graining adds to the pattern on this Virginia secretary made about 1810–1820. The heavy legs and pillars indicate the Empire influence. (Taylor and Dull, photography)

460. *Desk, late nineteenth century* The bottom half of this desk resembles the base of the secretary desk. The carved top "crowns" and the odd arrangement of cupboards indicate the Victorian influence. (Pensacola Historical Society, Pensacola, Florida)

461. *Accounting desk, nineteenth century* Specially designed desks were often used in stores. This accounting desk of waxed walnut was made about 1846–1860 in Bishop Hill, Illinois. (Index of American Design, Washington, D.C.)

462. *Schoolmaster's desk, nineteenth century* The top of this desk lifts, and papers are stored inside. This general shape, with or without a railing, is known as a schoolmaster's desk. (Western Reserve Historical Society, Cleveland, Ohio)

463. *Lift-top desk, date unknown* This unusual painted lift-top desk was made in Ontario, Canada. It is painted ocher with freehand black decorations. (Upper Canada Village, Morrisburg, Ontario, Canada)

13

Tables

History

TABLES HAVE BEEN IN USE since the earliest times, long before chairs. From the Egyptians on, every civilization found this furniture form useful.

During the Middle Ages tables were used principally for dining. A trestle-type table was set up for the meal and then removed. It lacked beauty and was not considered a stationary piece of furniture.

The early Puritans used a similar type of table with a pine top about 12 feet long, with supports made from oak.

The seventeenth century was really the era of the table, with a table for each special purpose. A game table was developed with scooped-out indentations for the chips, and small pullout shelves that held candles. These were made with three, four, or more sides to accommodate the special numbers of players needed for the many different games. Dressing, writing, sewing, and side tables were constructed. Even a small table was created to hold the teaset when tea was served. Tables that folded or closed in some manner were popular by the end of the seventeenth century.

American country tables can be recognized in many ways. They were usually of simple design and sturdy construction. The country furniture maker, in trying to copy most of the city styles, frequently overestimated his capabilities and produced very oddly proportioned furniture. He simplified the carved ornaments, made the turnings less intricate, and painted or gilded the decorations. The inlay he left for the more skilled city craftsman. Country pieces were made from native woods such as pine, walnut, cherry, maple, or the local fruitwoods. Mahogany was usually the mark of the city cabinetmaker. The frames of the table were made from hardwoods, with the tops made from pine, cherry, or maple. It is very rare to find turned legs of pine.

Tavern Tables

The name "tavern table" (Pictures 464–474) is modern, and refers to any lightweight table that could be easily moved and set before a guest in an inn or a tavern. Most pictured examples called "tavern tables" are made with no drawers or one small drawer. The turned legs were held by an H-type stretcher (Picture 470) or four stretchers. The top of the common tavern table extends over the edge of the legs and is rectangular. However, a few of the early ones had round tops.

The formal definition of a "tavern table" was given by Russell Kettle in his book about New England pine furniture. He wrote: "It [the tavern table] consisted of a joined frame of four, sometimes three legs, almost invariably turned, connected just above the feet by a circuit of stretchers, or a medial stretcher running between two end ones, either turned or plain. The top was usually rectangular, sometimes round, half round, or elliptical. There was a single drawer beneath the top. Usually the legs stood vertically on the floor but sometimes they slanted in."

EARLY, 1700–1750 (JACOBEAN, WILLIAM AND MARY)

The earliest American tavern tables were made in the Jacobean style. A few of them appear each year, previously unrecognized.

The table had a two- or three-board top, and may or may not have had a cleat under the top. The cleat is a piece of wood added to the underneath side of the top boards, running across the grain for additional support and to avoid warping.

The table may be up to 5 feet long and 30 inches wide, although most of them are smaller. The top extends over the legs from 6 inches to 8 inches. The side of the table, or the skirt, is usually plain, although in the best examples it is scalloped.

If there is a drawer in the tavern table it should be from 6 inches to 8 inches deep with a wooden turned knob. Occasionally a knob appears even when there is no drawer.

The four turned legs with ball feet are about 2 inches in diameter. The box stretcher, popular on the early tavern tables, was the customary four-stretcher arrangement with one stretcher on each side of the table and with each stretcher joining two legs.

The very earliest tavern tables had a special type of turning on the leg called a spiral turning.

The tavern table was made in all parts of the colonies, but a surprisingly large number of these tables have survived from the Pennsylvania area. The explanation may be because more tavern tables were made in Pennsylvania than elsewhere. Their legs were made from walnut, maple, or other hardwoods, with pine or other soft woods used for the top. A few are all pine and very light in weight.

A good table can be distinguished from a poor one by the turnings, the trim on the apron, the general proportion, and the type of wood used.

The local variations in the early tables can help in identifying a tavern table. Very rare are the Spanish foot and splayed leg. The splayed leg remained popular in the South until about 1790, when the Queen Anne and the Chippendale styles became the vogue.

The breadboard end is an indication of a better table regardless of age. A piece of wood was added to the end of the tabletop in the same manner as a breadboard. The grain of the wood runs in the opposite direction of the grain of the table boards, thus helping to keep the top from warping.

Queen Anne Tavern Table, 1725–1775

The tavern tables of the Queen Anne period were of many sizes, some quite large, from 5 feet to 8 feet in length. They had rectangular, oval, or round tops. The legs slightly tapered with a small pad foot and were typical of the Queen Anne period in formal furniture. *There was no stretcher.* The tavern table usually had a scalloped skirt and could have been made

with or without a drawer. The woods used were curly maple, plain maple, cherry, walnut, or pine. They appeared in all sections of the colonies but were most popular in the New England area.

1775–1800

The Chippendale styles influenced most of the formal furniture makers, but there is little indication of a Chippendale-style country version of the tavern table. Instead, the form gradually changed from the Queen Anne style to the nineteenth-century styles, which are adaptations of the earliest tavern tables.

Nineteenth-Century Tavern Tables

The nineteenth-century country furniture maker modeled his tables after the earlier versions. The tabletop often had two boards and was cleated, or, in good examples, had a breadboard end.

The tables ranged from 5 feet to 6 feet long and from 30 inches to 35 inches wide. The edge of the table had a plain skirt and no drawers. This simplification of the skirt and the omission of the drawer are just two of the ways the table became less elaborate in the nineteenth century.

The stretcher reappeared because the splayed leg was difficult to make and a stretcher was needed for structural support with a straight leg. A few skilled makers used the splayed leg and no stretcher, but most nineteenth-century tavern tables were made with the H stretcher or four stretchers.

The top and legs were usually made by using different hardwoods—maple, cherry, birch, and others; butternut, pine, and other soft woods were used for other parts. The tables were occasionally painted black or dark red.

Tavern tables are judged by their general appearance, proportion, turnings, or even lack of turnings.

Windsor Tables

A special version of the tavern table was made in a limited quantity during the eighteenth century. They were called Windsor tables (Picture 475) and were made with three or four legs that looked like the ones on a Windsor chair. They were made in New England and Philadelphia by Windsor chairmakers. The area of manufacture can be identified by comparing the turnings on the legs to those used on Windsor chairs.

Windsor tables are very rare, and almost all known examples are in museums.

TRESTLE TABLE

The trestle table (Pictures 476–482) is a long dinner table that was first used during the Middle Ages. The earliest known American versions date from 1650. The one-board plank top ranged up to 12 feet in length and was from 24 inches to 30 inches wide. The table-top was supported by two or three *T*-shaped trestles on a shoe foot. The name "trestle" refers to the single upright unit, not to the entire support for the table. To secure everything in place, a long board was placed through the upright trestles.

These tables were made of oak and maple. They were designed to be taken apart after each meal. This collapsible feature and their size were not appreciated by later generations. As a consequence they were not saved and are now very rare.

During the nineteenth century the Shakers made an adaptation of the early trestle table (Pictures 481, 482). Their version can be seen in most Shaker museums. (See Chapter 17, "Shaker Furniture.")

The trestle tables made during the eighteenth and early nineteenth centuries, to about 1840, are called New England survival-type trestle tables. They had a two-board top with the ends of the boards cleated. The trestle foot was much plainer than those used during the seventeenth century. The survival trestle table ranged from 4 feet to 6 feet in length, and was made entirely from pine or pine with maple trestles.

SAWBUCK TABLE

The sawbuck table was made during the late seventeenth and early eighteenth centuries. It had an *X*-shaped leg at each end and an *X*-shaped trestle. A plain horizontal stretcher joined the *X*-shaped ends. Usually one stretcher was placed at the center of the *X*, but occasionally one was placed at each side of the table, and at a height sufficiently convenient for it to be used as a footrest.

The long top was made from oak, walnut, or pine. Two boards were used with either cleated or bread-board ends. The *X*-shaped trestle had chamfered or slightly rounded edges.

A comparable table was made in the nineteenth century from 1800 to 1840. It was similar to the early sawbuck table but was lighter in weight, and the edges of the *X* trestle were not rounded. Its top ranged from 3 feet to 5 feet in length and from 26 inches to 32 inches in width. It was made from pine or had a pine top and a hardwood support.

GATELEG TABLE

The gateleg table (Pictures 483–486 has been made in all parts of the United States, but gained its original popularity in Europe. A "leggy" piece of furniture, it was originally designed during the early eighteenth century when turned legs were apparent on all shapes of furniture. A series of legs could be opened that would hold an extension or leaf.

The William and Mary style of gateleg table was made from 1690 to 1730. It had an oval or oblong top ranging from 3 feet to 6 feet in length, with six stationary legs and two swinging legs, all made of turned wood, as was the stretcher that joined the leg. Some early examples featured a Spanish foot; some contained a drawer that opened with a wooden knob. Gateleg tables were made from walnut, maple, or cherry.

Some unusual examples had six legs and two swinging gates held on two legs each. These and other arrangements of gates make this type of table very desirable.

The general style of the table remained the same during the eighteenth and nineteenth centuries. The construction details in the drawer, the method of joining large pieces of wood, and especially the type of turning will help to indicate age. Follow this general rule: the more elaborate the turnings, the earlier the table.

Northern tables had conventional eighteenth-century turnings with the vase and ball, the stretcher having several balls or other protuberances. The Southern turnings were less elaborate, with the stretcher almost a plain, undecorated piece of wood.

Most New England tables were made from maple or walnut. In Pennsylvania walnut was the usual material. In the South it is said that *only* walnut was used.

Gateleg tables are also judged by size, with the very large and the very small examples considered rare. Most gateleg tables range in width from 36 inches to 78 inches across. The character of the turnings, the number of feet (the more, the better), and the style of the turnings will help to indicate the age and desirability of the table.

BUTTERFLY TABLE

The butterfly table (Pictures 487, 488) is a type of drop-leaf table, first made in America about 1700 to 1730, that has been made ever since. It is American in design. The name is derived from the wing- or leaf-shaped bracket that holds up the table leaf. Instead of a pair of legs, as in the gateleg table, the bracket supports the leaf. The table was probably developed in Connecticut, with early examples being made in Massachusetts and New Hampshire.

A butterfly table must have splayed legs since the butterfly will not work properly if the legs are straight. Most of these tables have oval tops.

The bracket is a plain wing-shaped piece of wood from ½ inch to ⅝ of an inch thick. Be suspicious if the edge of the bracket is scalloped, for only a few old tables with elaborate carving at the edge of the bracket are known to exist.

The legs of the table were turned and a plain box stretcher was used. Some were made with ball feet. Usually it had a drawer whose bottom was wider than the top to allow it to slide between the slanted legs. Small wooden knobs were used on the drawer. Its height ranged from 25 inches to 27 inches. The top was maple or cherry, and the structural parts were of any type of wood.

Butterfly tables with more than one wing are rare, and tables with three or four wings are extremely rare.

DROP-LEAF TABLE

Any table with a leaf that drops down to the side, such as a gateleg or a butterfly table, is called a drop-leaf table (Pictures 483–500). There are many styles with simple mechanisms for supporting the leaf when opened.

Up to the Chippendale period the drop-leaf table was made in all styles. It was not a part of the formal furniture style of the Hepplewhite period, nor was it used in the later periods of formal furniture during the nineteenth century. It was, however, popular with country makers who used the older designs.

The Queen Anne drop-leaf table had two legs of typical Queen Anne shape that swung over to hold the leaf and were slightly curved to a small pad foot. The top of the table was either rectangular or oval.

The drop-leaf tables of the nineteenth century remained in the same style or adapted it by using a straight leg with occasional spool turnings. (See Chapter 18, "Spool Furniture.")

PEMBROKE TABLE

The name Pembroke came from an Englishman, the Earl of Pembroke. The Pembroke table (Picture 491) was popular from 1760 to 1820, and is still being made in both formal and country styles. It has a broad top with narrow drop leaves. (A special variation of the Pembroke table was made with a wide drop leaf and a narrow top and called a harvest table.) The fixed top of the eighteenth-century table ranges from 26 inches to 30 inches in length and from 16 inches to 18 inches in width. The leaves are half the width of the fixed top and are supported by inconspicuously shaped brackets. They often have slightly rounded corners. The end of the table has a straight and narrow skirt. Some have a drawer that was used to hold silverware. The four legs are square and most often with an **X** stretcher. The country table was made from cherry or curly maple, while mahogany was the wood for more formal styles.

The nineteenth-century examples are similar, but now spool turnings had gained popularity and the legs were turned. The drop leaf was shorter than before. These tables were made from cherry, pine, maple, or birch.

If you buy a drop-leaf table, be sure to question how comfortable a dining table it will make. When the leaves are up, will you be able to sit at a side or end without bumping into the structural supports under the top? This is a defect in many of these tables because they were not made originally for use as a dining-room piece.

PORRINGER TABLE (Picture 484)

A porringer table is the modern name applied to an early style. The corners of the tabletop were rounded like a porringer, and the rounded pieces were used to hold candles.

LAZY-SUSAN TABLE

Any table with a rotating tray in the center is called a lazy-susan table. Some authors call the lazy-susan table a farm or harvest table, but this is misleading. The cherry and maple lazy-susan tables of the Midwest were made in the 1860–1880 period. The legs are the best indication of age of a lazy-susan table.

TILT-TOP OR TIP-TOP TABLE

Any table with a single center leg and a top that tilts to an upright position is a tilt-top table (Pictures 501–505). It is basically a formal furniture style. (See Chapter 2, "Candlestands.")

HANDKERCHIEF TABLE (Picture 489)

A special drop-leaf table, made during the late eighteenth century, has been called a handkerchief table. The leaf drops and the corner points to the floor, making a triangular drop. The handkerchief table was very rare in formal as well as in country furniture.

TABLE CHAIRS OR CHAIR TABLE

A table chair or chair table (Pictures 530–536) was used during the seventeenth, eighteenth, and nineteenth centuries. It was an ingenious space-saving device that was a chair when the top was raised and a table when the top was down. It could be pushed against the wall to get it out of the way. The tabletop kept the draft off the person sitting in the chair.

The earliest chair tables (1675–1700) had square or turned uprights joined to square or flat arms on which the tabletop rested. The top was attached by means of a wooden pin that went through small boards, called cleats, which were attached to the underside of the tabletop. The top was round, square, or oblong, and was usually made from two boards. The legs were joined by a box stretcher.

Most of the early chair tables had pine tops and oak bases. Some, with elaborately turned stretchers, turned arms, or shaped tabletops, are still in existence. The chair part was made like any chair of its period.

SURVIVAL EXAMPLE, 1700–1825

The chair tables made during the eighteenth and early nineteenth centuries were less elaborate than those of the seventeenth century. The uprights were square. Some legs were joined by a box-type stretcher. A chair table usually had a round pine top with a seat made from maple or one of the other hardwoods.

HUTCH TABLE OR SETTLE TABLE

The name "hutch table" (Pictures 535–537) refers to a dual-purpose piece of furniture popular during the seventeenth and eighteenth centuries. If there is a chest under the tabletop and if the top tips back, the piece is called a hutch table. The hutch table resembles the table chair, but instead of a chair there is a chest under the tabletop. This style of furniture was made for so many years that it is difficult to date. The best indications of age are found in the shape of the leg and in the drawer construction. The hutch table was made as late as 1880, and copies are still being made.

464. *Tavern table, seventeenth century* Sometimes called a stretcher table, this Massachusetts piece was made of maple, oak, and pine about 1680–1700. The knob turnings are ebonized (painted black). Note the finial in the center of the shaped apron. (Courtesy of the Henry Ford Museum, Dearborn, Michigan)

465. *Tavern table, early eighteenth century* The box stretcher arrangement was used on this maple table with simple turned legs and no other distinguishing features. (The Metropolitan Museum of Art; gift of Mrs. Russell Sage, 1909)

466. *Tavern table, early eighteenth century* This is a typical tavern table made with an H stretcher and one drawer. Notice the mediocre turnings on the legs and the breadboard end on the tabletop. It has a pine top and a maple frame. (Metropolitan Museum of Art; gift of Mrs. Russell Sage, 1909)

467. *Tavern table, eighteenth century* The turned legs, the shaped top, and the unusual arrangement of stretchers at the top and bottom of the legs make this a fine example of an American turned leg table of about 1750. (Courtesy of National Park Service, Morristown National Historical Park, Morristown, New Jersey)

468. *Tavern table, eighteenth century* The turned maple legs and pine breadboard top are typical of tavern tables. Note the small ball foot and vase and ring turnings. (Index of American Design, Washington, D.C.)

469. *Tavern table, mid-eighteenth century* The rare stretcher with three crosspieces makes this a desirable table. Notice the drawer and turned legs. Made of Carolina pine, it was found in Virginia. (State Department of Archives and History, Raleigh, North Carolina; in Tryon Palace, New Bern, North Carolina)

470. *Tavern table, early nineteenth century*
A very crude country table of pine and oak with cleated top and splayed legs. Note the tabletop made of several boards and the method used to join the stretcher to the legs. (Sleepy Hollow Restorations, Inc., on the Tappan Zee, Tarrytown, New York)

471. *Tavern table, eighteenth century* The maple and curly maple used in this round-topped table add much to its beauty. The box stretcher and turned legs are well made. (Taylor and Dull, photography)

472. *Tavern table, eighteenth century* The oval top and triangular frame are unusual. This table was made of pine and stained walnut about 1725. (Index of American Design, Washington, D.C.)

474. *Tavern table, nineteenth century* The Spanish influence is noticed even in this crude hand-made table found near Santa Fe, New Mexico. It was painted many times. Note the mortise-and-tenon joints, cleated tabletop, and the odd scalloping on the stretchers. (Index of American Design, Washington, D.C.)

473. *Tavern table, nineteenth century* The Spanish influence is apparent in this New Mexican table of pine with hand-carved spindles. Tables were not needed by New Mexicans until chairs were introduced. (Collections of the Museum of New Mexico. Photograph by Laura Gilpin)

475. *Windsor table, eighteenth century* The Windsor table is very rare. This New England example was made of whitewood, maple, and ash. (Metropolitan Museum of Art; gift of Mrs. J. Insley Blair, 1947)

476. *Table, eighteenth century* The X-shaped structural brace of this table indicates it was made in the Hudson River Valley, New York. The pine table is painted gray. Note the stretcher construction. (Sleepy Hollow Restoration, Inc., on the Tappan Zee, Tarrytown, New York)

477. *Trestle table, seventeenth century* The pine top was easily removed from the oak frame of this New England table made about 1650. Note the T-shaped trestles and the long board that kept the trestles in place. This simple style continues in use for several hundred years. (Metropolitan Museum of Art; gift of Mrs. Russell Sage, 1909)

478. *Trestle table, seventeenth century* The maple top of the table is all one board. The oak framework has several boards between the upright trestles. It was made in Massachusetts about 1650. (Courtesy of the Henry Ford Museum, Dearborn, Michigan)

479. *Trestle table, eighteenth century* The trestles are cut with decorative curves and set into rail-like feet. The drawer is an unusual feature. This walnut table was made in Pennsylvania. (Index of American Design, Washington, D.C.; Metropolitan Museum of Art)

480. *Trestle table, nineteenth century* The carved pine and maple table was made in Pennsylvania about 1830. It has an oblong top decorated with geometric symbols. The trestles are shaped and held in a shaped rail-type foot. The board through the trestles is shaped. This is a most unusual nineteenth-century table, sometimes called a Conestoga table. (Taylor and Dull, photography)

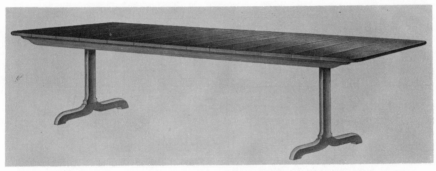

481. *Trestle table, nineteenth century* The Shakers of South Union, Kentucky, made this typical Shaker table from white oak, ash, and other hardwoods, then stained it red. It was made about 1838. (Index of American Design, Washington, D.C.)

482. *Trestle table, nineteenth century* Hickory and ash were oiled to finish this 1868 trestle table used in Kentucky by the Shakers. (Index of American Design, Washington, D.C.)

483. *Gateleg table, eighteenth century* This maple table has well-turned legs and feet. It is not unusual to find the feet missing on this sort of table. (Metropolitan Museum of Art; gift of Mrs. Russell Sage, 1909)

484. *Porringer table, unknown age*   The duck feet and porringer top of this Queen Anne table are made of maple. The table was found in Connecticut. (Old Sturbridge Village, Sturbridge, Massachusetts)

485. *Gateleg table, seventeenth century*   The turnings on this table are typical northern turnings. Notice the unusual foot that resembles the trestle. (Pilgrim Society, Plymouth, Massachusetts)

486. *Gateleg table, early eighteenth century*   The turnings of this Virginia-made gateleg table are southern style. The thick pad feet are also characteristic of southern Queen Anne pieces. The walnut table was made about 1710 to 1725. Notice the pine drawer. (Courtesy of the Henry Francis du Pont Winterthur Museum)

487. *Butterfly table, seventeenth century* The plain butterfly-shaped brackets supporting the table leaf gave this type of table its name. This maple table has box stretcher and long drop leaves. (Metropolitan Museum of Art; gift of Mrs. Russell Sage, 1909)

488. *Butterfly table, eighteenth century* This New England table has a drawer at one end. The feet and general shape of the table are indications of a skilled maker. (Metropolitan Museum of Art; gift of Mrs. Russell Sage, 1909)

489. *Drop-leaf table, eighteenth century* This corner table with the triangular drop leaf is called a "handkerchief" table. The table was made of mahogany in Philadelphia about 1750–1760. It is not a country piece. (Courtesy of Henry Francis du Pont Winterthur Museum)

490. *Pembroke table, eighteenth century* The details on this table, the pierced X stretcher, the small drawer, and the legs indicate that a mediocre city maker or a fine country furniture maker made this piece. It was made of cherry in Connecticut. (Taylor and Dull, photography)

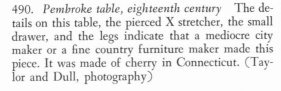

491. *Drop-leaf table, eighteenth century* This maple and pine table was made in Massachusetts about 1725 to 1740. It has the typical cabriole legs. Notice the scalloped skirt. (Courtesy of Henry Francis du Pont Winterthur Museum)

493. *Table, nineteenth century* The round drop-leaf table has a swing leg. The legs are tapered and slightly reeded in the Hepplewhite style. The top has a scrubbed surface, but the base retains much of its old red paint. (Old Sturbridge Village, Sturbridge, Massachusetts)

492. *Harvest table, nineteenth century* This pine table was made in New England. Notice the support for the leaves and the way the leg is shaped at the top where it joins the table. (Collection of Mr. and Mrs. R. N. Williams II, Philadelphia, Pennsylvania)

494. *Drop-leaf table, nineteenth century* This small table is sometimes called an occasional or bedside table. Notice the straight legs and wooden knobs and unadorned surfaces. This is a crude country piece made about 1820 in Rhode Island of stained cherry. (Index of American Design, Washington, D.C.)

495. *Drop-leaf table, nineteenth century* A Sheraton-style drop-leaf table with a curly-maple top made about 1820. Notice the reeded legs and the shaped corners of the table. (Western Reserve Historical Society, Cleveland, Ohio)

496. *Drop-leaf table, nineteenth century* The rear leg of the table swings out to hold the leaf. This is also called a folding-top table. Notice the spool-turned legs. The table was made of walnut, in Iowa, about 1850. (Index of American Design, Washington, D.C.)

497. *Drop-leaf table, nineteenth century* This unusual painted drop-leaf table was made about 1810–1820. In these two views the drop leaves are ornamented with baskets of flowers; the top shows scenes of mother and five daughters in a garden. The legs are painted with sponged design in a spiral pattern. This is a very desirable, unique collector's item. (Shelburne Museum, Inc. Photographer, Einars J. Mengis)

498. *Drop-leaf dining table, nineteenth century* A typical drop-leaf table with turned legs. Note the short drop leaf and small drawer. The table is made of pine. (Collection of Mr. and Mrs. R. N. Williams II, Philadelphia, Pennsylvania)

501. *Tilt-top table, eighteenth century* A square-topped tripod table of maple made about 1760–1780. (Courtesy of National Park Service, Morristown National Historical Park, Morristown, New Jersey)

499. *Drop-leaf table, mid-nineteenth century* The Canadian drop-leaf table was made before 1850, in eastern Ontario. The pine top is set on a maple frame and ash legs. The table is painted red. (Upper Canada Village, Morrisburg, Ontario)

500. *Folding-top table, seventeenth century* Called a refectory table, this unusual style has a top that opens, evidently to be supported by another table. It was made of turned ash and pine in Pennsylvania. Note the hardware. (Taylor and Dull, photography)

502. *Tilt-top table, eighteenth century* An octagonal-topped table made 1750–1755 with a painted stippled decoration on cherry wood. (Metropolitan Museum of Art; gift of Mrs. J. Insley Blair, 1945)

503. *Tilt-top table, nineteenth century* A New England–made table of maple painted red to imitate graining. It was made 1820–1830. (Courtesy of Henry Ford Museum, Dearborn, Michigan)

504. *Tilt-top table, nineteenth century (two views)* This three-legged table, made about 1850, has a cleated two-board top. (Historical Society of the Tarrytowns, Tarrytown, New York)

505. *Tilt-top table, nineteenth century* A maple table with a Victorian tripod base. (Cowlitz County Historical Museum, Kelso, Washington)

507. *Tripod table, late nineteenth century* A very crude table of spruce wood that is possibly factory made. (Cowlitz County Historical Museum, Kelso, Washington)

506. *Tripod table, nineteenth century* The cleated top and shaped stand are interesting on this pine table made about 1800 in Connecticut. (Index of American Design, Washington, D.C.)

508. *Tripod table, late nineteenth century* This table was made in Matagorda, Texas, in 1885, of Spanish cedar painted brown. Note the Victorian legs and round top.

509. *Tripod table, mid-nineteenth century* An oak and pine table found in Texas. It is 2 feet 4 inches high and 2 feet 8 inches wide. (Index of American Design, Washington, D.C.)

511. *Breakfast table, eighteenth century* A small round table with angled legs of a typical Queen Anne shape. The table was made of red gumwood in New York about 1725 to 1740. This fine table was the work of a skilled craftsman. (Courtesy of Henry Francis du Pont Winterthur Museum)

510. *Breakfast table, eighteenth century* This octagonal table is made of painted walnut. Notice the chamfered legs and the shaped skirt. The table was made in New England about 1720 to 1740. (Courtesy of Henry Francis du Pont Winterthur Museum)

513. *Side table, unknown date* Tiger-stripe maple was used to make this card table with a folding top. The fifth leg swings to hold the unfolded top. (Old Sturbridge Village, Sturbridge, Massachusetts)

512. *Queen Anne table, eighteenth century* A typical Queen Anne style of table made with cabriole leg, shaped skirt, duck foot. Many similar country versions of this table were made. Some had a folding top that could be extended and held by a swinging back leg. (Taylor and Dull, photography)

514. *Side table, Canadian, nineteenth century* The legs of this table were "ebonized" (painted black), but the tiger-maple top was given a natural finish. The table was made in Iroquois, Ontario, about 1820. The ebonizing of furniture was done in both the United States and Canada. (Upper Canada Village, Morrisburg, Ontario)

515. *Table, nineteenth century* Simple country table made in Texas in the mid-nineteenth century. Notice the two wide boards that form the top. The ends of the table top appear slightly curved because the boards have warped. (Witte Museum, San Antonio, Texas)

516. *Sheraton table, nineteenth century* This typical Sheraton-style worktable, of New England origin, was made of bird's eye maple about 1800. Note the decoration painted and incised and the typical round legs with turned tops. This is a very fine, formal example. (Metropolitan Museum of Art, Sansbury-Mills Fund, 1954)

517. *Table, nineteenth century* A table with two drawers or a "parlor stand." It is painted in bright colors. The "feathered" decoration is red-brown and yellow. The top and the drawer fronts are brilliant green with feathering in yellow. The table is of the Sheraton design. (Smithsonian Institution, United States National Museum, Washington, D.C.)

518. *Table, nineteenth century* A red-painted pine table made about 1800. Note the shaped skirt, the scalloped edge on the drawer, and the grooved legs. This is an excellent country piece. (Sturbridge Village, Sturbridge, Massachusetts)

519. *Table, nineteenth century* A one-drawer table of pine, probably made by the Shakers. The design has reduced the table to its simplest possible form. (Index of American Design, Washington, D.C.)

520. *Table, nineteenth century* A Shaker table of pine made with a drawer and shelf. It has typical Shaker simplicity of design. (Index of American Design, Washington, D.C.)

521. *Night stand, early nineteenth century* Walnut legs, cherry drawer, and burled maple top combine to form this Hepplewhite-style country stand. The angle of the legs adds to the grace of this well-designed piece made about 1800. (Western Reserve Historical Society, Cleveland, Ohio)

522. *Table, nineteenth century* A plain pine table made about 1800. The slant of the legs gives grace to the table. (Index of American Design, Washington, D.C.)

523. *End table, nineteenth century* Cherry wood was used to make this one-drawer Sheraton-style country night stand or end table. The round legs are typical of the Sheraton style popular about 1800–1820. (Western Reserve Historical Society, Cleveland, Ohio)

524. *Bedside table, nineteenth century* The one-drawer table was often used in the bedroom or living room. This table has spool-turned legs and a glass drawer knob. Many of the tables of this type were made in maple or cherry or pine. (Hale House, Western Reserve Historical Society, Cleveland, Ohio)

525. *Spool table, nineteenth century* The general shape of the table is typical of many spool tables of the 1815 to 1875 period. The turnings indicate the later part of the period. (Hale House, Western Reserve Historical Society, Cleveland, Ohio)

526. *Spool table, nineteenth century* The spool turnings used for the legs of this table were probably made originally to be cut into sections, drilled, and used as buttons. The table is typical of the spool furniture of the nineteenth century. (Hale House, Western Reserve Historical Society, Cleveland, Ohio)

527. *Table, nineteenth century* A rustic table made in Meadville, Pennsylvania, about 1870, by Joseph F. Haas. This type of rustic furniture, particularly cast-iron garden furniture, was popular for a short period. (Crawford County, Pennsylvania Historical Society)

528. *Table, painted, nineteenth century* A Sheraton-style table decorated by Elizabeth Paine Lombard, February, 1816. The table top is painted with baskets of fruit, grapes, leaves, and tendrils. The overall design is of flowers, fruit, birds, and foliage. The lettered name, a poem, and a townscape appear on the sides. This is a very unusual example of decorated country furniture. (Shelburne Museum, Inc. Photographer, Einars J. Mengis)

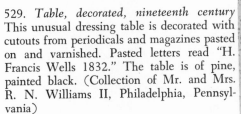

529. *Table, decorated, nineteenth century* This unusual dressing table is decorated with cutouts from periodicals and magazines pasted on and varnished. Pasted letters read "H. Francis Wells 1832." The table is of pine, painted black. (Collection of Mr. and Mrs. R. N. Williams II, Philadelphia, Pennsylvania)

530. *Chair table, eighteenth century* The top of this table bench flips up to form a large seat. Notice the oblong top of three boards and the breadboard ends, the solid sides to the bench, and the rail-like feet. Made about 1760–1765, it is sometimes called a hutch table. (State Department of Archives and History, Raleigh, North Carolina; in Tryon Palace, New Bern, North Carolina)

531. *Chair table, nineteenth century* A mahogany chair made in Carbondale, Pennsylvania, about 1833. This is the simplest form of chair table, with straight, unadorned legs, box stretcher, and a cleated top. (Index of American Design, Washington, D.C.)

533. *Hutch table, eighteenth century* A pine table with crude built-in storage area, rail feet, and a cleated top. (Courtesy of National Park Service, Morristown National Historical Park, Morristown, New Jersey)

532. *Chair table, late eighteenth or early nineteenth century* This oblong-topped chair table, shown with top up and down, painted black, has a four-board top. Note the spindles in the chair and the rough shaping of the saddle seat. (Shelburne Museum, Inc. Photographer, Einars J. Mengis)

535. *Hutch table, eighteenth century* (2 views) A pine and oak table attributed to Hudson River Valley, New York. Note the rail feet and shaped sides. (Sleepy Hollow Restorations, Inc., on the Tappan Zee, Tarrytown, New York)

534. *Hutch table, nineteenth century* A pine table made in the late eighteenth or early nineteenth century. Although it was found in a Canadian home, it is not different from those found in the eastern areas of the United States. (Upper Canada Village, Morrisburg, Ontario, Canada)

537. *Hutch table, nineteenth century* This New Mexican table is made of pine painted with blue tempera about 1830–1850. The southwestern designs are apparent. A typical cleat-and-pin arrangement is used to hold the top. (Index of American Design, Washington, D.C.)

536. *Hutch table, early eighteenth century* Because the opened table forms a settle bench, this is also called a settle table. The single-board rectangular top is held to a settle bottom with cleats and wooden pins. (Courtesy, Brooklyn Museum, Brooklyn, New York)

14

Washstands and Commode Tables

History

"COMMODE" IS THE NAME for a special chest of drawers that was popular in England during the eighteenth century. The term "commode table" has a different meaning. The commode table was used in the bedroom as a dressing table, with drawers for soap and towels, or perhaps for the slop jar. A shelf was available for the washbowl and pitcher.

To understand the design and use of a commode table, it is necessary to realize that toilet habits have radically changed with the use of indoor plumbing. Having no inside lavatories, our ancestors had to contrive acceptable indoor facilities. Bedrooms were equipped with a corner washstand holding soap and water. The toilet problem was solved by the use of a large covered chamber pot that was usually kept under the bed. Most well-to-do homes in the eighteenth century had servants who emptied the chamber pot daily. An adaptation of this system was used in the middle-class home where the washstand evolved into the commode table. The soap and water were kept in the top part of the table while a closed cupboard held the chamber pot.

Formal washstands (Picture 538) were made in the Chippendale, Hepplewhite, and later styles. Many had splashboards at the back of the table. Some had a hole in the top for the basin, a drawer, and a shelf. The formal furniture manufacturers made many of these corner washstands.

WASHSTAND WITH BOWL HOLE (Pictures 539–543)

The formal washstands of the eighteenth and nineteenth centuries took several shapes. Some were rectangular, but the corner stand was the most popular because it was a space saver. A hole was cut in the top of the stand so that a basin could fit into the top, thereby lessening the danger of spilling.

Such a washstand with a bowl hole was made in all the formal and country styles of the late eighteenth and nineteenth centuries. The finished table usually had a shelf for the pitcher and a drawer for supplies.

BEDSIDE TABLE (Pictures 544–547)

Many small bedside tables were used during the late eighteenth and early nineteenth centuries. Some of them held a basin and pitcher, while others were just small tables that held a candle or other source of light. Nothing in their design indicated the use of a washbowl.

Several of the bedside tables are shown, and more are included in the chapter on tables. All the design characteristics of the bedside table are similar to those of larger tables.

COMMON WASHSTAND (Picture 548)

The common country washstand was made from 1845 to 1890. It resembled a table with a drawer, except that it had a very low back and sides. A pitcher and bowl for water were kept on the top, while the drawer held soap and towels.

These stands were made from pine, poplar, or any of the local woods available. Some of them were painted.

TOWEL-BAR WASHSTAND (Pictures 542, 549, 551, 552)

The washstand with a towel bar at each side is closely related to the stands made by the formal cabinetmakers of the eighteenth century. Sometimes the top of the stand had a hole in the center for the washbowl. A shelf held the pitcher; a drawer under the shelf held towels. A towel bar was placed at each side of the stand, which often added to the decorative effect. Many of these stands were made of maple or cherry during the 1820–1850 period.

Lift-Top Commode (Picture 554)

The lift-top commode was a mid-nineteenth-century piece of furniture. When the top of the square chestlike commode was raised, it revealed a deep well where a washbowl and pitcher were stored. A small off-center drawer for towels and soap opened from the front of the piece. The bottom shelf, covered by a door, held the slop jar or chamber pot.

The lift-top commodes were made of pine, maple, and other local woods, and were usually painted. The lift-top commode is popular with decorators because the top section can be filled with plants. Reproductions are being made by several companies.

Victorian Country Furniture Commode

A late nineteenth-century version of the commode table now appears in altered form. It was originally made as a two-door chest with a top drawer.

A shaped backboard was the decorative feature of the Victorian commode. The backboard was curved or scalloped, and some of the elaborate pieces had added carved decorations. The stand was usually made from pine, painted or stained.

Many of the Victorian stands were stripped and have been refinished as old pine furniture. The backboard, which is one of the most obviously Victorian features, is removed and the stand sold as an early example of pine furniture. Careful examination of converted commodes will show the strip of wood across the back that was originally the bottom of the splashboard. An old commode table made with no splashboard would have a top made from one piece of wood.

538. *Washstand, eighteenth century* A formal Sheraton washstand made of mahogany and bird's-eye maple in the late eighteenth century. The corner form was often used because it was a space saver. Formal stands had shaped splashboards, shaped shelves, and inlay, as are found in this example. (Taylor and Dull, photography)

539. *Washstand or wig stand, nineteenth century* The two small round containers in the stand probably held powder for a wig. The cherry stand with brass hardware was made in Concord, Pennsylvania, probably about 1800–1810. (Mr. and Mrs. R. N. Williams II, Philadelphia, Pennsylvania)

540. *Washstand, nineteenth century* Pine was painted black and grained, then decorated with gilt stencil and yellow line trim to make this New England washstand about 1840. The large bowl was held in the hole; the pitcher stood on the bottom shelf. The drawer held other supplies. Note the shaped splashboard. (Courtesy of the Henry Ford Museum, Dearborn, Michigan) LEFT

541. *Washstand, nineteenth century* Plain pine stand painted dark brown, probably made in Texas in the middle 1800's. Straight legs and plain splashboard show that this was the work of an unskilled country maker. (Index of American Design, Washington, D.C.) RIGHT

543. *Commode table, nineteenth century* Poplar wood was used to make this unusual midwestern (probably Ohio) commode table. Notice the shaping of the shelf edge. The basin and pitcher were kept on the top shelf, the waste bowl below. Supplies were stored in the drawer. (Collection of William Pinney, Cleveland, Ohio)

542. *Washstand, nineteenth century* Unique homemade stand of Spanish cedar made in 1885, in Matagorda, Texas. The bowl hole and the shelf for the pitcher remain, but no splashboard was used. Spool turnings form legs and towel rack. (Index of American Design, Washington, D.C.)

544. *Bedside table, eighteenth century* Drop-leaf Sheraton bedside table made of maple, 29 inches high. Note the scallop on shelf edge and leaf. (Taylor and Dull, photography)

545. *Bedside table, nineteenth century* Unusual bedside table, probably to hold washbowl and pitcher. It is made of a combination of woods, stained to resemble mahogany, about 1800. (Index of American Design, Washington, D.C.)

546. *Washstand, nineteenth century* A Pennsylvania stand, made about 1830, of pine painted yellow with orange sponge decorations. This could also be called a bedside table.

547. *Table, nineteenth century* Pennsylvania pine table painted red with black trim, made about 1830. Gallery below table drawer and turned legs are unusual features. This may have been used in a bedroom or some other room in the home. (Courtesy of the Henry Ford Museum, Dearborn, Michigan)

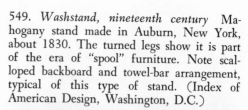

549. *Washstand, nineteenth century* Mahogany stand made in Auburn, New York, about 1830. The turned legs show it is part of the era of "spool" furniture. Note scalloped backboard and towel-bar arrangement, typical of this type of stand. (Index of American Design, Washington, D.C.)

548. *Washstand, nineteenth century* Curly-maple stand with opalescent Sandwich-glass type of knobs and made for use in Ohio about 1820–1830. Note the elaborate scrolls on the splashboard and the turned legs. (Summit County Historical Society, Akron, Ohio)

551. *Washstand, nineteenth century* Typical stand with towel racks made about 1850. This type of stand was used in all parts of the country. (Old Court House Museum, Vicksburg, Mississippi)

550. *Washstand, nineteenth century* Spool turnings were used to form the legs and the towel bars of this washstand made about 1840. This is a typical spool washstand; the turnings are factory made. (Western Reserve Historical Society, Cleveland, Ohio)

552. *Washstand, nineteenth century* Walnut washstand made in Maryville, Missouri, in 1874. Though the top is that of a typical one-drawer stand, the bottom resembles a Victorian chest of drawers. Note the hardware and notched side to form the leg. (Index of American Design, Washington, D.C.)

553. *Chest with towel bars, nineteenth century* Spool-turned towel bars indicate that the chest was used in a bedroom to hold a washbasin and pitcher. This type of chest was made about 1840 to 1865. (Hale House, Western Reserve Historical Society, Cleveland, Ohio)

554. *Lift-top commode, nineteenth century* The top of the commode opened to expose a well that held the bowl and pitcher. The small drawer held soap and towels; the bottom cupboard contained the other utensils. Notice the heavy pillars at the side of the chest, typical of Empire design. This chest was made of pine, about 1830. (Western Reserve Historical Society, Cleveland, Ohio)

555. *Commode, nineteenth century* This mahogany cabinet commode has a shelf behind the door. Notice the front trim and curved top edge. (Western Reserve Historical Society, Cleveland, Ohio)

556. *Washstand, nineteenth century* An infirmary washstand of stained pine made by Shaker craftsman in Mount Lebanon, New York, about 1830–1850. The splashboard arrangement is unusual. (Index of American Design, Washington, D.C.)

557. *Commode, nineteenth century* Commode, painted olive green with cream striping and gold design, made about 1800–1810. This style preceded the lift-top commode. (Courtesy of New-York Historical Society, New York City)

15

Workbenches, Kitchen Pieces, and Other Items

MANY PIECES OF EQUIPMENT that were used in the nineteenth-century home, store, or shop can now be found in the living room. Imagine placing your refrigerator or ironing board in the living room today. Yet, the equipment of the nineteenth century is now adapted to the uses of the twentieth century as furniture.

The ubiquitous cobbler's bench has become so popular it is reproduced by most of the "Early American" furniture makers today. Almost anything can be transformed into a usable piece of furniture, and we have included in this chapter cupboard pieces and small tablelike pieces most often used in a home today.

PIE CUPBOARD, TIN SAFE (Pictures 558–564)

The pie cupboard, tin safe, or meat safe was one type of nineteenth-century refrigerator. It was usually a large cabinet with shelves that could hold pies, bread, or even meat products. The most popular ones have pierced tin panels on the front doors, which ventilated the cabinet, kept out the insects, and added to the attractiveness of the piece. Most of the pierced tin pie safes were made in the Midwest and West after 1830. The skill shown in decorating the tin, the size of the boards, and the type of construction used all help to indicate the age of the pie safe. (See Chapter 19, "Furniture Construction.")

WATER BENCH, 1800–1860 (Picture 566)

A kitchen piece that was especially popular in Pennsylvania was the water bench. The shelf held a washbasin and a pail of water, with additional pails kept in the cupboard at the bottom. There were drawers that were used for soap and other cleaning materials.

The water bench, usually kitchen-counter height, was made from pine, poplar, cherry, or maple. Most of them were originally painted blue or red, although today most are seen in refinished pine.

DRY SINK, 1830–1900 (Pictures 567–570)

The dry sink was used in a kitchen that had no indoor plumbing. The "sink" was an open zinc-lined trough, with cupboards for storage below it. Some dry sinks had a top section with small drawers for silverware and a back splashboard.

A bowl of water was kept in the sink where the dishes were washed. The dry sinks rarely had legs and feet, but the sides were extended and slightly notched to resemble feet. Dry sinks were made from pine, maple, birch, poplar, or cherry, and were painted blue, green, brown, or gray. Some were left in an unfinished condition.

DOUGH TRAY (Pictures 572, 573)

The dough tray or kneading table was a necessity for baking bread. It was essential to have a place to knead the dough and also to store it while it was rising. The dough tray provided both. It was a large box with a reversible lid, which may or may not have stood on legs. The top was flat on one side, which was used for kneading, while the other side had several strips of wood carefully placed to hold the top while the dough was rising inside the tray. The tray was rectangular and about 12 inches deep. The top extended beyond its edges.

When legs were used, they were often turned and were angled out from the tray to afford firm support, just as the early Windsor chairs had legs that were askew. A scalloped or otherwise shaped skirt was often added to the tray.

Early Pennsylvania trays were often painted and decorated. Later dough trays in other areas were made of maple, walnut, or pine, with maple the most common after 1820.

JELLY CUPBOARD

The jelly cupboard, jam cupboard, or server is a small cupboard that was popular during the mid-nineteenth century. Made from maple, pine, cherry, or other local woods, it had two drawers above the two cupboard doors. In most areas of the country it was referred to as a small cupboard, except in the Midwest, where the name "jelly cupboard" is used.

COBBLER'S BENCH (Pictures 591–596)

The cobbler's bench was a specialized workbench made by the cobbler for use in his shop. At one end of the bench was a leather tray, while the other end contained drawers and shelves for tools. It is almost impossible to date a cobbler's bench from the style because each was individually constructed. A turned leg or a mushroom knob will occasionally help to indicate age. Most of them are scarred, dented, and marked by the hard use of the shoemaker.

CANDLE MOLD IN A STAND, CIRCA 1820–1880

Tin candle molds were made with tubes for six to twenty-four candles after 1750. Some of the larger molds were made and used in wooden frames in the nineteenth century. Most of the larger framed molds were made for use by a candlemaker, and not by the local housewife.

558. *Pie safe, nineteenth century* The pierced tin front on this pie safe has Gothic patterns. Notice how the sides are joined through the front corner. This southern pie safe was made about 1840. (Historic Mobile Preservation Society, Mobile, Alabama)

559. *Kitchen safe, mid-nineteenth century* The pierced tin doors are typical of the midwestern and western pie safes. Straight legs, porcelain knobs, and plain hinges indicate a kitchen piece. Safes of this type are judged mostly by the skill shown in piercing the tin. (Witte Museum, San Antonio, Texas)

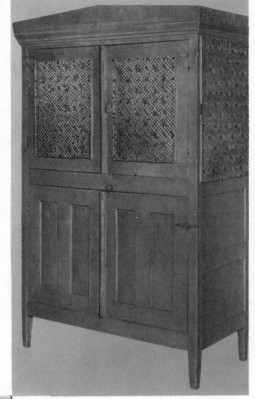

561. *Kitchen safe, nineteenth century* A unique Texas kitchen safe made about 1880 of Spanish cedar painted with dark yellow oil paint. The panels are covered with fabric. (Index of American Design, Washington, D.C.)

560. *Kitchen safe, nineteenth century* The Shakers of Shakertown, Kentucky, made this stained poplar kitchen safe about 1830. The many small pierced tin panels and the shaped feet and top molding show excellent workmanship. (Index of American Design, Washington, D.C.)

562. *Pine pie cupboard, Canadian, date unknown* The wooden grill permitted air circulation in this pine pie cupboard painted red-brown. The grill was painted green. Notice the molding and the details of the door construction. (Upper Canada Village, Morrisburg, Canada)

563. *Kitchen safe, late nineteenth century* This Texas-made pie safe had common screening in the doors and a porcelain knob. This is the least desirable type of country pie safe. (Witte Museum, San Antonio, Texas)

565. *Unventilated kitchen safe, late nineteenth century* This yellow pine kitchen safe was made in Marion County, Texas, about 1875. It had no ventilation and was used for storage of utensils, not food. Notice the simple door latch. The top drawer opens into a bin, perhaps for flour. (Index of American Design, Washington, D.C.)

564. *Kitchen safe, nineteenth century* The elaborate shape of the door openings (filled with screening) and the molding details show this to be the work of a good cabinetmaker. It may have been a closed cupboard adapted as a pie safe at a later date. The large round holes at the side furnish added ventilation. It was found in Texas. (Witte Museum, San Antonio, Texas)

566. *Pine water bench, early nineteenth century* The shaped edges of the sides and top and the cupboard doors show details used by a good country workman. The upper drawers held tableware and soap; the lower cabinets held basins and pails. The dishes were washed on the shelf. (Taylor and Dull, photography)

567. *Dry sink, nineteenth century* The Amish in central Ohio made this dry sink for use in a kitchen. The zinc liner was originally painted. It was made in the last half of the nineteenth century. (Western Reserve Historical Society, Cleveland, Ohio)

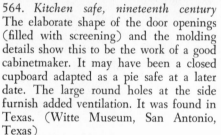

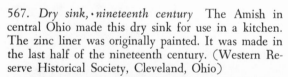

568. *Dry sink or Dutch sink* This Pennsylvania sink was made about 1820. The shaped back and legs add distinction. Notice the drain arrangement. Many of these sinks were lined with zinc. (Index of American Design, Washington, D.C.)

569. *Dry sink, nineteenth century* This dry sink was used in a Canadian kitchen in eastern Ontario. It is made of pine painted red. Notice the legs and shaped center of the apron. (Upper Canada Village, Morrisburg, Ontario)

570. *Dry sink, nineteenth century* The Shakers of Mount Lebanon, New York, made this small kitchen piece in the first half of the nineteenth century. It is curly maple and pearwood. (Index of American Design, Washington, D.C.)

571. *Sink bench, late nineteenth century* This unusual yellow-painted pine Gothic sink bench was probably made in Pennsylvania. The cathedral doors and unusual placement of the drawers make this a unique piece. The door latches are late machined examples. (Index of American Design, Washington, D.C.)

572. *Dough box, date unknown* The housewife put the dough inside this box to rise, or inverted the top to use it as a kneading board. This pine box, originally painted red, was used in Canada. (Upper Canada Village, Morrisburg, Ontario)

573. *Dough tray, nineteenth century* This pine dough tray was used at an Ohio farmhouse. It is typical of many similar dough boxes. Notice the turned legs. (Hale House, Western Reserve Historical Society, Cleveland, Ohio)

575. *Beaten-biscuit board, nineteenth century.* Poplar and pine were used to make this unusual kitchen table about 1840. The board was covered by the hinged top when not in use. It was used in Nashville, Tennessee. (Index of American Design, Washington, D.C.)

574. *Kitchen cabinet, nineteenth century* Kitchen furniture was made to be useful, and, as this cabinet shows, often there is not a special distinguishing feature. Cupboards of this type, which rested on the floor, are sometimes called "jam cupboards" or "servers." (Hale House, Western Reserve Historical Society, Cleveland, Ohio)

576. *Kitchen table, mid-nineteenth century* The walnut frame of this 1825–1850 table is stained dark reddish brown. The spool legs and large flour bins are unusual. It was used in Illinois. (Index of American Design, Washington, D.C.)

577. *Kitchen bench table, nineteenth century* A painted pine table made in Wilmington, Delaware, about 1860. Note the earlier style of the leg as part of the side. (Index of American Design, Washington, D.C.)

578. *Grain chest, nineteenth century* A pine or cottonwood chest with leather hinges, made in New Mexico, to hold grain. Notice the thick lumber, mortise-and-tenon joints, and panel construction. (Index of American Design, Washington, D.C.)

579. *Chest, nineteenth century* A New Mexican chest, probably for grain, made by a native for his own use. It has panel construction and a scalloped apron. (Index of American Design, Washington, D.C.)

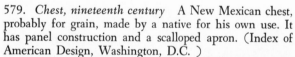

580. *Flour bin, late nineteenth century* Varnished pine was used to make this flour bin about 1865. There is no standard design for kitchen pieces such as a bin, and each was individually made and designed. (Index of American Design, Washington, D.C.)

582. *Woodbox, nineteenth century* Rectangular woodbox of pine painted dark red. It was made in Mount Lebanon, New York, by the Shaker community about 1828. This type of woodbox was made for several centuries by country makers in all parts of the country. (Index of American Design, Washington, D.C.)

581. *Woodbox, nineteenth century* The design for the woodbox has remained the same through the past three hundred years. The drawer is an unusual feature. This pine box was made about 1820 in Canterbury, New Hampshire, by the Shakers. (Index of American Design, Washington, D.C.)

583. *Sewing desk, nineteenth century* The South Union Shakers of Shakertown, Kentucky, made this sewing table for use in the community. Note the unusual way the drawer is supported by a small protrusion at the top edge. (Shaker Museum, Inc., Auburn, Kentucky)

584. *Sewing table, nineteenth century* Birch or maple was painted orange-red by the Shaker who made this table, about 1810–1840, at Mount Lebanon, New York. The leg shape is unusual for a Shaker table.

585. *Shaker tailoress's table, nineteenth century* This is a typical worktable with a drop leaf. The large top was needed when material was cut; the drawers held the sewing supplies. The wooden knobs and unadorned surfaces are a part of the Shaker tradition. (Golden Lamb Inn, Lebanon, Ohio)

586. *Shaker tailoress's table, nineteenth century* A maple table made about 1830 in the Hancock Community, Hancock, Massachusetts. This sewing cabinet has legs that are extensions of the side of the cabinet. (Index of American Design, Washington, D.C.)

587. *Tailor's bench, nineteenth century* Red-painted pine was fashioned into this crude bench about 1830 in Alabama. The cast hardware is Victorian. (Index of American Design, Washington, D.C.)

588. *Weaver's chest, nineteenth century* Shaker-made cupboard of pine made in 1810 at Mount Lebanon, New York. The lack of metal hardware and the straight lines are typical of the Shaker craftsmen. (Index of American Design, Washington, D.C.)

589. *Apothecary chest, nineteenth century* Pine was often used to make this type of herb storage chest. Each drawer held a different preparation. It was used in a kitchen or a store. (Collection of William Pinney, Cleveland, Ohio)

590. *Apothecary cabinet, nineteenth century* Drugs were stored in the drawers of this Shaker cabinet. Apothecary chests are usually of the simplest design—a collection of drawers with plain knobs. It was a storage piece for a shop, not a living-room piece. This chest was made of pine by the Shakers of Watervliet, New York. (Golden Lamb Inn, Lebanon, Ohio)

593. *Cobbler's bench* This cobbler liked a stand-up and sit-down work surface on his pine bench. Note that the legs are part of the sides, similar to the method used on chests. (Courtesy Lawrence Romaine, Weathercock House, Middleboro, Massachusetts)

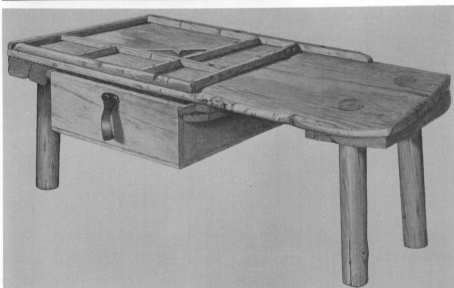

591. *Cobbler's bench, nineteenth century* This pine bench is lacking the leather seat area. It is the simplest of benches, with unfinished legs and a leather strap drawer handle. (Index of American Design, Washington, D.C.)

592. *Cobbler's bench, nineteenth century* Pine was used by the maker of this Pennsylvania cobbler's bench about 1825. Notice the trim on the edge of the tray. (Index of American Design, Washington, D.C.)

594. *Cobbler's bench* This elaborate cobbler's bench was made in New Haven, Connecticut. Notice the posts near the six small top drawers, the detail of the legs, and the turned knobs on the drawers. (Courtesy of New-York Historical Society, New York City)

595. *Cobbler's bench, nineteenth century* This cobbler's bench has unusual decorative "panels" at the side of the bench. Note the lack of drawer pulls. (Westchester County Historical Society, New York)

596. *Cobbler's bench, nineteenth century* Made for a cobbler's shop similar to this one used by the Shakers, the seated cobbler's bench was made in 1842. The saddlemaker's bench at the right was made in 1835. There is a leather-covered stool beside the standing bench. The cupboard and all the other pieces are made of pine. (Shaker Museum, Old Chatham, New York)

597. *Bench, circa 1840* A crude handmade wooden workbench made in the nineteenth century in Minnesota. (Olmsted County, Historical Society, Rochester, Minnesota)

599. *Shaving horse, nineteenth century* Shingles, butter tubs, and sap buckets were made with this shaving horse. This was a tool used in a barn or outdoors. (Castleton Historical Society Museum, Castleton, Vermont)

598. *Stitching horse* This goes back to pioneer days in Oregon, and is entirely homemade. A "stitching horse" was used for mending harness. The harnessmaker straddled the stool, fastened the leather in the wooden vise in front of him, and stitched back and forth from left to right. The vise is tightened or loosened by a foot pedal that is connected with the vise by a leather strap. The foot pedal will fit into any one of a series of notches in an iron bar fastened to the right front leg of the "horse." It is made of oak. (Cowlitz County Historical Museum, Kelso, Washington)

600. *Wood-carver's bench, late nineteenth century* This bench was made in Racine, Washington. (Index of American Design, Washington, D.C.)

601. *Milking stool, eighteenth century* This wooden bench has two straight legs that have not been smoothed. The other two legs are a forked tree branch. A hole in the handle was used to hang the bench on a hook when the bench was not in use. (Hagley Museum, Wilmington, Delaware)

602. *Wash bench or stool, nineteenth century* Bowls of water were placed on this blue painted wash bench when the dishes were washed. It was made in Zoar, Ohio, in the mid-nineteenth century. (Index of American Design, Washington, D.C.)

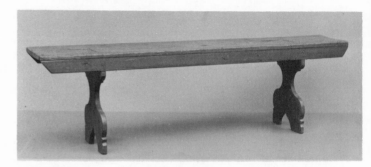

604. *Bench, eighteenth century* A yellow-pine bench painted red, made in Pennsylvania about 1725–1750. The leg style is found on tables of this period. (Metropolitan Museum of Art; gift of Mrs. Robert W. de Forest, 1933)

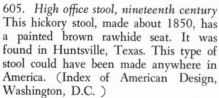

603. *Bed stool, Pennsylvania, 1790–1800* The top of the stool is made of poplar, the legs of maple, the rungs of oak, maple, and chestnut. (Index of American Design, Washington, D.C.)

605. *High office stool, nineteenth century* This hickory stool, made about 1850, has a painted brown rawhide seat. It was found in Huntsville, Texas. This type of stool could have been made anywhere in America. (Index of American Design, Washington, D.C.)

606. *Stool, nineteenth century* This high stool is made from tiger maple. The round legs end in the typical midwestern foot. This type of stool was made for several centuries. (Hale House, Western Reserve Historical Society, Cleveland, Ohio)

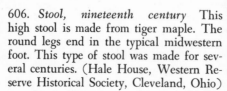

16

Pennsylvania Furniture

THE FOLK ART of the Pennsylvania German settlements in America has been the subject of many books and articles. The furniture made during the eighteenth and nineteenth centuries by the Pennsylvania settlers was one of the first forms of country furniture to interest the expert. Pennsylvania folk art and furniture have been collected by museums and antique lovers for many years.

The designs of the Pennsylvania Germans were actually the inspired adaptations made by many craftsmen who came to America from the Old World. The unsophisticated peasant designs, considered typical of the Pennsylvania Germans, are the result of mixing Old World memories with New World exuberance. At first, most of the tables, beds, and chairs were the quickest, crudest pieces that could be made to serve a specific need. By the late eighteenth century, however, the Pennsylvania Germans were concerned with attractive furnishings of fine quality. The cabinetmakers used walnut or cherry for the unpainted pieces, and maple, birch, hickory, and poplar for most of the painted pieces.

The painted designs on the Pennsylvania German furniture were the same designs popular in all Pennsylvania German art. Pottery, illustrated papers such as marriage and birth certificates, tinware, and other art forms featured the designs of tulips, unicorns, doves, hearts, and stylized flowers, and, between 1800 and 1830, the American eagle. Cupboards, chairs, and chests were sturdy and solid, with craftsman-like construction details and peasant gaiety of line and design.

Some of the finest Pennsylvania furniture pieces were made from walnut and inlaid with maple or holly designs or decorated with a striping of yellow paint.

The painted furniture made from softwoods was covered with a solid background paint of blue, green, yellow, or brown, with the later examples being painted gray. Unusual graining and stippling was used on nineteenth-century furniture (circa 1850–1880).

PLAIN CHEST, 1700–1830

The chest was an excellent storage piece and was used by the Pennsylvania Germans in many ways. The plain, unpainted chest was a part of the household furnishings and did not have the special significance of the bride's painted dower chest.

It was a typical chest with an overhanging lid, one or two drawers, and with feet that kept up with the changing styles. The ball, ogee bracket, and plain bracket foot were all used. Most of the chests were made of softwood and finished with oil or wax with an unpainted interior.

INLAID CHEST, 1700–1775

The fine inlaid walnut chests were similar in design to the plain chests but with more exacting cabinetwork. Flowers were often the motif for the inlay. When a name or initial is inlaid in the center, it is a dower marriage chest.

DOWER CHEST, 1750–1880

The dower chest, one of the most popular pieces of Pennsylvania furniture, was owned by a young girl who planned to be married. She filled it with quilts, coverlets, towels, and pillows to take to her new home.

The design of the chest varied in different parts of Pennsylvania, but most of them had an overhanging lid and plain bracket feet or no feet. The front of the chest was divided into two or three panels by the use of painted decorations. Sometimes an arch and pillars were painted to divide the panels. A design, such as stylized flowers, was painted inside each panel. The best dower chests have two matching end panels with the owner's name and date painted in the center panel.

They were made from pine, poplar, or other softwoods, and were painted red, green, blue, or yellow. Dower chests are still being made by using the old-time methods, but with careful examination the paint colors and pattern details will help in determining the recent examples.

TABLES

The Pennsylvania German table had turned legs and flat stretchers, which were popular with early craftsmen. Early German tables of the sawbuck design (See Chapter 13, "Tables") often had drawers of different sizes to hold the linen and cutlery.

The later tables (circa 1830) had no stretchers. The drawers were of equal size, and a carved apron was used on the edge of the table. Cherry drop-leaf tables were popular in the early nineteenth century.

CHESTS OF DRAWERS, 1800–1840

Chests of drawers made by the Pennsylvania Germans are not numerous. A few examples of unpainted walnut chests made in the eighteenth century can be seen in museums. The nineteenth-century chest was usually made from pine or another softwood, painted green or reddish brown and decorated with typical Pennsylvania German designs. It had four drawers, with the smallest at the top, and wooden knobs or brass rosettes for hardware. The legs of the chest were often short, turned, round legs.

CUPBOARDS, 1750–1850

The Pennsylvania German cupboard, or open-faced dresser, was a large, impressive piece of furniture made from oiled walnut (early) or painted pine. The top had open shelves and the bottom was made with a closed cupboard door and drawers. Elaborate early chests were made with molding trim, scallops, cutout notches that held the spoons on the shelf edges, formal or informal hardware, and any number of other exceptional details for country furniture. In general, the earlier the cupboard, the more extensive the trim and construction details. (See Chapter 11, "Cupboards.") The Pennsylvania Germans also made a closed cupboard that was similar to an open dresser. It was of painted pine.

PENNSYLVANIA CHAIRS

(See Chapter 6, "Chairs—Sheraton Fancy, or Painted.")

Other Nationality Groups

The eastern part of the United States was influenced by Holland and England, while in the West Spanish influences were predominant. The different backgrounds of the American settlers can be seen in the country furniture designs. The Shakers and Pennsylvania Germans are the largest special groups to have their own country furniture designs, although many small settlements exist where individual designs flourished.

A German settlement was started in Zoar, Ohio, in 1817. It was a resourceful community that prospered through business with their neighbors. The first furniture made at Zoar was typically German, but as the settlers became more like Midwesterners the furniture began to resemble the Empire styles popular in other communities. Zoarites made cupboards, tavern tables, chests of drawers, beds, kitchen and Windsor chairs.

The furniture was made from cherry, poplar, walnut, pine, maple, or hickory. It was rarely painted unless it was painted to resemble wood graining.

Amana, Iowa, was settled by another group from Germany, Switzerland, Holland, and France in 1855. The furniture made at Amana reflects the heritage of all these settlements.

The Gnadenau settlement in Kansas, the German-Russian Mennonite settlers who moved to Kansas in the 1870's, and many other special nationality settlements can be found in the United States, each with unique furniture, yet resembling other country furniture.

(Picture references: Candlestands, 40, 52, 54, 55; Chairs, rocking, 101; Chairs, painted, 146, 147, 166, 171, 172, 173, 182; Chairs, slat-back, 198, 199, 205, 263, 267; Chairs, Windsor, 282, 301, 303, 312, 319; Chests, 343, 344, 350, 351, 352, 353, 354, 355, 356, 368, 369; Cradles, 394; Cupboards, 398, 408, 410, 419; Tables, 479, 480, 500; Washstands, 547; Workbenches, 568, 571, 592, 603, 604.)

607. The painted chests and trestle table are interesting examples of the Pennsylvania· German art seen in this room. The walls, from a home built in 1783, are painted with mottled blue paint. This is a room filled with eighteenth-century furnishings from Pennsylvania: wainscot chairs made before 1750, dower chests, and fractur paintings on the walls. (Courtesy of the Henry Francis du Pont Winterthur Museum)

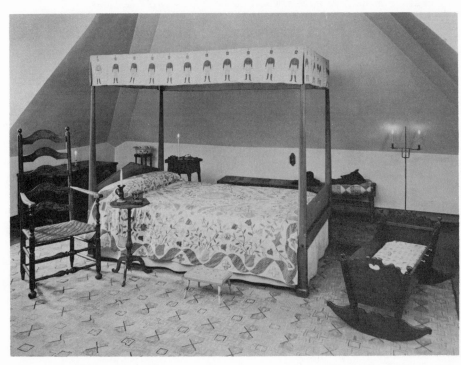

608. The Lebanon Bedroom features a pencil-post bed with attractive hangings picturing Hessian soldiers. The ladder-back chair has five curved slats. This is a Pennsylvania German bedroom of the eighteenth century. (Courtesy of Henry Francis du Pont Winterthur Museum)

609. The Pennsylvania German furnishings of this room are fine examples of the eighteenth-century workmanship of the group. Notice the side chairs with the heart pierced through the back. A painted chest is between the windows, and a walnut "schrank" used for storage is at one end of the room. Notice the sawbuck table. (Courtesy of the Henry Francis du Pont Winterthur Museum)

17

Shaker Furniture

IT IS VIRTUALLY IMPOSSIBLE to furnish a history of Shaker furniture in one chapter. Many books have been written about the furniture of this unique religious sect that added so much to the American way of life. The furniture designed and made by the Shakers reflected their religious beliefs. The simplicity of their designs and the ingenuity of their other inventions indicate their resourcefulness.

Picture the style and design of Shaker furniture when it was made in nineteenth-century America. Compare some of the finest, simplest Shaker pieces with the overdone Victorian furniture that was in high style at the same time. Certainly the Shakers were a group with courage and individuality.

Many types of wood were used in Shaker pieces because the furniture was made in various Shaker settlements that were scattered through the United States from the East Coast to the Midwest. Most of the pieces were made from old-growth pine, but maple, cherry, apple, and pear woods were also used. Maple was used for the slender units such as pegs, knobs, posts, rungs, or slats of chairs. Cherry was the favored wood for tabletops, while ash and hickory were used in the bent pieces such as rockers, rungs, slats, and arms.

Shaker design and workmanship are easily recognized because there is an individual quality of the work that stamps every Shaker piece as truly Shaker. One of the chief characteristics of all Shaker furniture is that it was made light in weight so it could be moved for cleaning. The Shakers were taught to treat everything with care and, having few children, rarely abused their furniture. Thus it could be more fragile than many pieces made for the average family.

Because their religion required a Shaker to attempt perfection at all times, Shaker furniture could never be found with poor finishings, unfinished back wood, sloppy paint, or uneven parts.

The earliest chairs and tables were painted or stained red. Later, the Shakers used a very light stain so that the grain of the wood showed. There is never any veneer on a piece of Shaker furniture, nor was heavy lacquer used. The earliest chair seats were made of rush, splint, or straw, while the later ones used the characteristic woven tape seats.

One feature that is most easily identified is the acorn-shaped finial used on the chairs. The leg of the chair was tapered, and there was no foot. Rockers were popular, many of them with a special tilting device invented by the Shakers. Shaker chairs had many other built-in features, such as drawers built underneath the sewing chair, and a rod across the back of the top of the chair, which was primarily used for a folded blanket or cushion ties.

DINING CHAIRS

Most of the dining chairs had one slat across the back, and were so low that they could be pushed under the table when not in use. They were about 25 inches in height from the top slat to the floor, and 16 inches from the seat to the floor. The seat was wider in the front than at the back. A two-slat style was made wider than the one-slat chair, with the top slat 26 inches from the floor and the chair front 16½ inches from the floor. Most of the low one-slat dining chairs were made at Hancock, Massachusetts, or West Pittsfield, Massachusetts. The two-slat chairs were made later at Mount Lebanon, New York; Watervliet, New York; Canterbury, New Hampshire; and Groveland, New York.

SIDE CHAIRS

Shaker side chairs were made for men or women, but the sister's chair had a lower seat than the brother's. The back of the chair often slanted back and made a surprisingly comfortable wooden-backed chair. If there were arms on the chair, they had mushroom knobs at the end.

Rocking chairs were numerous because of the large number of old Shakers living in their community. The straight lines, backs, taped seats, acorn finials, and other Shaker designs also appeared on the rockers. There were five types of rockers with each one named for its special feature: the scroll-arm, rolled-arm, front-upright with mushroom ends, cross-rail, and armless-sewing rockers.

TABLES

The Shakers made a trestle-type table with a shoe foot during the 1800-1860 period. They also made a sawbuck table that was used in the kitchen and for ironing.

CHESTS

The Shaker chests were made with simple molded edges. There was never any brass hardware. The wooden knobs on the drawers were mushroom turned.

Sharply angled bracket feet were used, and narrow cupboard doors were held with ingenious wrought-iron catches. Many of the chests, cupboards, and cabinets were built into the room.

Much of the Shaker furniture was made for sale to people living outside the Shaker settlement. The checkerboard tape seats in many colors were probably the result of their desire to please the customer. Red, yellow, or green colors were also used to finish wooden pieces.

As the strength of the Shaker religion dwindled, the influences of the outside world became more apparent in their furniture. Particularly in some of the southern settlements, the furniture styles changed into combinations of Shaker and outside designs, and the lightweight simple lines disappeared.

(Picture references: Beds, 12, 13; Candlesticks, 50; Chairs, rocking, 85, 102, 109; Chairs, slat-back, 208, 209; Chairs, Windsor, 324; Cupboards, 429; Desks, 458; Tables 481, 482, 519, 520; Washstands, 556; Workbenches, 560, 570, 581, 582, 583, 584, 585, 586, 588, 590, 596.)

610. The Shakers placed their furniture in clean, uncluttered rooms. The pegboard and built-in storage units are typical of Shaker rooms. Notice the rocking chair and the bed, as well as the lack of curtains and rugs. (Courtesy of the Henry Francis du Pont Winterthur Museum)

611. In this Shaker kitchen at the Shaker Village in Hancock, Massachusetts, are the tools and tables used by the cooks. The simple lines and expert finishing details appear on each piece of furniture. (Hancock Village, Massachusetts)

18

Spool Furniture

NEW TYPES OF MACHINERY made the development of spool furniture possible by the American furniture manufacturers of the nineteenth century. While the single-blade turning lathe had been in use for many years, the multiple-blade lathe for making wooden buttons and spools was not developed until about 1815. A clever cabinetmaker, realizing the decorative qualities of the elaborate turnings, began to use the spool-turned wood as a part of furniture. Examine a spool-turned bed and notice how the turnings resemble a stack of empty thread spools placed one above the other. The original spool turnings were sliced apart and drilled through the middle. The furniture turnings were lengths of these uncut spools.

Dating spool furniture is just a matter of common sense. Because it was easier to make long straight lengths of turnings, that was the first type of spool furniture made.

Beds made with button or spool turnings were popular about 1830. The headboards and footboards were of the same height, ranging from 36 inches to 42 inches. A few of them had finials at the tip of the bedposts. Strips of turnings were joined at sharp, unrounded corners. The low-post spool-turned bed was popular during the time the famous singer Jenny Lind was traveling in the United States. Her name was given to the bed.

These beds were made from pine, maple, or birch, and were usually painted. They had wooden slats that were used to hold the mattress in place, while the supporting frame was held in place with countersunk screws.

The spool furniture of the 1850 period was made with rounded corners because the furniture makers developed a method of bending the spool turnings, which were usually made from stained hardwood. The headboard and footboard had curved corners.

The tall-post spool bed is a regional style usually found in the Midwest and the South. These beds had spool-turned posts from 5½ feet to 7 feet high. A full tester was over some beds, while others had finials on high posts. This midwestern spool furniture was made from maple, walnut, cherry, poplar, cottonwood, and occasionally mahogany. If the wood had an attractive color, it was given a natural finish, but the pine and other softwoods were stained or painted.

Spool turnings were used in most types of furniture, including chairs, stools, benches, settees, single and double beds, hatracks, music stands, and tables. The style was so popular by 1840 that many factories just made and sold turnings to cabinetmakers. At the same time some furniture was being decorated with split turnings. A piece of the spool-turned wood was sliced in half. The half turnings were painted, then glued or nailed to the furniture as added decoration.

(Picture references: Beds, 21, 22, 23, 24; Chests, 346; Cupboards, 414; Tables, 524, 525, 526; Washstands, 549, 550, 553; Workbenches, 577.)

19

Furniture Construction

DATING COUNTRY FURNITURE purely by design is always difficult because the country cabinetmaker used the same designs for many years. The methods of construction changed through the years with new types of nails, screws, saws, lathes, and new methods of joining wood. Country makers were slow to adopt the new methods, as they were reluctant to replace some of their tools and supplies.

HARDWARE, NAILS

Three types of nails are found in country furniture. The hand-forged nail, the oldest type, was in use until about 1870. It can still be purchased at local hardware stores. The machine-cut nail was made from 1790 to 1870 but was not used in quantity until about 1815. The machine-cut nail was made by slicing a strip of metal about ⅛ of an inch thick. The head and the shank were about the same size, and square. The early hand-forged nails were hammered, with marks often showing on the square heads and shanks.

Today's style of wire nail with a round head and a circular shank was first made about 1870.

SCREWS

Screws are not new. Blunt end wood screws were made and used in the colonies during the early eighteenth century. Long before the first American furniture was made, they were used on European furniture. Early handmade screws were made from brass or iron, with very irregular spirals. The shallow and often off-center slot in the head was cut by a saw. Almost every screw was of a different length.

The first machine-made screw was produced about 1815. It had a blunt end with spirals that were even and regular. The gimlet, or pointed screw, was made about 1846. Many furniture makers, however, felt that the gimlet would not hold as well as the blunt screw, and continued to use blunt screws long after the development of the pointed screw.

Screws that held braces on chairs or cleats under tabletops are almost never replaced. Those holding hinges on doors or hardware on drawers were often lost and replaced by the later types of screws. Common sense should help you decide if a screw could have logically worked loose after 150 years and have to be replaced. If you remove a screw that is original, the hole in the wood should have only one set of spiral tracks.

HINGES

Wrought-iron hinges used on country furniture are poor indications of age. Canadian country cabinets made during the 1870's have fine handmade rattail hinges made in the manner popular in Pennsylvania one hundred years earlier. The butterfly, rattail, **H** and **L** hinges are still being made, appear on reproduction furniture, and can be obtained in many hardware stores. It is helpful to know when each type of hinge was first used, but useless to try to date any piece from the hardware alone.

KNOBS AND BRASSES

Brasses were not used on most country furniture. The style of the formal furniture was copied by the country makers, so the design of the hardware can be some indication of age. Small teardrop-style handles were used during the William and Mary and the early Queen Anne periods to about 1750. The large Chippendale-type brasses were popular to about 1775. Bail handles were used by many country makers from 1760 to 1800, and the oval Hepplewhite and Sheraton hardwares were used until about 1830.

Most of the country furniture was made with either wooden, glass, or brass knobs. The earliest (seventeenth-century) wooden knobs were turned and egg-shaped. The mushroom-turned knob was popular about 1800 to 1840. Carved wooden knobs shaped like leaves or fruit were used during the early Victorian era, about 1840 to 1875.

It was easy for the country makers to produce a wooden knob that was attached with a metal spike. Later a screw was used whose age helps determine the age of the knob.

Brass rosette-shaped knobs made with a screw back that went through a hole in the wooden drawer front were popular from about 1800 to 1840. While the earliest examples were bulbous, by the 1830's stamped disklike knobs were used on furniture.

Pressed glass knobs were popular from 1820 to 1840. They were made from clear glass or in opalescent blue, green, or yellow. Many of the knobs were made by the famous Boston and Sandwich Glass Company, and many copies have been produced.

DRAWER

Common sense is the best beginning when examining a piece of country furniture with drawers. Normal signs of wear will appear after a hundred years, and particular attention should be paid to the slides on the bottom of the drawer. If they are worn, the drawer is loose. Pieces are often found with thin strips of wood added to the bottom of the drawer. The edges and corners of the drawers should be nicked by many years of wear.

Construction features must be examined. Unless a piece of furniture has been made from fancy grained maple or other decorative wood, the drawer should be the same as the rest of the piece of furniture. The side, back, and bottom of a drawer were usually made from woods such as pine, spruce, yellow poplar, or white wood. English furniture was often made with oak drawers.

The interior of an early drawer was never shellacked or varnished. The bottom of the exterior of the drawer was often rough, with the marks of the jack plane easily visible. The drawer bottom was often made from a thick piece of lumber that was cut to fit into narrow grooves in the sides of the drawer.

DOVETAILING

The corner joints of a drawer are called dovetails. The type of dovetailing changed through the years. Eighteenth-century country furniture was made using dovetails up to two inches in width. By the early nineteenth century the joint was approximately one inch wide, and the dovetails in a drawer were uni-

form in size. In the early nineteenth century there were often four to five small dovetail joints in a drawer, depending on the size of the drawer. Early factory pieces were made with dovetails having rounded ends (1840).

MORTISE AND TENON

The mortise-and-tenon joint was used to join various pieces of wood, such as the leg of a chair to a seat. A tenon or slot was cut into a piece of wood, and the other piece of wood was shaped to fit into the slot. A quarter-inch hole was drilled through the two pieces, and a wooden pin was inserted to hold the mortise and tenon together.

The pins on early pieces were hand carved and many-sided. The machine-made pins of the nineteenth century were perfectly round. Some mortise-and-tenon joints were made without a pin, with glues developed to hold a joint secure. The dovetail is really a specially sized mortise-and-tenon joint.

OTHER FEATURES

There are other special features in the construction of country furniture. The pegs were usually made from hickory or ash that was cut to shape. Some pegs were oblong or square; none were perfectly round. The turned pegs on old country furniture should not be perfectly round but slightly oval because of the shrinkage of the wood. A calipers is a great help in determining whether a leg or a knob is round.

Chests of drawers from England were made with dust boards, a board placed between the drawers. In American chests of drawers there were no dust boards.

If a chest of drawers was made before the 1880's, the back of the chest was usually made from random-width wood. The boards were thicker than today's, and ranged up to 24 inches in width. The backboards often had knots, but they were always small since the large ones fell out when the wood dried.

TOOL MARKS

A little study is needed in identifying the marks of early tools. The backboard of a large piece of country furniture was usually left in rough condition, with slight ridges and hollows left by the wide-bladed jack plane that was used until about 1835.

Saw marks are always a good indication of age.

The up-and-down pit saw left straight tracks, while the circular saw left wide circular arcs on the wood. The circular saw was not used until the 1840's; thus any piece of furniture with circular saw marks must date after 1840.

PAINT AND FINISH

Paint is very little help in determining the age of country furniture. Certain muted colors, such as brick red and blue green, were used by early furniture makers. Many of these colors are still being used. Today's bright colors and pastels were not popular then.

The patina or color of the wood on an unpainted piece of country furniture is hard to identify. There is very little difference between the patina of a table-top that is fifty years old and one that is 150 years old. Artificially aged wood is different in color, with more orange or gray caused by the method of aging. It is wise to learn the true appearance of old wood. If the inside of a drawer is as dark as the top of the chest or if the bottom of the tabletop is the same color as the top, beware! Wood changes color slowly, and the exposure to light and air will hasten the process. Covered areas will not darken quickly.

GLASS

The early glass used in cupboard doors was wavy, bubbly, and often slightly blue in color. Sheet window glass was in use by the middle of the Victorian era. Be suspicious if all the windows of an early nineteenth-century piece are sheet glass or if all the windows are bull's-eye or bubbled glass. Accidents can happen, and any piece of furniture with a glass door that has remained in perfect shape for one hundred years or more is remarkable.

GLASS KNOBS

Glass knobs were used from about 1815 to 1840. The pressed glass knobs were made in many colors by several factories, but most of them were made of clear glass, opal, or white glass. Some glass knobs were made with a screw end similar to the top of a screw-top jar. Other glass knobs had screws that were held by plaster of Paris. A third type had a screw going through the entire knob, which was held by a screw-head in front and a bolt at the back.

Some of the better furniture had cut-glass knobs. The glass was backed with foil and set in a metal frame or cup attached to the screw.

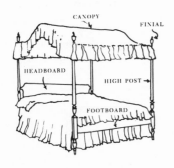

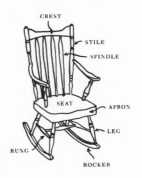

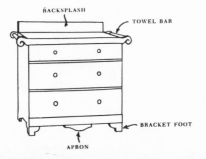

20

Bibliography

Accessories

Freeman, Larry. *Light on Old Lamps*. Watkins Glen, N.Y.: Century House Americana, 1944.

Gould, Mary Earle. *Early American Wooden Ware*. Rutland, Vt.: Charles E. Tuttle Company, 1962.

Hayward, Arthur. *Colonial Lighting*. Boston, Mass. B. J. Brimmer Co., 1923.

Jenkins, Dorothy. *A Fortune in the Junk Pile*. New York: Crown Publishers, 1963.

Speare, Elizabeth George. *Life in Colonial America*. New York: Random House, 1963.

Thwing, Leroy L. *Flickering Flames: A History of Domestic Lighting Through the Ages*. Rutland, Vt.: Charles E. Tuttle Company, 1958.

General Books on Furniture

Brooklyn Museum. *Country Style*. Exhibition, 1956.

Burroughs, P. H. *Southern Antiques*. Richmond, Va.: Garrett and Massie, 1931.

Chamberlain, Narcissa. *Old Rooms for New Living*. New York: Hastings House, 1953.

Christensen, Erwin. *Index of American Design*. New York: The Macmillan Company, 1950.

Comstock, Helen. *The Concise Encyclopedia of American Antiques*. New York: Hawthorn Books, 1958.

Downs, Joseph. *American Furniture: Queen Anne and Chippendale Periods*. New York: The Macmillan Company, 1952.

Drepperd, Carl. *Handbook of Antique Chairs*. New York: Doubleday & Company, 1948.

———— *Primer of American Antiques*. Garden City, N.Y.: Doubleday & Company, 1952.

Dyer, Walter A., and Esther S. Fraser. *The Rocking Chair: An American Institution*. New York: Century Company, 1928.

Grotz, George. *The New Antiques: Knowing and Buying Victorian Furniture*. Garden City, N.Y.: Doubleday & Company, 1964.

Kettell, Russell. *The Pine Furniture of Early New England*. New York: Dover Publications, 1929.

Lazeare, James. *Primitive Pine Furniture*. Watkins Glen, N.Y.: Century House, 1957.

Lockwood, Luke Vincent. *Colonial Furniture in America*. New York: Castel Books, 3 vols., Charles Scribner's Sons, 1926.

Marsh, Moreton. *The Easy Expert in Collecting and Restoring American Antiques*. Philadelphia: J. B. Lippincott Company, 1959.

Miller, Edgar George. *American Antique Furniture*. New York: Barrows and Company, 1948; Greystone Press, 1950.

Naetzer, Donald P. *Country Furniture and Accessories*. Fairport, N.Y.: Robert Cuttis, 1962.

Nutting, Wallace. *Furniture Treasury*. New York: The Macmillan Company, 3 vols., 1949.

Ormsbee, Thomas. *Collecting Antiques in America*. New York: Deerfield Books, 1936, 1962.

————. *Field Guide to Early American Furniture*. Boston: Little Brown and Company, 1951.

————. *Field Guide to American Victorian Furniture*. Boston: Little Brown and Company, 1952.

————. *Know Your Heirlooms*. New York: The McBride Company, 1956.

————. *A Storehouse of Antiques*. New York: Dodd, Mead & Company, 1947.

Sack, Albert. *Fine Points of Furniture*. New York: Crown Publishers, 1950, 1960.

"Three Centuries of Furniture," Cornell Extension Bulletin, Cornell University, Ithaca, N.Y.: November, 1950.

Painted Chairs

Lea, Zilla Rider. *The Ornamented Chair: Its Development in America*. Rutland, Vt.: Charles E. Tuttle Company, 1960.

Regional Differences in Furniture

CANADA

MacLaren, George. *Antique Furniture by Nova Scotian Craftsmen*. Toronto: Ryerson Press, 1961.

Minhinnick, Jeanne. *Furniture in Upper Canada Village*. Toronto: Ryerson Press, 1964.

Palardy, Jean. *The Early Furniture of French Canada*. The Macmillan Company of Canada, 1963.

Stevens, Gerald. *In a Canadian Attic*. Toronto: Ryerson Press, 1963.

PENNSYLVANIA

Licthten, Frances. *Folk Art of Rural Pennsylvania*. New York: Charles Scribner's Sons, 1946.

Robacker, Earl F. *Pennsylvania Dutch Stuff*. Philadelphia: University of Pennsylvania Press, 1944.

SHAKER

Andrews, E. D., and F. Andrews. *Shaker Furniture*. New Haven: Yale University Press, 1937, 1950.

Philadelphia Museum Bulletin, "The Shakers and Their Arts and Crafts." Spring, 1962.

Windsor Chairs

Nutting, Wallace. *American Windsors*. Framingham and Boston: Old American Company, 1917.

Ormsbee, Thomas. *The Windsor Chair*. New York: Hearthside Press, 1962.

Apple peelers

Needed in every kitchen because peeled apples were used in pies or dried as an important part of the diet. The earliest peelers were made of clever arrangements of wooden gears; later, cast-iron peelers were developed (616, 617).

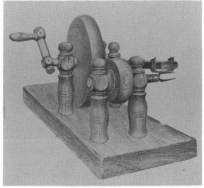

616. Red oak apple peeler made in Wilmington, Delaware, about 1840. (Index of American Design, Washington, D.C.)

617. Cast-iron peeler made about 1880.

Box stretcher

The arrangement of four stretchers between the legs of a table or chair to form a boxlike shape. See picture 468.

BOXES

All sizes and shapes were needed for the country home. Wooden, tin, and paper boxes held valuable papers, tea and spices, clothes, or just odds and ends (618–620).

618. A wooden candle box painted in gay colors. (Metropolitan Museum of Art; gift of Mr. Robert W. de Forest)

620. Oval boxes made by the Shakers during the nineteenth century. The more "fingers" and metal rivets in the overlap, the newer the box. These are made of pine and maple, unpainted or stained blue, red, yellow, or green. (Index of American Design, Washington, D.C.)

619. Bonnet box or cap box made of thinly split cedar about 1780. It is sewn together with rattan, and painted. Many bonnet boxes were covered with specially designed wallpaper. (Metropolitan Museum of Art)

Boxes, elongated

Hung on the wall and used for many purposes in the farm home. Spoon racks, candle sconces, saltboxes, pipe and tobacco boxes and matchboxes all are similar in size and shape (621–626).

621. About 1750 this saltbox was made of yellow pine and painted red. (Metropolitan Museum of Art; gift of Mrs. Robert W. de Forest)

623. Spoon rack with a small box, probably for cleaning compound, made of walnut about 1820. (Index of American Design, Washington, D.C.)

626. Candle sconce or candle wall holder made by the Shakers from stained pine in the nineteenth century. (Index of American Design, Washington, D.C.)

624. Assorted nineteenth-century saltboxes. (Garth)

622. Wooden pipe and tobacco box made of pine in the early nineteenth century. The drawer held the tobacco; the top section held the long-stemmed clay pipe. (Metropolitan Museum of Art; gift of Mrs. Russell Sage, 1909)

Breadboard end

The reinforced construction method to keep a long wooden board, usually a tabletop, from warping. A board was run the width of the top against the grain of the other boards in the same manner as today's breadboard. See picture 466.

625. Painted tin match holder of the 1860's. (Ray and Lee Grover)

CABRIOLE LEG

Curved leg said to resemble the outline of a curved animal leg. See picture 512.

Chopping knife

Important for the success of any cook. This mid-nineteenth-century knife was made from sheet iron (627).

627. (Index of American Design, Washington, D.C.)

CHURNS

Assorted sizes and shapes, all were used to make butter by agitating the cream (628–630).

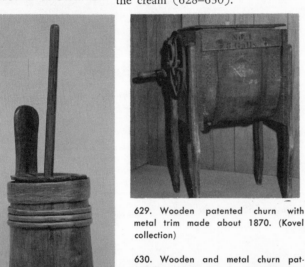

629. Wooden patented churn with metal trim made about 1870. (Kovel collection)

630. Wooden and metal churn patented in 1870. (Kovel collection)

628. Wooden dasher churn bound with wooden hoops. (Metropolitan Museum of Art; gift of Mrs. Russell Sage, 1909)

Cleat

A piece of wood attached to the back of a board to brace or strengthen it. See picture 531.

Clock reel or bankwinder

A wooden device used to wind the thread to be spun. The housewife of 1800 had one of these to use (631).

CLOCKS

All kinds were used in the country home. The wag-on-the-wall was part of a do-it-yourself idea. The clock could be cased later and made into a grandfather's clock or tall case clock. The nineteenth-century clockmaker made many types of shelf clocks, some with wooden works, some with brass works, and many with painted glass fronts (632–636).

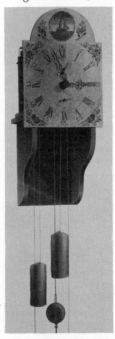

FROM LEFT TO RIGHT

632. Wag-on-the-wall clock with wooden dial and wooden works, made by the Shrewsbury Clock Company about 1800.

633. Grandfather's clock or hall clock or tall case clock made about 1821–1834 by Luman Watson of Cincinnnati, Ohio.

634. Shelf clock made by Ephraim Downs about 1816–1834. LEFT

635. Shelf clock made by Birge and Fuller of Bristol, Connecticut, about 1845. It is made of mahogany with a decalcomania design on the glass. RIGHT

636. Shelf clock made by Chauncey Jerome of New Haven, Connecticut, about 1865. It has a walnut case with a reverse glass painting. (Index of American Design, Washington, D.C.)

Drying rack

Made of wood, this item was needed in the days before the automatic dryer. This pine rack was used in Texas about 1850 (637).

637. (Pensacola Historical Society, Pensacola, Florida)

Ember carrier

When the fire went out, it was a serious problem if your nearest neighbor was miles down the road. Someone had to run down the road with this ember carrier, fill it with glowing coals from the neighbor's fireplace, and scurry back home before the coals died. Tin and wood were used in this midwestern piece of the mid-nineteenth century (640).

Eggboiler

Used in the nineteenth century by the well-organized housewife who served hot eggs at breakfast. The tin boiler was filled with hot water, eggs were put in the rack, and the eggs cooked at the table (638, 639). (Index of American Design, Washington, D.C.)

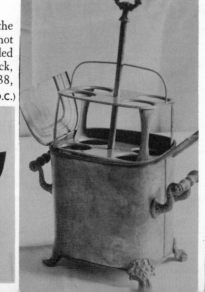

Ember holder or hoopskirt lifter

This expanding scissors had two jobs. It seems strange that it would be used to raise the edge of milady's skirt, but that is one of the stories attached to this item. It is certain that this scissors-like tool was used to lift glowing coals from the fire to light a pipe or to send to a neighbor whose fire had died (641).

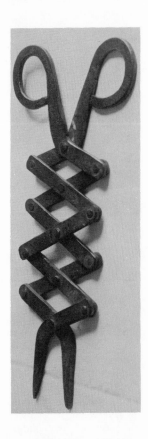

Feather duster

Used to keep the house clean. Turkey feathers quickly dusted away the dirt (642). (Kovel collection)

FLUTING

A special type of grooving used to decorate furniture. See picture 418.

FLYTRAP

Flies and bugs are always a problem, but the country kitchen had a novel flytrap. This pottery flypot was baited with sugar. Poor little flies crawled into the holes and could never find the way out (643).

Foot warmers

Cold feet were a problem that could be solved in many ways. Pierced tin and wood were used to make the foot warmers of about 1800. Pottery was used in the nineteenth century. Hot coals or hot water were kept in the warmer, on top of which milady put her cold feet (644, 645).

644. A wooden and metal warmer made in the nineteenth century to hold coals.

645. Late nineteenth-century pottery foot warmers that held hot water.

FRAME

The wooden skeleton of a piece of furniture.

Goffering iron

For making goffered wafers or waffles. The inside was decorated with patterns that were repeated on the waffle. Originally a Swedish idea, the goffering iron is found in all parts of the United States (646).

H STRETCHER

Arrangement of stretchers between the legs of tables and chairs that form an H shape. See picture.

Ice tongs

Refrigerators were unknown, but because ice was needed to preserve food, ice tongs were needed in every home. The ice was cut from the pond in winter and stored at the icehouse for summer use. These ice tongs were made about 1855 in Wisconsin (647).

647. Index of American Design, Washington, D.C.)

237

IRONS

Sadirons, fluting irons, tailor's irons, flatirons, and crimping irons all meant a muscular, exhausted housewife in the nineteenth century. The iron of the day was filled with charcoal or heated on a stove. It was hot and heavy (648–652).

651. Fluting iron made in 1866. The iron was used for pleating women's dresses. (Kovel collection)

652. Fluting or crimping iron of about 1870. (Kovel collection)

648. Charcoal-burning sadiron of about 1860, sometimes called a tailor's iron.

649. Charcoal-filled sadiron of lighter weight.

650. Flatiron of the late nineteenth century. One heated on the stove while another was in use. (Kovel collection)

KEY

To tighten and twist the ropes on the bed (653).

653. (Old Sturbridge Village, Sturbridge, Massachusetts)

Kitchen gadgets

654. (Metropolitan Museum of Art, Sylmaris Collection; gift of George Coe Graves, 1930)

Found in every early American kitchen. Pots and pans, molds and skimmers were used. Even this toy kitchen of the late eighteenth century is completely equipped with the kitchen utensils of the day (654).

KNEE

See picture 614.

Lamps

All sorts were used for light and were needed in every room. Fuels and shapes varied (655–661).

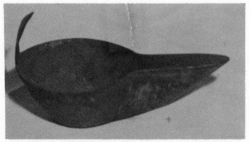

655. First of the lighting devices of the settlers was this simple type of "pan lamp" or "crusie." Cavemen used these. Any oil that was handy served as the fuel; a wick dangled from the spout. Settlers burned animal and vegetable fats in these lamps—any kind but pig fat, which had an awful odor.

656. Put a half-round metal piece to hold the wick in a pan lamp and you have made a "Betty lamp." The wick support kept the fat from seeping out of the lamp and dripping on the floor, an improvement even the housewife of the Middle Ages appreciated. This type of covered Betty lamp on a stand was made about 1850. (Ray and Lee Grover)

657. Some lanterns were made for torchlight parades. This tinned sheet-iron lantern was made about 1860 for use at the end of a wooden pole. A candle inside supplied the light. "Wide-Awake" clubs of Republicans paraded with these lanterns during the campaign. (Index of American Design, Washington, D.C.)

658. A candle furnished the light indoors for the eighteenth-century housewife. This tin sconce could be hung on the wall. The polished tin back reflected the candle to double the light. (Index of American Design, Washington, D.C.)

659. Lanterns were used to light the way from the house to the barn. This New England lantern of iron was made about 1770. (Index of American Design, Washington, D.C.)

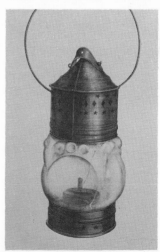

660. Paul Revere never used a lantern like this, but it has his name. The pierced tin lantern was common in the eighteenth and nineteenth centuries. A candle inside the lantern shed dim light through the tiny slits in the tin-sided lantern. Paul Revere would never have known how the British were coming if he had depended on this dim light source. The real lantern hung in the church had glass sides. (Index of American Design, Washington, D.C.)

661. The peg lamp was a thrifty colonist's clever way to increase the light at small cost. The peg lamp was placed in any candlestick. This raised the light source and gave a larger lamp at a small cost. Any lamp made to fit into a candlestick can be called a "peg lamp" or "stump lamp" or "socket lamp." This glass peg lamp was fitted into the brass candlestick about 1810. (Index of American Design, Washington, D.C.)

Maple sugar mold

Found in special areas of the country. Regional products caused inventive settlers to make their own tools. This nineteenth-century maple-sugar mold comes apart to release the sticks of maple sweetener (662).

Pie lifter

Bend a piece of wire, add a handle, and you have a replica of this nineteenth-century pie lifter. The hook catches the edge of the pie and forms a handle to lift the pie from the oven (663).

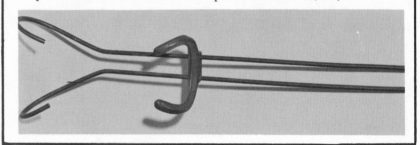

Mortise and tenon

See Chapter 19, "Furniture Construction."

PAD FOOT

The simple flattened end of a cabriole leg. See picture 486.

Pitchfork

Made from one long branch of wood. The prongs were made by slitting the branch and bracing the prong with other wooden pins (664). (Kovel collection)

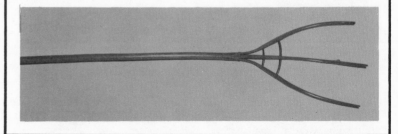

Potato basket or salad basket

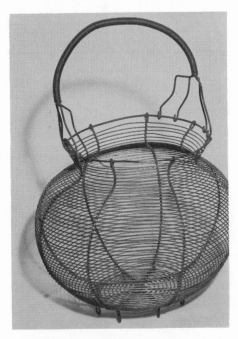

665. This double-purpose kitchen utensil was used by the nineteenth-century housewife. The wire basket held potatoes in a pot of boiling water or held greens under the pump water when they needed washing.

Potato digger

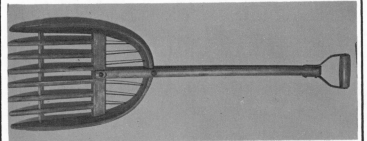

666. A wooden tool made at Zoar, Ohio, about 1850. (Ray and Lee Grover)

POTS AND PANS

Made of heavy metal to swing over the glowing fire. Large copper pots and cast-iron pots of all sizes were used in the country home (667–669).

667. Copper pan with iron handles that was used to make candy about 1865.

668. Mid-nineteenth century cast-iron kettle with feet.

669. Muffin pan of cast iron with shaped muffin holes. (All from Index of American Design, Washington, D.C.)

REEDING

A special type of carving made with round, raised sections, supposedly to resemble bundles of reeds.

Sausage stuffers

Needed to make the delicious sausage of the farmhouse kitchens. Styles in stuffers varied as often as the seasoning in the sausage. Wooden presses or sausage mills were made in the eighteenth century. Tin stuffers with long snouts and heavy iron stuffers with long handles were products of the nineteenth century (670–672).

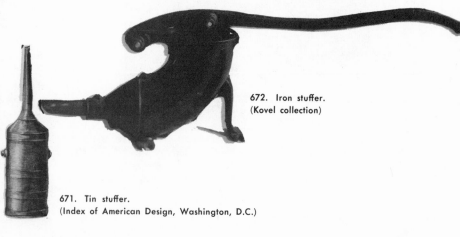

670. Wooden press.
(Metropolitan Museum of Art)

672. Iron stuffer.
(Kovel collection)

671. Tin stuffer.
(Index of American Design, Washington, D.C.)

Sifter

Cooking problems were the same in the nineteenth-century kitchen (673, 674), and sifting flour was one of the many jobs for the housewife.

674. Improvements in the sifter show in this 1864 version made of cedar wood and screening.
(Index of American Design, Washington, D.C.)

673. The copper and tin screen sifter might have been used about 1800.

SKIRT

See picture 615.

SPADE FOOT

The foot at the bottom of a leg of a chair or table that resembles a spade. Usually found on English, not American pieces.

Spice chest

This walnut chest was patented in 1866. The lower section revolved like a lazy susan (675).

675. (Shelburne Museum, Shelburne, Vermont)

Spool turning

Specially shaped turnings made at first to be cut apart into thread spool or buttons. The turnings were used on mid-nineteenth-century spool furniture. See Chapter 18, "Spool Furniture."

TEAPOT

This pot is made of iron for use on the old wood-burning stove or over the fireplace embers (680) (Kovel collection)

Spinning wheels

These wheels spun wool or linen. Small wheels were used to spin flax and sometimes wool. The large wheels were made for wool alone. The spinner sat to spin flax, but for wool she walked, often twenty miles a day, back and forth by the wheel (676–678).

676. Eighteenth-century spinning wheel for flax. (Metropolitan Museum of Art; gift of Mrs. Russell Sage, 1909)

677. Flax wheel. (Historical Society of the Tarrytowns, Tarrytown, New York)

678. Nineteenth-century walnut spinning wheel made about 1850 in Texas. (Index of American Design, Washington, D.C.)

TOASTER

Toasted bread for breakfast is a centuries-old tradition, and every well-equipped cooking fireplace had a toaster. The wrought-iron, handmade, and individually designed toaster was made in the mid-eighteenth and early nineteenth centuries. The toasters were placed in front of the fire; then the top rack revolved to brown toast evenly (681–684).

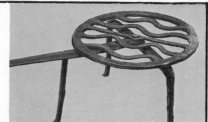

683. Round wrought-iron revolving rack made in the late eighteenth century in Pennsylvania. (Index of American Design, Washington, D.C.)

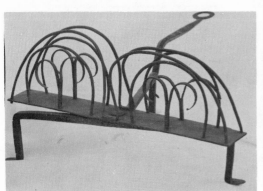

681. Wrought-iron revolving toaster with penny feet.

682. Eighteenth-century wrought-iron toast rack from Connecticut. (Index of American Design, Washington, D.C.)

684. Wooden-handled toast holder with iron wire trefoils made in the nineteenth century. (Index of American Design, Washington, D.C.)

Toleware

The colorful painted tin of the country home that served as well as pottery and glass, which were scarce and fragile, Pennsylvania painted tin of the early nineteenth century is today's cherished American folk art (685).

685. (Index of American Design, Washington, D.C.)

TRAMMEL

This metal or wooden device held the bubbling pot over the fireplace (686).

686. (Metropolitan Museum of Art; gift of Mrs. Russell Sage)

TRESTLE

See Chapter 13, "Tables."

Turned

Means shaped on a lathe. Any chair with turned decoration or turned parts can be called a turned chair.

Woodenware or treenware

Made from the wood that was plentiful and free for the taking in the nineteenth century. Many kitchen utensils were made from wood. Burl, the tough knotted wood, was used for bowls and spoons because it did not warp or crack (687–691).

687. The maple burl scoop is made of one piece of wood. The boat-shaped pine dish held soap. (Old Sturbridge Village, Sturbridge, Massachusetts)

688. Treenware is any type of small turned woodenware like these nineteenth-century boxes and vases. (Taylor and Dull, photography)

689. Carved butter molds like this one of cherry added patterns to the homemade butter.

690. This wooden potato masher may also have been used as a wooden pestle to grind spices. (Index of American Design, Washington, D.C.)

691. Indians taught the early settlers to make corn mortars from a hollowed log. A wooden pestle was used with the mortar. (Historic Mobile Preservation Society, Mobile, Alabama)

x stretcher   An arrangement of stretchers between legs of table and chair that form an X shape.

INDEX

Numerals refer to page numbers EXCEPT those in bold-face type, which refer to picture-figure numbers.

accounting desk, 461
acorn finial, 225
Adam style, 186
Adams, 59
Alabama, 587
Alford, Alfred, 62
Alford and Company, 62
Alford, Arba Jr., 62
American Standard rocker, 39
Amish, 567
angel-wing slat, 61; 182, 183
angle of hole, 113
animal foot, 17
ankle, 17
apothecary chest, see chest, apothecary
Appalachian Mountains, 85
Arizona, 84
Arkansas, chair, 230
armless sewing rocker, 226
arms, rocking-chair, 38
arrow, 173–77
  back, 61, 113, 115, 116; 309–12
  design, 154
  spindle, 105–10
artificially grained, 59

back, Windsor, 113
ball, feet, 132, 133, 134; 198, 330
ball-type handle, 133
balloon back, 61; 292
Baltimore, 61
baluster back, 25
bamboo, 61, 117; 187, 292, 302
  turnings, 60, 113, 114, 116; 62, 141, 295, 302, 320, 323, 327
banc lit, see bench bed
bannister back, 60, 83, 115
bannister-back chair, see Chapter 3
beaten-biscuit board, 575
beds, see Chapter 1
bedside table, 200; 544, 545
bench, 602–4
  bed, 30, 31
  rocker, see mammy bench
  tailors, 587
  work, 595
Bergen County, New Jersey, 84
bird cage, 323, 327
  back, 162
bird's eye maple, 61
Birge and Fuller, 236
blanket chest, 357–62, 364, 366, 373–81
  Pennsylvania, 133
  survival example, 134
bobbin-shaped turnings, 114
bonnet cabinet, 425, 426
bootjack chair, 276
Boston rocker, 38, 39, 60, 62; 99, 100, 112–18, 120–24, 307
bowback Windsor, 114, 115; 290–97
box cradle, 396
box stretcher, 178, 181; 465, 487
brace back, 115
bracket feet, 133, 134; 349, 354, 359
brasses, 227
breadboard end, 178, 179; 466, 468, 530
breakfast table, 510, 511
Brewster, 25; 67, 68
bulbous turnings, 71
Burlington rocker, 97
butt hinge, 156
butterfly table, 180; 487, 488
button back, 60; 153

cabinet, kitchen, 574
cabriole, 2, 30
  leg, 133; 10, 436
California, 84; 383
  Mission bench, 253
  Mission chair, 244–49
  Mission style, 85
  Santa Barbara, 337

camp bed, 34
Canada, 107, 111, 200, 572
Canadian, 19, 29–31, 83, 140, 206–8, 534; see also Ontario, Canada
  candlestand, 47, 48
  chair, 251, 252
  chest, 341, 378
  rocker, 94
  settee, 321
candlestand, see Chapter 2
cane back, 30
  chair, 83
  seat, 38, 39, 60; 125, 141
caning, 25
cannon ball, 16–18
canopy, 1, 2; 385
captain's chair, 112, 115, 116; 316, 317
Carver, 25, 83; 62–65
casters, 2, 134
cellarette, 440, 441
"Central," 84
chair
  formal, see Chapter 4
  painted, see Chapter 6
  Pennsylvania, see Chapter 6
  seat, 38
  Sheraton fancy, see Chapter 6
  table 181; 530–32
chairs, Pennsylvania, see Chapter 6
Chalk, Jule, 180
chamfered, 179
Charles the Second chair, 30
Chases, Samuel, 178
checkered diagonal rushing, 85
checkered rush, 85
chest
  apothecary, 589, 590
  dower, see dower chest
  grain, 578, 579
  inlaid, Pennsylvania, 221
  one-drawer, 271, 370
  of drawers, 338–49
    Chippendale, 133
    Pennsylvania, 222
  -on-chest, 133; 336, 337
  on frame, 132, 133; 331–35
  Pennsylvania, 221
  seventeenth and eighteenth century, 132
  Shaker, 226
  Weavers, 588
chests, see Chapter 9
child's bed, 32
  chair, 228–30, 232; 293, 297, 314
children's Windsor, 326
china cabinet, 155
Chippendale, 2, 3, 17, 30, 83, 178, 180, 200; 79, 80, 81, 341, 354, 358, 369, 372, 446
  style foot, 353, 360, 375
  type slant-front desk, 167
churning chair, 224
Cincinnati, 59
circular saw, 231
claw and ball foot, 2, 30
cleat, 174–76, 229; 470, 504, 506, 531, 536, 537
Cleopatra barge chair, 59, 60
closed cupboard, 156; 406–14, 564
closed dresser, 155
club foot, 30
cobbler's bench, 207; 591–96
  light, 17
  shop, 596
  table, 44
Colorado, 84
comb-back Windsor, 112, 113, 114, 115; 279–82
commode, 200
  lift top, 201; 554
  nineteenth century, 555, 557
  table, 200, see Chapter 14; 543
  Victorian, 201
Conestoga table, 480
Connecticut, 39, 85, 112, 132, 180,

244; 1, 32, 57, 264, 265, 288, 329, 340, 448, 484, 490, 506
  Barkhamsted, 62
  Cheshire, 62
  Guilford, 334, 366
  Hartford, 298
  Hitchcocksville, 59
  Killingworth, 158
  New Haven, 593
  Riverton, 62
  Unionville, 62
construction
  banister-back chair, 25
  furniture, see Chapter 19, 229
  rocking-chair, 37
corn-shuck seat, 234
corner cabinet, 155, 156
corner chair, 86; 259–62
corner cupboard, 415–23
  closed, 428, 429
cornhusk seat, 85
cornucopia, 60
"Côte de Beaupré," 251
countersunk screws, 228
court cupboard, 155
cow horns, 86
cowhide seat, 222, 223, 226
Cowlitz County, Washington, 91
cradle
  settee, see mammy bench
  Windsor, 327
cradle-shaped rocker, 38
cradles, see Chapter 10; 384–96
Creole chair, 234
crest, 26, 59
crib, 24
crossbands, 59
cross-bar feet, 39
crossbars, 17
cross rail, rocker, Shaker, 226
crown top, 149
cupboards, see Chapter 11, 132; 596
  Pennsylvania, 222
cupid's bow, 115
curly maple, 37, 61; 3, 459, 471
cut-out slat, 164, 165
cylinder front, 170

daybed, 26; 27
decadent period, 59, 60
Deckman, George, 179
Delaware, 84; 98, 296
  Wilmington, 114, 576
dentil molding, 343
desks, see Chapter 12
diagonal rushing, 201
diamond-shaped splat, 152, 166
dining chair, Shaker, 225
Directoire, 1
Dominy, Nathaniel, 76
"donkey ear," 228
double stretcher, 116
dough box, 205; 572, 573
dough tray, see dough box
dovetail, 133, 228
dowels, 85
dower chest, Pennsylvania, 132, 133, 134, 221, 222; 350–56, 368, 369, 607
Downs, Ephraim, 236
drawer construction, 230
drawshave, 114
dresser, 155; 407
dressing table, 177
drop-leaf table, 180; 490, 491, 493–99
drop-lid desk, 169, 170
dry sink, 205; 567–70
duck foot, 75, 76
dust board, 230
Dutch foot, 30

eagle, 60
  back, 150
early period, 59, 60
"ears," 114
East, 224

ebonized, 464, 514
Economites, 303, 312
elm, soaked, 390
Empire, 8, 38, 39, 60, 83, 112, 134, 156, 168; 144, 459, 554
  bed, 2, 3; 35
end table, 523
England, Berkshire district, 112
English chair, 250
exposed hinge, 155; 412
extension of top slat, 61

fall front, 169, 170
  desk, 169, 170; 453
false drawer, 134
fan-back Windsor, 115; 71, 283–87, 301
fancy chairs, see Chapter 6, 115
feathered decoration, 363
feet shoes, 17
"felly," 112
fiddle back, 39, 60; 77, 120–24
fiddle-shaped splat, 39
field bed, 2; 33, 34
firehouse Windsor, 115, 116; 313–15
flat-top desk, 169
flattened stiles, 59
Flemish-type chair, 33
Florida, 206, 222, 224
  Allenhurst, 268
  Ferandina, 221
  Mascot, 219
  Pensacola, 220
flour bin, 580
fluted, 2, 237; 4
fly whisk, 205
foil, 231
fold over, 170
folding
  chair, 86; 175
  rocking, 129
  top table, 496, 500
foot
  contoured, 17
  flat, 17
  T-bar, 17
  tripod, 17
formal chair, see Chapter 4
frames, bed, 1
Franklín, Benjamin, 37; 205
French, 61
French Canadian, 84, 85; see Canadian
French foot, 133, 169
French-style chair, 251
fretwork, 59
front upright with mushroom ends, rocker, Shaker, 226

game table, 177
gateleg table, 179; 483, 485, 486
Gautier, Andrew, 112
Georgia, Fitzgerald, 275
German, 222
Giddings, Deacon Thomas, 340
gimlet, 229
glass, 231
  knobs, 231
Gnadenau, 222
gold stripes, 59
gooseneck rocker, 127
Gothic, 571
  pattern, 558
  type chair, 86
  type chest, 382
grain chest, see chest, grain
grained, 375, 378, 419
grapevine, 60
Greek revival, 136
green wood, 113, 114
Guilford chest, 132

H.C. Co., 62
H-hinge, 156; 400, 417
H-stretcher, 78, 114, 174, 175, 466
Haas, Joseph, 527

Hadley chest, 132, 133; **328**
half-banister, 25
handgrip, 59, 60
    crest, **156**
handkerchief table, 181; **489**
handle-grip crest, **138**
hanging cradle, **395**
hardware on cabinets, 156
Hartford, Connecticut, 73
harvest table, 180; **492**
Haskin, S., 184
hasp, 59
HaubeKaeschtle, **425**
headboard, 1, 2
headrest, **131**
Hepplewhite, 2, 17, 83, 133, 156, 170, 180, 200, 299; 3, 186, 340, 341, 342, 415, 433, 434, 439
hide seat, 89
highboy, 133
hinge, 229; *see* rat tail, H, exposed
Hitchcock, 59, 62; **132**
    Alford and Company, 62; **156**
    Lambert, 39, 62
    type, 60, 61, 62, 83, 116, 134
        chair, 149, 150, 152–56, 161, 165
Hitchcocksville, Connecticut, 59, 62
hollowed log, 86
hood, 255, 256
hooded cradle, **391**
hooklike finial, 84
hoop-back Windsor, 115; **288, 289**
horned chairs, **274**
horse
    shaving, **599, 600**
    stitching, **598**
Hudson Valley chair, 145
Hull, John, 158
huntboard, 156; **437–39**
hunt table, 156
hutch cupboard, 155
hutch table, 181; **533–37**

Ile d'Orléans-type chair, 85; **250–52**
Illinois, 212, 577
    Bishop Hill, **461**
    rocker, **90**
Indiana, 39; **241**
inlaid, 17
Iowa, **110**
    Amana, 222
    Des Moines, **306**
Ipswich chest, 132
iron
    candlestand, 54
    catch, 3
ironing chair, **209**

jack plane, 230
jam cupboard, 208; **574**
jelly cupboard, 208
Jenny Lind bed, 3; **22**
Jerome, Chauncey, 236
Jones, John, 112

"kas" cupboard, 155
Kentucky, **482**
    Lexington, 112
    Logan County, **209**
    Shakerton, **560, 583**
    South Union, **481**
Kettle, Russell, 177
keyhole, 133, 134
kitchen
    bench table, *see* table
    cabinet, *see* cabinet, kitchen
    chair, 115
    pieces, *see* Chapter 15
    safe, **558–65**
    table, *see* table, kitchen
    Windsor, 116; **306, 311**
kneading table, 207
knee, **614**
kneehole desk, 169
knife-blade rocker, 38
knobs, 229
    on beds, 2
knots, 112, 230

ladder-back chair, *see* Chapter 7, 30, 81, 84, 115; **88, 609**
Langdon, J., 78
lathe, 113, 114, 228
lazy susan table, 180, 181
Lebanon, Ohio, **109**
legs, Windsor chair, 113
lift-top chest, **352, 353**
lift-top desk, 170
Lincoln, Abraham, 39
Lincoln rocker, 39; **127**
Little Boston rocker, 39
Lloyd, William, 434
log chair, **273**
Lombard, Elizabeth Paine, **528**
loopback Windsor, 115; **290–97**
Louisiana, 16
    New Orleans, 276
lowback Windsor, 114; **277, 278**
lyre-shaped, 123, 124

mahogany, 2
Maine, 85; **392**
    Groveland, 225
    Livermore, **339**
mammy bench, 39, 62; **132–35**
manufacture of Windsors, 112
Maryland, 84
    Annapolis, 178
Massachusetts, 39, 59, 83, 85, 112, 180; **67, 78, 464, 478, 491**
    Canterbury, 225
    Cape Cod, **374**
    Gloucester, **365**
    Hadley, 37
    Hancock, 225; **586, 611**
    Marlborough, **367**
    Springfield, 434
    Sterling, 168
    West Pittsfield, 225
match holder, **234**
meat safe, 207
metal bolt cover, bed, 2
Mexican, 84
Michigan, 457
    chest, **424**
    Kalamazoo, **388**
Midwest, 228; **135, 223, 606**
Midwestern
    chair, 213–15, 227, 228, 262, 295, 313
    jelly cupboard, 208
    kitchen safe, **559**
    rocker, 39, 87
    table, lazy susan, 181
milking stool, **601**
Minnesota, 266, 450, 595
    Marine, **121**
Mission Purisima Concepcion de Maria Santissima, California, 253
Mission San Miguel Arcangel, 244
Mission style, 85
Mississippi
    bed, **23**
    Vicksburg, **8**
Missouri, **456**
    Maryville, **552**
molding on cabinets, 156
Morse, E., 339
mortise and tenon, 1, 2, 84, 132, 230; **235**
mushroom, 224; **102**
    ends, **195, 196**
    handles, **342**
    knobs, 26, 229; **69, 348**

N backward, 62
nails, 229
    square head, 229
nationality groups, 222
Nevada, Panaca, **20**
New England, 83, 84, 115, 156, 178, 239; **65, 95, 105–7, 119, 132, 164, 188, 194, 197, 202, 280, 281, 284, 286, 287, 291, 292, 294, 313, 332, 333, 335, 336, 402, 406, 475, 477, 492, 503, 510, 516, 540**
    armchair, Windsor, 115; **299, 300**

bed, 4
candlestand, 60
    rocking chair, 39
    settle, **258**
    sideboard, 435
    survival-type trestle table, 179
    table, 179
New Hampshire, 39, 85, 180; **106, 375**
    Barrington-Strafford, **82**
    Canterbury, 324, **581**
    Portsmouth, 78
New Jersey, 26, 84, 114, 115
    Bergen County, **409**
New Mexico, 84; **235, 473, 537, 578, 579**
    bench, **254**
    chair, **249**
    Santa Fe, **474**
    Trampas, **248**
New York, 39, 114–16; **28, 75, 105, 194, 288, 364, 511**
    Canaan, **371**
    Dobbs Ferry, **423**
    Hudson River Valley, **476, 535**
    Long Island, **376**
    Mount Lebanon, 225; **12, 13, 85, 102, 429, 458, 556, 570, 582, 584, 588**
    New York City, 59; **148, 186**
    Schoharie, 5, **46**
    Watervliet, 225; **590**
night stand, **521, 523**
North Carolina, **411**
    Pedquimans County, 71
"northern" chair, 83, 84
    table, gateleg, 179
    turnings, **485**
notched shelf, 155, 222; **398**
notched side as foot, 134, 207; **268, 375**
novelty chair, 86
nurse rocker, 39
nursing chair, 39

octagonal top, 39, 49
ogee bracket foot, 221
Ohio, 39, 59; **86, 96, 108, 109, 115, 167, 305, 420, 548, 573**
    chest, **361**
    Cuyahoga County, **304**
    dry sink, **567**
    Lancaster, 170
    Zoar, 220, 241; **179–81, 425, 426, 602**; *see also* Zoarites
oil paint, 61
Ontario, Canada, 9, 14, 18, 126, 159, 174, 175, 184, 463, 499; *see also* Canadian
    Belleville, **140**
    dry sink, **569**
    Iroquois, **514**
open cupboard, 155; **398–405**
Oregon, **598**
    Oregon City, **310**

pad foot, 240
paint, 229
painted graining, **147, 148**
panel construction, **579**
panel, dower chest, 222
    painted chest, **351**
parlor stand, **517**
patent rocker, 130
patina, 231
peg foot candlestand, **55**
pegs, 132, 230
Pembroke table, 177; **490**
pencil
    post, 3; **6**
Pennsylvania, 39, 83, 84, 170, 178, 244; **27, 101, 115, 120, 198, 199, 205, 263, 264, 282, 301, 319, 343, 344, 373, 394, 398, 407, 408, 410, 417, 419, 433, 479, 480, 500, 571, 592, 603, 604**
    candlestand, 40, 52, 54, 55
    Carbondale, **531**
    chair style, 61

chest, 132
    of drawers, 222
    Concord, **539**
    dough tray, 208
    dower chest, 350–56, 368, 369
    dry sink, **568**
    Economy, 303, 312
    furniture, *see* Chapter 16
    German, **607–9**
        designs, 221
    inlaid chest, 221
    Meadville, **527**
    painted chair, 146, 147, 171–73, 182–84, 188
    Pittsburgh, 59
    plain chest, 221
    table, 179, 222
    washstand, **546, 547**
    waterbench, 207
"penny" feet, 54
period of stenciling, 59, 60
pewter cupboard, 155
Philadelphia, 2, 37, 112, 114, 115, 117, 178; **10, 289, 320, 489**
    Phyfe, Duncan, 84; **235**
pie cupboard, 207; **562**, *see* kitchen safe
    Canadian, **562**
pie safe, *see* kitchen safe
pierced tin, 207
Pilgrim, 83, 132
Pilgrim furniture, 1, 151; **384**
pillow, 59, 60
pillow-grip, 155, 157, 166
pillow-shape hand grip, *see* pillow grip
pins, 230
pin-type hinge, **431**
    wooden, 85
plank seat, 60; **143, 158, 160, 170, 172, 174, 177**
plate-guard rail, **403**
platform rocker, 130
porringer
    table, 180; **484**
    top, 48
post and socket, 84
Pratt, Joel, Jun., 168
press cupboard, 155; **397**
pressed-glass knob, 230
"priest" chair, 85; **244**
Prince of Wales feather, **140**
pullout, 170
    writing shelf, 169
Puritans, tables, 169

Quebec, 84, 85
Queen Anne, 17, 25, 86, 178, 229; **74–78, 511, 512**
    bed, 2
    chair, 30
    dropleaf table, 180
    table, **484, 486**

rabbit ear, 84; **213, 228, 311**
random-width boards, 230
Rank, Johann, **355**
rat-tail hinge, **398, 401, 425**
ratchet candlestand, 17; **58, 61**
rawhide, 20, 90
    seat, 84; **103, 212, 215, 223, 225–27, 238, 240**
    thong, 85
rectangular center slat, **156**
    construction, 132, 155; **330**
    crest, **158**
red graining, 60
reeding, 169, 242
refectory table, **500**
regional differences
    in chair style, 61
    Connecticut, Windsor, 116
    eighteenth-century turnings, 116
    New England, Windsor, 117; **279**
    Philadelphia, Windsor, 116; **282**
reverse banister back, 25
riverboat, 59
Rhode Island, 112; **299, 494**
rockers, 37, 113

rocking
  bench, combination, *see* mammy bench
  chair, *see* Chapter 5
  Shaker, 226
rod back, 115, 116; 301–6
roll front seat, 60
roll-over bed, 3
roll top, 59, 60, 169; 153, 154, 165
rolled-arm rocker, Shaker, 226
rolled seat, 61; 113, 115, 117, 118, 120, 121, 124
rolling crest, 38
roman numerals, bed, 2
rope, 212
  bed, 1, 2; 21
  lacing, bed, 3
ropelike trim, 418
rosette, 113
rosette on Boston rocker, 38
rosette knob, 230
roundabout chair, 259
rounded chair seat, 60; 138, 155
rush, 86
rush seat, 30, 60, 84, 85; 62, 63, 66, 69, 74–77, 80, 81, 137, 139, 142, 161, 190, 199, 202, 231, 262
rustic table, 527

saddlemaker's bench, 596
Saint Lawrence, 85; 207, 251
salamander, 84
  slat, 200
Salem rocker, 39; 118
salt box, 234
Santa Barbara Mission, 246
sausage turned, 84; 68–70, 192
Savery, William, 37
sawbuck table, 179, 226
saw marks, 231
Saxton, 97
scalloped
  apron, 438, 441
  shelves, 155, 156
  skirt, 178, 207
  trim, 401, 403
school-master's desk, 169, 170; 453, 462
school seat, 268
schrank, 608
screw
  mechanism, 57
  -top stand, 56
  -type candlestand, 17; 42–44
screws, 1, 2, 227
  countersunk, 3
scroll-arm rocker, Shaker, 226
scroll-eared top crest, 286
sea chest, 365
seasoned wood, 114
seat, chair, 85
seat construction, Windsor, 113
seat, Windsor, 112
secretary desk, 170; 454–57, 459
  bookcase type, 170
Seltzer, Christian, 354
  John, 353
serpentine, 133
  slat, 84
server, 208; 574
settee, 39
  painted, 187
  Windsor, 319–24
settle, 255–58
  bed, 28, 29
  bench, high back, 85, 86
  table, 181; 536
sewing
  chair, Shaker, 225
  desk, *see* table, sewing
  rocker, 39
  table, *see* table, sewing
Shaker, 26, 38, 39, 83, 85, 179, *see* Chapter 17; 69, 85, 102, 109, 208, 209, 211, 262, 324, 371, 379, 458, 481, 482, 519, 520, 550, 566, 570, 581–86, 588, 610, 611
  bed, 12, 13

box, 233, 234
candlestand, 50
design, 225
furniture, type of wood, 225
Shelburne
  rocker, 97
  Vermont, 97
shell-like dome, 156
Sheraton, 3, 59, 156, 227; 2, 6, 190, 219, 523
  bed, 2; 28
  fancy chair, 112; 136–43, 163, 164, 167
  table, 495
shield, 60
shield back, 82, 136
side table, 177
sideboard, 155, 156; 433–37
sidechair, Shaker, 225
sink bench, 571
sixty-degree back curve, 113
slant-front desk
  eighteenth century, 443, 444
  nineteenth century, 169; 450
  on frame, 451
  Queen Anne, 445
slant-front Hepplewhite desk, 169; 447, 448
slant-lid desk, 452
slanted-top desk, 169
slat back, nineteenth century, 85
slat-back chairs, *see* Chapter 7; 191–239
slat, bed, 3
slat, pierced, 30; 79
slats, 1; 13, 14, 25
Sleepy Hollow, 39
sleigh bed, 1, 3; 35–37
sleigh cradle, 151; 392
slip seat, 30
Smith, Eliakim, 37
snake feet, 49
socket, 38, 114
South, 230
South Carolina, Charleston, 62
"southern," 83
Southern
  chair, 178, 269
  cupboard, 412, 422
  hunt board, 439
  pie safe, 558
  regional chair style, 61
  sideboard, 156
  slat-back chair, 85
  table, 179
    gateleg, 179
  turnings, 486
southwestern
  chair, 84; 223, 235, 238–40
    style, 236, 237
  cupboard, 413
spade feet, 2, 242; 434
Spanish, 84, 85; 235, 473, 474
  feet, 26, 178, 179; 259
  influence, 247
spindle with knobs, 171
spindles, Windsor, 112
splint seat, 85; 94, 203, 211
split-ash seat, 204
split-bottom seat, 211
split-hickory seat, 92
split turnings, 228
spool
  bed, 3, 228, 21–24
  furniture, Chapter 18; 408, 414, 577
spool table, 524–26
  turning, 180, 243; 131, 346, 496, 542, 549, 550, 553
spoon notches, 155
  rack, 234
spring rocker, 130
square
  drawer in desk, 169
  leg, 85
  peg, 208
  post, 83, 84; 92, 128, 239, 240, 244, 248, 253
  seat, 59

steamboat fancies, 59
Steel, A., 320
stencil decoration, 139, 152–60, 171, 174–76, 180, 189
stencil decorations, bed, 30, 31
stencils, 38, 39, 59, 60, 61; 104, 105, 112, 115, 116, 119, 121
step down, 309
  crest rail, 116
  slat, 61
step top, 38; 119
Stephens (N.R.) Chair Factory (1832), 362
stick construction, 114
stool, 603, 605, 606
  milking, 601
straight rushing, 85
sugar chest, 156; 441, 442
sunburst, 169
Sunflower chest, 329
styles, bed, 2
styles, Windsor, 114

T-bar, 17
T-base candlestand, 41
T-shaped trestle, 179; 477
table
  kitchen, 576
    bench, 577
  Pennsylvania, 222
  sewing, 177; 583–86
  Shaker, 226
    tailoress, *see* table, sewing
table chair, 181
tables, *see* Chapter 13
tables, *see* butterfly, dropleaf, hand-kerchief, hutch, gateleg, Pembroke, Queen Anne, table chair, tavern tilt top, trestle, sawbuck, settle, Windsor
tables, history of, 177
tailor's bench, *see* bench, tailor's
tambour
  desk, 170
  front, 169
tape seat, 85, 226
tavern table, 177; 464–74
  Jacobean, William and Mary, 177
  nineteenth century, 178
  Queen Anne, 178
Tennessee, 372, 442
  Nashville, 485, 575
tent bed, 34
Texas, 84, 86, 236; 92, 93, 103, 128, 223, 227, 389, 454, 515, 541
  Austin, chair, 261
  Bastrop, 413
  bed, 25, 26, 36, 37
  chair, 237
  chest, 346
  Clarksville, 386
  Fredericksburg, 225, 396
  Houston County, 360
  Huntsville, 226, 349, 605
  Indianola, 347
  kitchen safe, 561, 563–65
  Loredo, 428
  Marion County, 565
  Marshall, 387
  Matagorda, 508, 542
  Nacogdoches, 432
  Quihi, 238, 239
  San Antonio, 414
  San Augustine, 431, 455
tiger maple, 83, 184, 513, 606
till, 134
tilt-top candlestand, 17
tilt-top table, 181; 501–5
tilting chair, 38
  Shaker, 225
tin safe, 207
tip-top table, 181
toilet habits, 200
tool marks, 230
transparent color, 61
transparent oil, 60
tray-top candlestand, 61
trestle table, 179, 226; 477–82

tripod
  candlestand, 17
  leg, 42, 43, 45, 46, 49, 50
  table, 508, 509
trundle bed, 3; 38
trustee's desk, 458
turkey work, 250
turned, 244
  ball, 60
turnip feet, 357
turtle back, 60; 149
twin beds, 3
two-slat chair, 83

under-the-eaves bed, 3
Utah
  chair, 231, 233
  Salt Lake City, 131, 169
  Willard, 313

valance, 134
valanced skirt, 133
vase-shaped splat, 30, 39
Vermont, 39
  Braintree, 395
Victorian, 86, 112; 125, 185, 505, 508
  bed, 1, 2
  candlestands, 17
  chair, 83, 242, 307, 308, 318, 343
  chests, 134
  desk, 460
  fancy chair, 162
  novelty chair, 86
Virginia, 331, 436, 437, 469
  bed, 11

wagon seat, 86; 263–67
wagon-wheel makers, 112
wainscot chair, 25; 607
Wallace, Victor, 310
wardrobe, 431, 432
Washington, 124, 215
  Martha, 290
  Racine, 600
washstands, *see* Chapter 14; 538–41
  with bowl hole, 200
  common, 200
  towel bar, 200; 549–53
water bench, 566
Watson, Luman, 235
weaver's chest, *see* chest, weaver
weaver's stand, 17; 41
wedge, 113, 114
Wells, Francis H., 529
West Indies, 112
West, pierced tin, 207
Western pie safe, 559
wheelwrights, 112
wig stand, 539
William and Mary, 134, 229; 72, 76
  blanket chest, 330
  chest of drawers, 132
  gateleg table, 179
Windsor, 39, 61; 95–97, 100, 118, 176
  chair, *see* Chapter 8, 207; 44
  table, 178; 475
wing armrest, 232
Wisconsin, 237
  Racine, 273
woodbox, 581, 582
workbench, *see* Chapter 15
woven corn shuck seat, 269
woven splint seat, 210
writing arm Windsor, 115; 98, 278
writing table, 177
wrought-iron hinge, 133
wrought-iron strap hinge, 357

x-shaped foot, 40
x-shaped leg, 179
x-shaped trestle, 179; 476
x stretcher, 180, 245; 292, 490

Young, Brigham, 131, 169

zinc-lined trough, 207
zinc liner, 567, 568
Zoarites, 222; 15, 425, 426